THE OPEN QUESTION

THE OPEN QUESTION

BEN HOGAN AND GOLF'S MOST ENDURING CONTROVERSY

Peter May

ROWMAN & LITTLEFIELD
Lanham • Boulder • New York • London

Published by Rowman & Littlefield
An imprint of The Rowman & Littlefield Publishing Group, Inc.
4501 Forbes Boulevard, Suite 200, Lanham, Maryland 20706
www.rowman.com

6 Tinworth Street, London, SE11 5AL, United Kingdom

Distributed by NATIONAL BOOK NETWORK

British Library Cataloguing in Publication Information Available

Library of Congress Cataloging-in-Publication Data

Names: May, Peter, 1951 February 7– author.
Title: The Open question : Ben Hogan and golf's most enduring controversy / Peter
    May.
Description: Lanham : Rowman & Littlefield, [2021] | Includes bibliographical
    references and index. | Summary: "This book provides the first in-depth look at the
    controversial Hale-America National Open, won by Ben Hogan in 1942 against the
    backdrop of the wartime home front. Peter May champions Hogan's claim that it
    should have counted as an official US Open, which would have given him a record
    five US Open titles."—Provided by publisher.
Identifiers: LCCN 2020042785 (print) | LCCN 2020042786 (ebook) | ISBN
    9781538137093 (cloth) | ISBN 9781538137109 (epub)
Subjects: LCSH: Hogan, Ben, 1912–1997. | Hale-America National Open (Golf
    tournament)—History. | Golf—Tournaments—United States—History—20th
    century. | Golf—United States—History—20th century.
Classification: LCC GV970.3.B46 M39 2021 (print) | LCC GV970.3.B46 (ebook) |
    DDC 796.3520973—dc23
LC record available at https://lccn.loc.gov/2020042785
LC ebook record available at https://lccn.loc.gov/2020042786

To Tara Valente, Victoria Nenno, Travis Puterbaugh, Nathan Myers, Kathy Shoemaker, Norm Richards, Nancy Rasmussen, Courtney Chartier, and all the overworked and underappreciated archivists, historians, and librarians who make it possible for us to do our work. Thank you!

CONTENTS

PROLOGUE

June 19, 1955:
The Olympic Club, San Francisco

Father's Day dawned cool and overcast, typical weather for the Bay Area in mid-June. The average temperature for June is 67 degrees, only 6 degrees warmer than in January.

The two individuals who later that day would participate in an 18-hole play-off to determine the US Open champion both wore sweaters, as they had done in previous rounds due to the pervasive damp conditions. By the time they teed off at 2:00 p.m., the sun had materialized but did not bring with it a summertime warmth. The high temperature that day would reach 58 degrees.

The two golfers had completed the 72 holes with identical scores of 287, 7 over par across the treacherous Olympic Club layout. But while their scores were the same, the two individuals could not have been more different.

One, Ben Hogan, was the dominant player of his time. He had already won four official US Opens and, nearing the age of 43, was hoping to become the first to win five. The other, Jack Fleck, was a club pro from Davenport, Iowa. He idolized Hogan. He played with golf clubs designed by Ben Hogan, including two wedges that Hogan had given him prior to the start of the tournament. Fleck had never won a professional tournament.

Hogan had finished his final round well before Fleck and had assumed, as did most everyone else at the tournament, that he would emerge victorious. He had given his golf ball to a United States Golf Association official at the end of his round for what he figured would be a spot in the USGA Museum as winner of an unprecedented five US Opens. But Fleck caught Hogan with a birdie on the 18th hole in the gloaming of Saturday—and after NBC Television had gone off the air declaring Hogan the winner—prompting the 18-hole playoff on Sunday.

The USGA, which sponsors the Open, approaches its signature event with an almost Darwinian zeal. Until recently it favored the old, traditional courses such as Olympic, which has hosted five US Opens. The 1955 US Open was its first. The organization prefers lightning-fast greens, punitive rough conditions, and tight fairways.

Until 1965, the last two rounds of the tournament were played on the same day—Saturday—making it an endurance test as well. The British Open likes to call its winner the "Champion Golfer." The US Open could well deem its winner the "Champion Survivor."

Originally, the USGA decreed that playoffs, like the one Hogan and Fleck were about to engage in, be 36 holes. The association later shortened it to 18 holes and, in 2018, decided that the cumulative scores of 2 extra holes would be enough to determine a champion.

Hogan had wanted things to end on Saturday. When he heard that Fleck needed two birdies in the final four holes to force a tie, Hogan remarked that he hoped Fleck made one birdie—or three. He was exhausted. He knew all about the rigors required of a US Open champion, having won at Riviera outside Los Angeles in 1948. He had also won in 1950—after nearly being killed in an automobile accident in February 1949—and in 1951 and 1953.

Hogan had also won the 1951 and 1953 Masters Tournaments; the 1946 and 1948 PGA (Professional Golfers' Association) Championships, which were match-play events; and in his only appearance in the tournament, the 1953 British Open at demanding Carnoustie. He was the pre-eminent golfer of his time.

Fleck, nearly nine years younger than Hogan, was only nine years old when Hogan first turned professional in 1930. Fleck had had little success on the PGA Tour and, in fact, would win only twice more, in 1960 at the Phoenix Open and in 1961 at the Bakersfield Open. Hogan had won 64 times on the PGA Tour prior to that memorable afternoon by San Francisco Bay. One of those 64 wins had been a US Open playoff victory in 1950 at Merion over Lloyd Mangrum and George Fazio.

That this was a mismatch on paper was inarguable. The great golf writer Herbert Warren Wind called Fleck "a pro with just the suspicion of a reputation." As an aside, Wind noted that Fleck had shot an 87 in a practice round.

Yet, as he approached the first tee, Fleck later recalled, "I was never nervous." How could he be?

While Hogan was a daunting adversary, and the Olympic Club a demanding layout, Fleck had faced a far greater challenge 11 years earlier—the Third Reich. When Operation Overlord was launched on June 6, 1944, Jack Fleck was there. As World War II veteran Mangrum observed, "I don't suppose that any of the pro and amateur golfers who were combat soldiers, Marines or sailors will soon be able to think of a three-foot putt as one of the really bad troubles in life."

Fleck had joined the US Naval Reserves in September 1942. He had spent three years in the Reserve Officer Training Corps (ROTC) in high school in Iowa and eventually became a quartermaster, or a noncommissioned petty officer. He traveled on the luxury liner *Queen Elizabeth*, which had been converted to a troop ship, bound for England along with thousands of US Army troops.

Fleck was placed on a British-made rocket-launching ship, the 406, and went on maneuvers in the English Channel, training with tank landing ships (LSTs) while keeping a watch out for German submarines. He watched one night as an LST was sunk by torpedoes and saw stacks of bodies on the dock when returning home from maneuvers.

Originally, Fleck and his boat left England on June 5, but inclement weather forced them to turn back. The next day they launched again. The target was enemy troops trying to stop the Allied assault on Utah Beach. At dawn, the ship was 500 yards from shore, launching its 5-inch rockets to try and clean out machine-gun nests, mortar sites, mines, and pillboxes.

After the beachhead was secured, the ship returned to England, its war duty far from over. From England, Fleck and his shipmates sailed for Italy, then to the island of Corsica and, finally, to assist in another invasion of France, this one from the south. It would be called Operation Dragoon. Its objectives were two ports in southern France—Marseille and Toulon.

At first, Dragoon was supposed to be held simultaneously with Overlord. But due to a lack of ships, supplies, and soldiers, Dragoon was postponed. By the time it was launched in mid-August, Allied war planners had learned not only from Normandy, but also from a beach landing in Anzio, Italy. As a result, casualties were far fewer and German resistance much less severe.

With Dragoon finished, Fleck's ship sailed to Sicily and was turned over to the British Navy. He returned to his base, then went to North Africa, and then to the United States after being informed his mother was terminally ill. He got back to Iowa just in time to say his last good-bye.

Fleck was then assigned to a new crew to take over a rocket-launching ship for what everyone assumed would be a large-scale invasion of Japan. The ships underwent maneuvers off the Carolinas and then set off for the Pacific Theater. Fleck's ship went through the Panama Canal, stopped for supplies in San Diego, and then headed out for Pearl Harbor. It never arrived. On the way, word had come that Japan had surrendered, and the ship was ordered back to San Diego.

Fleck left the Naval Reserves in December 1945, one of millions to serve his country in World War II. Less than a decade later, he would be the centerpiece of one the most memorable upsets not only in the history of the US Open—but in the history of professional sports.

On the morning of the playoff, Fleck did his stretching exercises "and a few minutes of meditation and prayer." He took a walk along the beach "for peace, quiet and prayer." Fleck told Hogan that he had seen the motorcycle police and ambulance driving to the scene of Hogan's horrific accident in 1949, but had not known the accident involved Hogan until the following morning.

"So no matter what the outcome is today," Fleck told the taciturn Hogan, "good luck and play well."

Hogan never led in the playoff. Fleck's par at the fifth hole gave him a one-stroke lead. He was three strokes ahead after 10 holes. Hogan did not win a hole until the 11th but had shaved the deficit to a single stroke after the 17th hole. By now, an estimated crowd of 6,000 was following the golfers.

Then, on the 18th tee, Hogan did the unforgivable. Of the many possible miscues in golf, Hogan regarded the hook as the most egregious. As a young pro trying to make it on the PGA Tour, he battled his tendency to hook, which, in turn, made it difficult to score well. Once he learned to get rid of his hook, Hogan found success on the tour.

"Ben Hogan would rather let a black widow spider crawl around inside his shirt than hit a hook," said Claude Harmon, the 1948 Masters champion.

But Hogan appeared to slip as he drove his tee ball well left into the damp, thick, unforgiving rough. It took him two shots just to get his ball back into the fairway and he ended up making a double-bogey 6. Fleck scored a routine par and won the playoff with a 69 to Hogan's 72.

In the locker room after the presentation ceremony, Hogan puffed on a cigarette while sipping an iced tea. He had earlier announced his retirement from competitive golf, although he would continue to appear in the marquee events. As he sat, chatting with a few golf writers, one of them remarked, "Tough luck Ben. It would have been your fifth Open."

Hogan had a one-word response: "Sixth."

ABOUT THIS BOOK

Ben Hogan had made similar remarks after winning the US Open in 1950 and 1951. After returning to his home in Fort Worth, Texas, he ventured over to Colonial Country Club, where he reminded friends of how many US Opens he thought he had won. He was congratulated for winning his second in 1950. "Third," he said. He was congratulated for winning his third in 1951. "Fourth," he said.

Hogan went to his grave in 1997 believing he had won ten major professional golf championships, including a record five US Open titles. He was not alone in that assessment.

On more than one occasion, Hogan reminded those in his company that he always considered his victory in the 1942 Hale America National Open Golf Tournament as the first of five US Open championships.

"I have heard Mr. Hogan talk about it. I can tell you from personal experience that Mr. Hogan considered it (the Hale America) a US Open win," said Robert Stennett, the executive director of the Ben Hogan Foundation. Stennett told the golf podcast *No Laying Up* that "whenever you would ask Mr. Hogan about how many US Opens he won, he would say five, not four."

Hogan told Hall of Famer Nick Faldo at a 1992 luncheon in Fort Worth, Texas, that he knew what it took to win a US Open—something Faldo never achieved—and that he had five medals to prove it. One of those medals had been given to him after he won the Hale America Tournament. The only difference in the medal he received was the lack of a blue background for the group of stars on the front and the inscription on the back of the medal, which referenced the Hale America. Otherwise, the medal looks just like the ones he was given after winning in 1948, 1950, 1951, and 1953.

The USGA, which runs the US Open and also cosponsored the Hale America Tournament, has, for nearly eight decades, continued to classify its 1942 "National Open Tournament" as just another tournament. Or as a wartime substitute for the US Open. It is a controversial position in that many in the golf community—not just Hogan—believe that to be a wrong that should have been righted a long time ago.

The Hall of Fame golf writer Dan Jenkins was probably the most forceful and persistent to have championed Hogan's insistence that the Hale America count as a US Open and major championship victory. Prior to his death in 2019, Jenkins said, "I've spent a whole career arguing that that should count as his tenth major and fifth US Open."

Longtime *Golf Digest* writer Ron Sirak took up the cause on the 75th anniversary of Hogan's triumph—the 2017 US Open at Erin Hills—to again urge the USGA to change its stance and formally recognize the Hale America for what Sirak and others have long believed it to be: the de facto 1942 United States Open. He called the inability to do so a "major mistake" and that the USGA "should acknowledge that Ben Hogan won the US Open five times, not four."

This book will examine Hogan's claim by revisiting that weekend in June 1942 and challenging some of the USGA's assertions that the Hale America was not worthy of a US Open. It will present an opportunity for the reader to engage in this debate, either by reigniting the issue for those who have long fought for Hogan to be recognized, or by exposing it to a whole generation of golf fans who are unfamiliar with the story or the surrounding controversy.

One of the obligations of those who have a grasp of the past is to remind those who do not of what came before them. There's a generation of golf fans who think Tiger Woods is the embodiment and sole icon of the game. But before Tiger there was Jack Nicklaus, and before Nicklaus there was Arnold Palmer, and before Palmer there was this fellow called Ben Hogan. The Hale America National Open is a story that has never been told in detail, only in passing.

In the early 1940s, professional golf had a number of colorful personalities, virtually all of whom played in the Hale America Tournament. The stories of four of them—Hogan, Hale America runner-up Jimmy Demaret, 1946 US Open champion Lloyd Mangrum, and the legendary Bobby Jones—will be interwoven in between rounds of the tournament.

This is not in any sense purporting to be a biography of any of those individuals, only snapshots into their respective lives. There are several biographies of Jones and Hogan. Demaret wrote his autobiography. Mangrum wrote an instructional book (as did the other three) that included a dedication from Bing Crosby, who called Mangrum "a great player and a wonderful fellow." Their careers in golf and war will be examined with particular attention to their roles in World War II. Jones left his lucrative law practice in Atlanta and insisted he be sent to the European theater despite his age (40) and celebrity status. He ended up participating in D-Day. Mangrum joined the celebrated 90th Infantry Division, the so-called Tough 'Ombres, as it made its way across France and into Germany and Czechoslovakia in the spring of 1945. Hogan (the Army Air Corps) and Demaret (the Navy) both served stateside.

Also interwoven will be the stories of some of the other, lesser-known personalities who populated professional golf in that era: Sam Byrd, the baseball player-turned-PGA golfer; Jug McSpaden, the perennial runner-up; Craig Wood, a late-blooming winner whose litany of close calls would make Greg Norman blush; Jim Ferrier, the Australian who came to the United States as a sports writer and quickly turned into one of the top players; and the remarkable golfing family from New York, the Turnesas.

The Hale America was the last professional tournament in which Bobby Jones participated, other than the Masters, which he started in the 1930s and played until 1948. Jones had retired from competitive golf in 1930 and was 8 years older than Demaret, 10 years older than Hogan, and 12 years older than Mangrum.

But while Jones was making a comeback of sorts at the Hale America, the careers of the other three were just getting started. Mangrum, Hogan, and Demaret were all born in Texas, and not one of them possessed a high school diploma. All three are in the World Golf Hall of Fame, as is Jones. Demaret became the first three-time winner of the Masters. Mangrum won the first official US Open after World War II.

And then there was Hogan. In the four years after suffering a near-fatal car accident, Hogan won three US Opens, two Masters, and one British Open. It remains to this day one of the greatest comeback stories in sports.

Prior to the 2019 Masters, itself a terrific comeback story, Tiger Woods was asked if he thought a victory in the tournament would rank as golf's greatest comeback story.

"One of the greatest comebacks in all of sports is the gentleman who won here, Mr. Hogan," Woods said. "I mean, he got hit by a bus and came back and won major championships." Woods won the Masters after years of battling knee and back woes, which necessitated a number of surgeries.

Prior to his automobile accident, Hogan had won two PGA Championships as well as his first "official" US Open in 1948 at the Riviera Country Club. In Hogan's mind, Riviera was not the first, but the second. And as years went on, and victories accumulated, the quest to have the Hale America recognized as an official US Open only intensified.

Hogan had emerged from World War II to become his generation's greatest golfer. He was even more dominant in the early 1950s after his brush with death, although he couldn't participate in as many tournaments because of the lingering effects of the accident. But he was no less proficient than on that June weekend in 1942 at Chicago's Ridgemoor Country Club. In his mind, his triumph there deserves to be officially recognized for what it was and for what he always thought it should be.

ACKNOWLEDGMENTS

In June 2017, Justin Thomas was en route to what could have been the lowest-scoring round in the history of the US Open. He ended up with a 63, which matched the lowest-scoring round in the long history of the tournament. Watching it, celebrated writer Dan Jenkins tweeted, "Nine-under 63 by Justin Thomas. Hogan shot a 10-under 62 in the 1943 [*sic*] National Open. The USGA doesn't count it, but I do and Hogan did."

I wondered what on earth he was referring to. I did some research and discovered the 1942 Hale America Tournament, of which I was unaware. With the help of Dan's daughter, *Washington Post* columnist Sally Jenkins, I connected with Dan via email. We went back and forth a few times, and I became determined to tell this story. So the first and foremost acknowledgment goes to the late Mr. Jenkins. This book would never have happened had I not read that tweet.

There are also many golf historians, librarians, archivists, and ardent fans and collectors to thank for making this project come to life. Tara Valente and Victoria Nenno at the USGA couldn't have been more helpful. Thanks to them, I now know what Dropbox is! Travis Puterbaugh at the World Golf Hall of Fame provided much-appreciated assistance, as did Nathan Myers at Augusta National. Kathy Shoemaker and Courtney Chartier at Emory University guided me through the Emory archives and even saved some digital prints that had expired. Nancy Rasmussen, the woman who runs the reunions for the 90th Infantry Division, was invaluable in getting me in touch with the division historians. Michelle Kopfer at the Eisenhower Presidential Library provided me with the correspondence between the 34th president and Bobby

Jones. Golf historians Tony Parker and Jeff Martin also provided valuable insights. Michelle Press at Getty Images helped me navigate the intimidating world of licensed photography. Sam Smith was there, as always.

It helps me to acknowledge the many others who assisted with this book by breaking this down by the four main characters.

BEN HOGAN

Hogan collector John Seidenstein was instrumental to the entire project, giving me access to his trove of Hogan memorabilia and offering to read parts of the manuscript. He has forgotten more about Hogan than I'll ever know. Similarly, Mark Baron also was quite helpful, particularly with Hogan's war records. They were otherwise unobtainable. Hogan expert Martin Davis offered his considerable advice. Karen Wright of the Ben Hogan Museum provided stories about the man and his legacy. Jody Vasquez helped me with introductions at the Colonial Country Club as well as providing background on his days as a Hogan ball shagger. Dow Finsterwald Jr., the head pro at Colonial, personally guided me through the Ben Hogan Room and the replica of Hogan's office. Jon Kane, the general manager of Ridgemoor Country Club, took time to give me a ride around the course while showing me a number of Hogan photographs from the Hale America Tournament that adorn the clubhouse. He also provided me with a book on Ridgemoor's history, which had more detail on the Hale America than any other book I have come across.

BOBBY JONES

It goes without saying that any research or history involving Bobby Jones starts and ends with the great Sidney Matthew. He could not have been more helpful, and made numerous suggestions that I hope will illuminate this part of Jones's remarkable life. My thanks to Catherine Lewis as well. She, too, is a fountain of Jones information as well as an excellent proofreader. Jake Brusch at Emory provided an entrée to the invaluable Ms. Lewis, and the redoubtable Hank Klibanoff introduced me to Jake. Klibanoff, a former *Boston Globe* colleague, is a professor at Emory. I also want to thank Bob Jones IV for his thoughts during a number of interviews. Stephen Lowe was a huge help in allowing me to read Jones's war records and correspondences from Jones's time in Europe. Steve Reid also was incredibly helpful in piecing together Jones's 1944 visit to Royal

Lytham and his correspondence with the club about his famous shot out of the bunker of the 71st hole of the 1926 British Open.

LLOYD MANGRUM

In trying to get to the bottom of Lloyd Mangrum's war years, the indefatigable Norm Richards was indispensable. As the 90th Division's association assistant historian, Richards was able to navigate the Office of Military Personnel Records in St. Louis on my behalf to try and set the Mangrum record straight. He went to enormous lengths to find and copy all the Morning Reports, which enabled me to piece together where Mangrum was and when he was there. A lot is still unknown but, thanks to Norm, a lot more is now known. Mangrum's granddaughter Jean Schuessler also was helpful in tracking down various pieces of her grandfather's war years. David Barrett and Guy Yocum provided assistance on Mangrum's background. No one has ever written a real biography of this man. He is worth it.

JIMMY DEMARET

Of all the characters in this book, Demaret is the one I'd like to have a beer with, just to listen to his stories. The Office of Military Personnel Records was able to provide documents from Demaret's days in the US Navy. Unlike US Army files, many of which were destroyed in a 1973 fire, the Navy files remained largely undamaged. Demaret himself provided much of the personal information here thanks to his book, *My Partner, Ben Hogan*. To call the man self-effacing would be an understatement. Todd Robbins at Wee Burn Country Club provided information on Demaret's time there. Greg Hansen of the Arizona Daily Star provided the background on Demaret's memorable 14 during the 1952 Tucson Open.

Thanks also to the people who really made this book possible: my literary agent, Colleen Mohyde, and Christen Karniski, Erinn Slanina, Lara Hahn, and Veronica Jurgena from Rowman & Littlefield. Laura Hibbler, Chloe Gerson, and Dzintra Lacis at Brandeis University helped me re-enter the old world of reading microfilm rolls. Friends and family keep you grounded and level-headed in times like these; my thanks to my children, Tim, Patrick, and Katie; my brothers, Todd and Andy; and my sister, Ellie. Tom and Kathi Mullin and

ACKNOWLEDGMENTS

Doug and Sue Noyes provided wine, laughs, and support. And as is true in all phases of life, my thanks to Eileen McNamara for her counsel, advice, and support throughout a pandemic, self-quarantine, cancer surgery, the death of two beloved dogs, the arrival of a new (and exhausting) dog, the discovery of *A French Village*, and many months of Zoom, sweat pants, stretch pants, quitters, and noncollared, loose-fitting T-shirts. How did that happen?

I

ELEVEN MONTHS

1

MAY 1941 TO JANUARY 1942

The USGA Giveth and the USGA Taketh Away

There never has been a National Open golf tournament of the United States. What is this tournament we call the National Open? It's the USGA National Open.

—Gene Sarazen, winner of the
USGA National Open in 1922 and 1932

In May 1941, World War II was raging on three continents. In the United States, golf remained in full swing with no obvious danger signs ahead.

The United States may have been sending war materiel to England, the free French, and Russia, but the hostilities and casualties seemed worlds away to a country protected by vast seas on both coasts. The PGA Tour schedule ran from the first week in January to the last week in December, with 30 official tournaments—and a few more that offered money if no "official" designation.

All the big names in the sport—Hogan, Snead, Nelson, Mangrum, Demaret—and others crisscrossed the country, competing for nearly $170,000 in total purses, an increase of more than $50,000 from the year before. There was no golf in England, which had been at war since 1939, so there was no British Open, no British Amateur, and no Ryder Cup, although the United States did stage a Ryder Cup of sorts at the Detroit Golf Club in August to raise money for the Red Cross and the United Service Organizations (USO).

All the contemporary stars at the time showed up in Detroit and were divided into two teams, one captained by the great amateur Bobby Jones, who had retired from golf in 1930 but still played in the Masters every year, and the other by the also-retired Walter Hagen, who had captained every American Ryder Cup team since the competition started in 1927. More than 20,000 fans attended as the PGA Tour accommodated by leaving a week open in the schedule between the Rochester and Hershey Opens. The real Ryder Cup did not return until 1947.

Hogan continued to dominate the PGA Tour, though he finished a distant fourth in the Masters to champion Craig Wood who, months later, would add the US Open to his list of important victories. The US Open that year was held in Fort Worth, Texas, at Colonial Country Club. It was the first time in the history of the event—which had begun in 1895—that the sponsoring United States Golf Association had ventured as far west and south to stage its pre-eminent event. When Wood left Fort Worth after his US Open victory, he flew to Oklahoma City for an exhibition. That is what players did in those days for extra cash. With him he had the 18-inch USGA Trophy given to the US Open champion. Little did he know that it would be five years before another one would be handed out.

Craig Wood was equal parts late bloomer and heartbreak kid. He was one of the more popular players on the tour. Born and raised in Lake Placid, New York, Wood had learned how to wield an ax at an early age. His father was a foreman for a local timber company.

Wood graduated from Rider College in New Jersey and won several tournaments in the state before making it big on the PGA Tour. He is enshrined in the World Golf Hall of Fame. He became the first man to win the Masters and the US Open in the same year, a feat later duplicated by Ben Hogan, Jack Nicklaus, Tiger Woods, and Jordan Spieth. From 1928 to 1944, Wood won 21 times.

But it was the devastating losses that defined Wood's storied career. He became the first golfer to lose each of what are now considered the four majors in a playoff. He would be alone in that distinction until Greg Norman matched him in 1993.

The most celebrated of Wood's playoff defeats in a major had to be the 1935 Masters. He had finished second the year before, in the inaugural Masters (then called the Augusta Invitational) when Horton Smith made a birdie on the 71st hole to earn a one-shot victory. The following year, Wood was in control on the final day when Gene Sarazen recorded his "shot heard 'round the world," the double eagle on the 15th hole. The shot enabled Sarazen to tie Wood, forcing a 36-hole playoff, which Sarazen won by five shots. That was the only time the Masters had a 36-hole playoff. Wood finally broke through at Augusta in 1941, at the age of 39, becoming the tournament's first wire-to-wire champion and defeating Byron Nelson by three shots. Wood played in 25 Masters tournaments. The win in 1941 marked the third and final time he would finish in the top three.

In 1939, Wood had been gifted a spot in a three-way playoff in the US Open with Nelson and Denny Shute when tournament leader and would-be champion Sam Snead blew up on the 72nd hole, taking an 8. In the playoff, Wood had a one-shot lead over Nelson going to the 18th hole, but Nelson evened things with a birdie. So the two players returned to the Philadelphia Country Club on Monday for another 18-hole playoff (Shute had been eliminated after the first 18 holes). Nelson built an early five-stroke lead, helped by an eagle on the fourth hole, and won by three shots.

Wood finally got his US Open victory two years later at Colonial, defeating Shute by three strokes and Ben Hogan by five. Wood not only claimed his second major, but got revenge on Shute, who had beaten him in a playoff at the 1933 British Open at St. Andrews. That playoff got off to a bad start for Wood when he hit his ball into the Swilcan Burn that cuts across the first fairway, just short of the green. He took a double bogey and also double-bogeyed the second to quickly fall four shots behind. Shute, who won three majors in the 1930s, including consecutive PGA Championships in 1936–1937, comfortably won the 36-hole playoff by five shots. Shute's back-to-back PGA titles would not be equaled for 63 years, or until Tiger Woods won the 1999 and 2000 titles. Shute was inducted into the World Golf Hall of Fame in 2008.

In the following year—1934—Wood lost the PGA Championship in a playoff to Paul Runyan, one of the many golfers Wood had mentored along the way. Runyan had even been an assistant pro under Wood in New Jersey. The two went the customary 36 holes in the final and finished even. Runyan won on the second playoff hole. Wood had now lost a major in a playoff for three straight years.

At Colonial in 1941, Wood would have none of the drama. It wasn't as clean as his Masters win had been two months earlier, but the three-shot cushion provided him with serenity and satisfaction as he made his way to the 18th green on that Saturday afternoon in sweltering Fort Worth. He put an exclamation point on his round with a birdie on 18.

No one could say then, or now, that Wood hadn't earned it. Or deserved it.

Wood received $1,000 for winning, and he promptly announced he would spend $100 on a national defense bond. Although the United States was not at war yet, the government had started to issue defense bonds in May 1941. Wood's popularity among his peers was such that a number of his competitors offered to pitch in and pay the $100 so that Wood could keep his entire check.

Wood refused. "I want this bond myself and it will mean even more to me because it was bought with the money awarded in this fine tournament," he said.

Wood turned 40 in November 1941 and was too old to be considered for the draft when the United States did enter the war. (He was four months older than Bobby Jones, who likewise had not been considered draft eligible by Uncle Sam.) He also was fighting off a nagging back injury, which at one point he thought might have precluded him from competing at Colonial. He wore a polo corset during the three-day tournament and his back held up. Wood became the US Open's oldest champion and, in the eyes of the sponsoring USGA, the tournament's last champion until 1946.

In the month between Wood's wins at Augusta and Colonial, the USGA decided which club would host its 1942 US Open. This was 13 months before the start of the tournament, an unthinkable time frame today, when the USGA designates Open venues seven years down the road.

The choice was a familiar one to golf aficionados: Interlachen Country Club outside Minneapolis. The course had a track record of success, having successfully hosted one of the more historic US Opens in 1930, won by Bobby Jones for the third leg of his Grand Slam. It had also hosted the 1935 US Women's Amateur, won by Glenna Collett Vare, who nudged out Interlachen member and future Hall of Famer Patty Berg, 3 and 2. Berg was only 17 years old. That was the last of the record six US Amateurs won by Vare.

Minnesotans were predictably jubilant with the USGA's decision. Bernard Swanson of the *Minneapolis Morning Tribune* called the US Open "the World Series of the fairway sport" and the *Star-Journal* called it the "blue ribbon event of all golfing extravaganzas." Interlachen had submitted its bid in the fall of 1940 for either the 1942 or 1943 Opens, confident that its success 10 years earlier would lead to a favorable decision. The club had hoped to stage the 1942 tournament in July rather than June, due to the late-starting golf season in the Twin Cities area. The USGA had allowed a date change in 1930. It did not do so this time, holding firm to its traditional dates in the middle of June.

The 1930 tournament set records for attendance and overall interest, given the magnetic presence of Jones, who had won both the British Open and British Amateur prior to the US Open and received a ticker tape parade in New York City before leaving. Club officials even considered asking Jones to play an exhibition prior to the start of the 1942 tournament.

No one at either the USGA headquarters in New York or the Interlachen clubhouse in Minnesota had any concerns about the success of the 1942 US Open. The club had done it before. It would do it again. The president of the club, Bill White Jr., visited the 1941 Open at Colonial for some advance planning and tips for what he and everyone else figured would be a seamless transition to 1942, even without the dashing presence of Jones.

"The golf overlords will learn again that Minneapolis will do an outstanding job of staging and supporting the National Open next year," wrote Charles Johnson of the *Minneapolis Star-Journal*. (He later urged Interlachen to send notices to surrounding clubs reminding them of the "do's and don'ts" of proper golf course etiquette.)

Interlachen was right out of Central Casting as far as the USGA was concerned. It had all the necessities—the stately Tudor clubhouse, the Donald Ross–designed course, the previous experience of hosting a US Open. It may not have been one of the bluebloods of the East like Baltusrol, Oakmont, Winged Foot, or Merion, but it was precisely the kind of place that attracts the USGA. It had cachet.

Interlachen was founded in 1909, and five years later was hosting the Western Open, one of the top tournaments of the time. Ross, the Scottish-born golf course architect-designer whose list of course designs include Seminole in Florida, East Lake in Georgia, Worcester in Massachusetts (site of the first Ryder Cup in 1927), Oakland Hills in Michigan, Oak Hill in New York, and three Pinehurst courses in North Carolina, including the famed No. 2, was hired in the 1920s to do a course redesign. The club paid for Ross's fee by assessing each member $50.

The timing of the 1930 US Open could not have been any more fortuitous for the club. When the golf year started, Jones had already won nine "majors"— three US Opens, two British Opens, and four US Amateurs. Suspense continued to build when he won the first of what then were deemed to be the four majors, the British Amateur, at St. Andrews in May by trouncing England's Roger Wethered, 7 and 6 in the finals. Three weeks later, he won the British Open at Royal Liverpool by two shots over Americans Leo Diegel and MacDonald Smith. That tournament ended on June 20, which traditionally was around the time that the US Open was contested.

The tournament was rescheduled to mid-July, enabling Jones to continue his quest for the Grand Slam. He got the hero's welcome in New York City and then headed out to Minneapolis. Interlachen was overwhelmed by the attention. There were 90 reporters covering the tournament. There had to be space set aside for Western Union and others transmitting over the wires. A special scoreboard was constructed, which received numbers via messenger. Interlachen could deal with that. It had no say in the weather. And it was hot.

Jones's biographer, O. B. Keeler, called it a "Turkish-bath heat that rose from the pretty little lakes set artistically about the countryside." After a sweltering first round, in which he shot 71, Jones could not even unknot his tie. Keeler had to cut it off with a knife. The heat abated for the second round and Jones's 73. He was two strokes off the lead. He would have been more off had it not been for his famous "lily pad shot" on the ninth hole. Jones got distracted by crowd movement in his backswing and topped his second shot. His ball headed straight for a pond that fronts the green. Observers said it hit a lily pad and skipped to the other side of the pond, just short of the green. Jones ended up making birdie.

With the heat wave finally broken for the 36-hole final on Saturday, Jones took command, setting the course record with a 68 in the morning. It was the lowest round he ever shot in a US Open. The 68 propelled him to a five-stroke lead heading into the final round. He played unevenly and caught a break when a rules official said a lost ball was likely to have been lost in a hazard, costing just a one-stroke penalty. He had a one-stroke lead going to the 18th hole, then rolled in a 40-foot birdie putt to win the tournament by two shots.

It had been a grueling stretch. Jones lost 17 pounds during the week. But the galleries who showed up at Interlachen and dutifully followed Jones around the course, got to see something that would never happen again: Bobby Jones, unquestionably the greatest golfer on the planet, defeating what was deemed to be the strongest field in golf for the very last time. He later would complete the Grand Slam at fabled Merion in September, defeating Eugene Homans, 8 and 7 in a lopsided US Amateur finale. He had made his national debut in 1916 at the same club as a 14 year old, and won the first of his five US Amateur titles there in 1924.

So Interlachen had the Jones connection, and the club reported that it made $15,000 in profits. The club got positive reviews from that most demanding of groups—the golfing press. One writer said the Interlachen experience helped "to dissipate the aroma of snobbishness." The USGA gave Interlachen the US Women's Amateur five years later, which announced to the world the arrival of local favorite Berg. Only a high school junior, Patty Berg's runner-up finish launched a spectacular career which saw her win the first US Women's Open in 1946 (the only time it was a match-play event) and the Western Open seven times. She was one of the founding members of what is now the LPGA and was inducted into the World Golf Hall of Fame in 1974.

So Interlachen had a strong and proven track record when it asked to host either the 1942 or 1943 US Open. When approval came, there was one final part of the agreement that didn't get a lot of attention at the time. The USGA agreed to give Interlachen first crack at the US Open should the 1942 tournament be canceled. The club had the right of first refusal should the country be called to war. At that point, it seemed almost like a superfluous add-on.

Then came December 7, 1941—and everything changed.

The Japanese sneak attack on Pearl Harbor killed more than 2,400 US personnel, including 68 civilians. The following day, President Franklin D. Roosevelt delivered his historic "Day of Infamy" speech and Congress declared war on the Empire of Japan. The United States at last had entered World War II.

Thirty-two days after the war declaration, the USGA Executive Committee assembled in New York City and the headline from the minutes of that meeting tell the whole story: War Time Aim Is to Serve the Nation. Under the headline were two words that resonated all the way back to Minneapolis—and beyond: Championship Canceled.

In this case, the organization that sets the rules for the game of golf was an outlier. The PGA Tour, separate from the USGA, announced its intention to play on and had already started its winter run through California. The Los Angeles Open, which would be won by Ben Hogan, was in progress while the USGA committee of 17 met in the organization's main office on East 57th Street.

President Roosevelt had already suggested that baseball continue, saying, "6,000 athletes will provide a vital morale boost for US workers and soldiers." At the heart of the committee meeting, as detailed in the minutes, was whether to follow baseball's lead. While it was suggested during the discussion that the organization reach out to the government for guidance, the board took it upon itself to act independently and unilaterally.

"The association has a clear duty to set an example vividly and quickly for the game of golf, that it would be better for the Association to devote its energies to something more useful than Championships," the notes read. "Usual championships in war-time would be hollow and perhaps improper, and that clubs where Championships are scheduled should be advised promptly of any possible change in plans."

The clubs in question would include Interlachen, as well as the clubs hosting the US Women's Amateur, the US Men's Amateur, and the US Pubinx Championship. At that time, those were the only 4 tournaments over which the USGA held sway. In 2019, the organization conducted 14.

Frankly, the idea of any sport continuing at this time seemed almost ridiculous. Things were not going well for the United States in the Pacific Theater. While Germany and Italy quickly joined Japan in declaring war on the United States, it would be 6 months before US Marines launched the first assault in the Pacific and 10 months before the country sent its soldiers across the Atlantic.

The Pacific Theater already provided a relentless drumbeat of devastating and demoralizing losses for the United States. Before the end of 1941, the Japanese had seized Guam and Wake Islands, and had forced General Douglas MacArthur, commander of US Armed Forces in the Far East, out of the main part of the Philippines. His air force had been decimated by the Japanese the day after Pearl Harbor. The British had surrendered Hong Kong, and Manila was captured a week before the USGA Executive Committee met in New York.

So the idea of staging its events seemed, as the USGA had noted, "hollow and perhaps improper." The organization had canceled the US Open in 1917 and 1918, the two years the United States had fought in World War I. USGA President Harold Pierce told the group that he felt the organization should cancel all of its tournaments not just for 1942, but for the duration of the war, and devote its efforts to war relief.

Fielding Wallace, an executive committee member from Augusta, Georgia, proposed that all four tournaments be canceled. Francis Ouimet, who won the 1913 US Open as an amateur and ushered in a wave of popularity for the game, seconded the motion. Pierce asked for a voice vote and got no dissenters. The committee then issued a resolution stating that "the main aim of golfers and golf organizations should be to contribute the greatest possible service to the Nation for the duration of the war."

The cancellation decision was announced the following day, January 10, at the USGA's annual meeting, held at the Waldorf-Astoria hotel. The USGA also decided to allow amateurs to be eligible to receive up to $100 in war bonds without jeopardizing their amateur status.

The decision did not prompt other golf organizations to follow suit. The Masters vowed to continue in April 1942, with tournament chairman Clifford Roberts originally saying he expected 88 players. The PGA Tour continued without interruption. It still had not selected a site for its annual championship, but would eventually settle on Seaview Country Club in New Jersey. The tournament would be played in May.

Interlachen officials greeted the USGA's decision as inevitable, with club president White saying it was "the right thing to do. The war will hurt golf and everything else, and we'd much rather call it off than stage a mediocre tournament." But he really had no say in the matter. There would be no 1942 US Open for Interlachen. That was the call of the USGA, not the club.

But *Minneapolis Morning Tribune* columnist Bernard Swanson wrote that "the USGA is coming in for more and more heat in its hasty action. . . . The governing body of amateur golf certainly lost caste by its cancellations, just at a time when the President and others in authority are encouraging more and bigger sports promotions."

Perhaps the harshest criticism of the USGA's decision came from one of its own decorated champions, future Hall of Famer and two-time US Open winner Gene Sarazen. He had already achieved the modern-day Grand Slam and, like Jones, would turn 40 in 1942. Sarazen had played in 22 consecutive US Opens when he got the news about the 1942 cancellation. He was not about to let it slide without comment.

"There never has been a National Open golf tournament of the United States," he told the *New York Times* in late January. "What is this tournament we call the National Open? It's the USGA National Open. That's the way their literature describes it. It's the USGA's own tournament. It's the same as John Jones starting a tournament and calling it the John Jones National Open tournament. Really, it's a private affair, with the USGA reserving the right to deny entry."

Sarazen then offered what he thought was a reasonable solution, one that would look more and more like what the Hale America National Open would become: "Now that the USGA has called off its own open tournament, for why I don't know unless they are taking it for granted conditions now are the same as in 1917, there is a chance for the PGA to step in and hold a National Open which anyone could enter who had the money to get there.

"It wouldn't be the PGA National Open championship," he continued. "It would be the National Open championship sponsored by the PGA. Defense bonds could be awarded instead of cash prizes and the proceeds would go to charity. It wouldn't be anyone's private National Open. Just a National Open? Right?"

Shortly after the cancellation, Thomas McMahon, president of the Chicago District Golf Association, and Lowell Rutherford, the organization's vice president, took a train to New York City to meet with the USGA. They proposed that the dates for the 1942 US Open be used to stage a war relief fundraiser in the Chicago area. The new USGA president, George Blossom, was from Chicago and the idea appealed to him. It also got Fred Corcoran's imprimatur. He was the tournament manager for the PGA.

McMahon similarly convinced the USGA not to stage the tournament at Interlachen, given Chicago's more centralized and accessible location. And, he told the USGA, his group would handle all the logistics and grunt work. The USGA could stick to entries, rules, and qualifying. The PGA would supply the manpower.

On January 21, the USGA announced what it deemed to be a wartime substitute for the US Open. It would be called the Hale America National Open and it would be played June 18–21 at a club in the Chicago area. The USGA also was urging member clubs across the country to stage their own Hale America tournaments on holiday weekends over the summer and fall, with proceeds going to the Red Cross.

The "Hale" was the idea of John B. Kelly, a wealthy weekend golfer from Philadelphia who, despite his riches, was much more Main Street than Main Line. He was 53 at the time and a case can be made that he was as responsible as any single individual for keeping golf and the PGA alive during World War II.

He volunteered to help the war effort and was given a rather bizarre title—Assistant Director of Civilian Defense in Charge of Physical Fitness. Basically, it was left up to John Kelly which sports would continue to be played during the war. Baseball, of course, was not going to be touched. But golf was different. It was perceived as a rich man's game played at elitist country clubs. You needed rubber for golf balls and steel for golf clubs, and those commodities were directed to the war effort. Several courses, including Augusta National, turned their fairways into pastures for cows or vegetable gardens.

Still, Kelly looked at golf and instead of seeing men in ties and knickers having a gin and tonic on the 19th hole, he saw the previous 18 holes as an excellent opportunity for exercise. So he advised the USGA, which had already canceled its tournaments, to instead sponsor these Hale America tournaments on holiday weekends throughout the summer. "Hale" meant hearty. "Hale" meant healthy.

"Eight million people will be going into the Armed Forces. My job is to look after 124 million who won't or can't go. They can keep fit by playing golf," Kelly said.

Kelly had some credibility in the athletics field, having won two rowing gold medals at the 1920 Olympics in Antwerp and a third gold four years later at the Paris Olympics. He also was the father of a Philadelphia woman who a decade later would become famous as an actress and then as the wife of the Prince of Monaco—Grace Kelly.

Chicago was a logical choice to hold the Hale America, in part due to its rich golf history. Business tycoon Charles Macdonald opened the Chicago Golf Club in 1892. It is believed to be the first 18-hole course in the United States and was selected by the USGA to host its third US Open in 1897. The club hosted it again in 1900 and 1911. Chicago-area clubs hosted nine US Opens from 1895 through 1933.

Having secured the tournament and the dates, all McMahon needed to do was provide a venue. The Chicago District Golf Association held a board meeting on January 22 where McMahon told its members that Ridgemoor Country Club officials had offered to host the Hale America. All that was needed was the Ridgemoor board's approval, which came shortly thereafter. The CDGA then announced on January 27 that Ridgemoor would host the first (and last) Hale America National Open.

The CDGA thought Ridgemoor to be the closest golf course of championship caliber to the heart of the city. It was also only a 15-minute drive from the north and west sides of the city. It had been in business since 1905, though it had never hosted a USGA event.

"It has always enjoyed a reputation of being one of the best groomed courses in the district," noted a release from the Tournament Committee. The club also had a traditional clubhouse, surrounded by large porches. The course played to a par 72 over 6,500 yards. (In 1942, Augusta National played at 6,800 yards.) It was enclosed by a wire fence that helped with protection and security.

Even though the USGA had canceled all its 1942 tournaments, the organization was heavily into promoting its one big professional golf event of that year, an event in which it had more than just a passing interest and organizational hand.

While the CDGA went to work on the nitty-gritty details such as tickets, parking, and publicity—McMahon established 24 committees for the tournament—it was the USGA that devoted the bulk of its attention to setting the stage for the Hale America. It jumped in headfirst, starting with the January 21 announcement that the tournament would be played in Chicago. And before anyone got the wrong idea, Joe Dey, the USGA's executive secretary, said that the Hale America would *not* be considered as a legitimate US Open by his organization. "The tournament will not be a championship, as the USGA has decided that its usual national championships should not properly be held in wartime," Dey said. "Rather, the Hale America Open will be a patriotic demonstration similar to an open patriotic tournament held by the USGA in 1917, but on a much wider basis."

The original intent was to get as many entries as possible. The USGA charged a $5 entry fee for professionals and any amateur with a handicap of 6 or less. Then, the USGA did what it had done every year since 1924—stage qualifying rounds across the country, just like they did for regular US Opens. There were to be 36 holes of local qualifying at 69 sites and, for those who made it out, another 54 holes of sectional qualifying. (Due to the Covid-19 pandemic in 2020, the USGA dispensed with qualifying rounds, and the US Open was played in September of that year rather than the originally scheduled weekend in June.)

Organizers figured on an eventual field of around 100 for what was to be a four-day, 72-hole event (like today's US Open, but not like the US Opens of the time, when the final 36 holes were contested on Saturday.) The top players in the game all received special exemptions from qualifying, but were told to attempt to play money-raising exhibitions during the time of sectional qualifying.

There was one intriguing name on the exemption list: Robert T. Jones Jr. He also was the first to accept, wiring USGA Tournament Director Francis Ouimet on January 22 that he would come out of retirement to lend his name to the worthy cause. The *Chicago Tribune* cited Jones's entry into "what undoubtedly will be the biggest fairway-and-green show ever conducted in American golf."

Other than his yearly forays at Augusta National for the Masters, Jones had not played a competitive round of golf since retiring in 1930. But he was still a marquee name in the sport and would be voted golf's greatest player for the first 50 years of the twentieth century. And given that there was no 36-hole cut, another departure from normal US Open rules, Jones would be around all weekend.

The USGA had its eyes on raising as much money as it could for USO, a charity that serves active-duty military, and the Naval Relief. One of the earliest proposals had invitations going out to Bing Crosby and Bob Hope to draw even larger crowds. Crosby was a decent golfer; Hope, not so much. Jimmy Demaret once said of Hope's game, "He has an excellent short game. Unfortunately, it's off the tee."

The *Chicago Tribune* also noted that new USGA President Blossom dispelled any possibility that the tournament winner would be seen as the 1942 US Open champion by the organization. And the CDGA said whoever won the tournament would also be declared the winner of the 1942 Chicago Open, which had been slotted for that weekend once the USGA canceled its Open at Interlachen.

So in the space of 18 days, the USGA had canceled the 1942 US Open, set in motion a replacement tournament, and chosen a site nowhere near Minneapolis. The USGA would not return to the Twin Cities for a US Open until 1970, but it would not be to Interlachen. By then, the folks at Interlachen had moved on. They still had the memory of 1930, the club's last US Open, and Bobby Jones's last one as well. Not a bad marker in the club's history book.

2

APRIL TO JUNE 1942

Augusta, Seaview, and East Lake

The Masters always has been a classically important competition, rivaling in its own unique mode the Open Championship of the United States. This year, by force of circumstance, it stands alone.

—1942 Augusta National Golf Club release

As the PGA Tour rolled along in the spring of 1942, the USGA was preparing to host the Hale America Tournament with all the pre-tournament steps particular to an official US Open. The organization conducted only one professional tournament in the early 1940s and had a very specific format for its official US Opens. Its format for the Hale America would be similar and different at the same time.

The USGA started by organizing the two rounds of qualifying for the Hale America. It exempted PGA Championship contests from the local, or first stage, of qualifying because the dates conflicted. It also exempted those who applied to participate in local qualifying in California, where only sectional qualifying was being conducted.

All entries were due by May 13.

The USGA made it clear that the $5 entry fee would go into a tournament fund, from which the organization would purchase US War Savings Bonds. At least $1,200 in war bonds, worth around $1,000, would be set aside for the Hale America champion with the USGA anticipating an overall purse of around

$6,000. (The war bonds matured in 10 years and were sold at a 75 percent discount.) The USGA would purchase any bonds left over and distribute the revenue to the two organizations that were designated as official beneficiaries—the Navy Relief Society and the USO.

The USGA also hoped to raise sufficient revenue from the second round of qualifying to pay the five top professionals. That money would come from admission fees.

Setting up the qualifying rounds was a truly national endeavor. Local qualifying, which consisted of 36 holes of stroke play, was scheduled for May 25 with the exception of two locales—Denver and Sheridan, Wyoming—where play was to be held the day before. Eighty golf courses in 37 states, the District of Columbia, and Canada were originally selected as sites for local qualifying. One of those 80 courses was Interlachen Country Club. Also on the list were regular US Open sites such as Oakmont Country Club outside Pittsburgh and Cherry Hills Country Club outside Denver. The actual number of sites was trimmed to 69.

The USGA designated the Atlanta Athletic Club, which would host the 1976 US Open, as the site for both local and sectional qualifying in Georgia. But by the time the first qualifying rounds were played in late May, the Georgia venue had shifted to East Lake Country Club, the Atlanta home course of Bobby Jones. And although Jones had been exempted from qualifying, he decided he would play in all five rounds, if for no other reason than to sharpen his game.

But before Jones would hit the links at East Lake, there was the matter of the 1942 Masters to which he needed to devote his attention. Jones not only was president of Augusta National Golf Club, which he founded and helped design, but also ran the tournament along with Clifford Roberts, the general chairman of the event.

If there had been any doubt about playing the 1942 tournament after the USGA canceled the US Open, it was put to rest in early February when Roberts sent a note to "Press and Radio" with a list of the players invited to participate in the 1942 Masters. It was clear then that Augusta was not only going to host the 1942 Masters, but considered it the premier medal play event of the year.

"While we may not have expected it originally," Roberts wrote, "we have created a tournament of such importance that we are bound to see it continue." It did indeed continue—until it was canceled in 1943. It didn't return until 1946.

Roberts's list of invitees numbered 84. The high number was due to invitations going out to previous Masters champions, previous US Open champions, previous PGA Championship winners, and any player who had won a US Amateur or a British Amateur championship. Additionally, the top 30 finishers in the 1941 Masters and US Open as well as all quarterfinalists from the 1941 US Amateur and PGA Championship were on the list.

Roberts said he expected an additional four invitations to be sent out, three to professionals and one to an amateur. However, Roberts noted, the field may be as low as 50, "as some of the older champions on our Invitation List no longer play competitive golf." Some would also be in the military.

The 1941 Masters had ended up with a field of 50, 3 of whom withdrew. The only times the Masters' field had exceeded 50 finishers since the tournament launched in 1934 was in the first two years and again in 1940. So a field of 50 was around the norm for that time.

Roberts also said revenues from the tournament would help to pay for a driving range and putting green at nearby Fort Gordon. Augusta National pledged to contribute enough funds to finance maintenance, equipment, and 1,000 golf balls. "It's our idea that soldiers cannot very often come to a golf course, but golf can come to them," he said.

Twenty-three amateurs were invited; only three showed up, and one of those was Jones himself. Of the twenty former US Open champions invited, only seven showed up. All previous Masters winners were in the field, including four players—Byron Nelson, defender Craig Wood, Gene Sarazen, and Ralph Guldahl—who also had won US Opens.

But even with the trimmed-down field, the big names and top money winners all teed up on April 9. Whatever the 1942 Masters lacked in terms of attendance, it more than made up for it with the talent on hand. You could purchase a ticket for $5.50, which entitled you to attend all four practice rounds and all four days of the tournament.

"The Masters always has been a classically important competition, rivaling in its own unique mode the Open Championship of the United States," noted the club in a release. "This year, by force of circumstance, it stands alone." The release then added that the 1942 Masters "must inevitably be the No. 1 golfing competition."

No one could argue that it didn't live up to its advance billing. Perhaps sensing that this would be the final Masters until the war ended, the cream rose to the top over the four days—and even that wasn't enough to produce a champion. In addition to a splendid field, for the first time the Masters experimented with ropes to contain the large galleries—or what the club always calls "the patrons." When the USGA finally got around to roping off galleries, it was during the 1954 US Open at Baltusrol, as Joe Dey remembered it. "We had special crews going up and down the line telling people that play would be stopped if they did not stay behind the ropes," Dey recalled. "We made it clear that we meant it. And it worked." Dey would later say that he got the idea from the Masters and that roping off galleries "revolutionized tournament golf, or at least the spectating of it."

Byron Nelson led for much of the 1942 tournament, but at the end of 72 holes, he and Ben Hogan were tied at 280. The two had played in a memorable Christmas caddy tournament at Glen Garden in Fort Worth 15 years earlier. They would do so again on Monday to determine the 1942 Masters champion.

While the ending of the Masters had an air of predictability about it—Hogan and Nelson were the tournament favorites—the first two rounds had not produced what could charitably be described as an epic leaderboard. Hogan was only 1 under par after rounds of 73 and 70 and trailed Nelson by eight shots. One of the real eyebrow-raisers was a first-round 72 turned in by Jones, his best first-round score since the Masters began in 1934.

First-round leaders Paul Runyan and two-time Masters winner Horton Smith were three shots closer. Jimmy Demaret, the 1940 champion, was also five behind Byron Nelson, who was being chased by Sam Byrd, a former New York Yankees outfielder who had turned to golf. Byrd was one shot back.

Among the early casualties was Lloyd Mangrum, author of the course-record 64 in 1940. He opened with a 74 and then took ill while playing his second round and withdrew. Denny Shute withdrew two days later after a third-round 81, meaning only 40 players completed all four rounds.

Hogan made his move on Moving Day, as Saturday is sometimes called on the PGA Tour. There was only one round under 70 on what was a windy day—and Hogan had it with a sterling 67. But it still left him three shots astern of Nelson, who matched par at 72. But there was no one between them as they teed off on Sunday. Hogan said his round on Saturday was the best "managing" he had ever done on a golf course.

Hogan would become famous for many things—unending practice sessions, laser-like concentration, almost flawless accuracy—but he also was one of the first, if not *the* first, to talk about course management, now a staple. As he put it later in life, "Once you have the ability to propel the golf ball, it all becomes about course management. If you don't have that, you have no chance."

Jack Burke Jr., the winner of the 1956 Masters, said, "I'll never forget what Hogan told me. He said, 'you think this is a game of stick and ball? It isn't. It's a game of adjustments, a game of constant change and adjustment. It's a game of stick, ball and field.'"

There was no television available in those days, and it was the rare tournament that lumped the leaders in the final group on the final day. Organizers liked to balance the big names, regardless of where they stood on the leaderboard. So Hogan played ahead of Nelson on the final day. He shot a 70 to finish at 280, 8 under par.

Nelson struggled to a 73 but nearly won the tournament on the 72nd hole with a 15-foot birdie putt. So the two Texans would reconnect the following afternoon for an 18-hole playoff.

Hogan had already lost twice in head-to-head professional competitions with Nelson. In the 1940 Texas Open, the two went an extra 18 holes and Nelson beat Hogan by a single shot. A year later, at the PGA Championship at Cherry Hills outside Denver, Nelson eliminated Hogan in the quarterfinals. Nelson would lose the final to Vic Ghezzi.

You might think Hogan was due to beat his old caddying buddy. Or even overdue. And Nelson seemed ready to finally crack after double-bogeying the first hole and quickly falling three shots behind after just four holes. But Nelson gained two shots on the par-3 sixth (a birdie to Hogan's bogey) and two more at the eighth (an eagle to Hogan's par) and led by one shot after nine holes.

Nelson increased his lead to three strokes through 13 holes and still led by two as the two players stood on the 18th tee. Nelson played it safe, knowing he likely could win with a bogey, as 18 had been the sixth most difficult of the tournament, yielding only 10 birdies. He made a bogey. Hogan made a par. Nelson thus had his second Masters, having also won in 1937. Hogan was runner-up, a bridesmaid, and it would be some time before he officially put an end to that unflattering moniker in major tournaments.

That also was the last time those two ever went head-to-head in a tournament. Nelson never lost to Hogan in a playoff or match-play event, and he never lost when he went head-to-head with Sam Snead.

But in 1946, Nelson bought a ranch in Texas and basically retired at the age of 34. He would occasionally surface for big tournaments, but he had had his run in 1945, winning 18 times, including 11 in a row. Then again, he didn't do too terribly in 1946, winning 5 times. He won once more, in 1951, at the Bing Crosby Pro-Am. It was the 52nd win of his illustrious, Hall of Fame career.

Jones, meanwhile, stumbled after his encouraging opening round and finished 24 shots off the winning score. He was never serious about contending or winning the Masters. But as he walked off the course after a final-round 78, he was asked about his plans to play in the Hale America in two months.

"I think I could get back in shape but I'm a little too busy now to get in enough golf to really get set," he said. "I'd need a lot of practice and maybe a swing on the winter tour."

The success of the Masters provided a much-needed boost to war-weary America, which was getting bombarded by bad news from the Pacific Theater on an almost daily basis. In February 1942, the British stronghold of Singapore, the "Gibraltar of the East," had surrendered to the Japanese. US and Filipino forces were pinned down at the end of the Bataan Peninsula in the Philippines. It was a succession of losses as bad as—or even worse than—any other time in the country's history.

The day the Masters started, the American and Filipino holdouts at Bataan surrendered to the Japanese and the following day, the infamous Bataan Death March began. More than 75,000 Allied prisoners of war, including 12,000 Americans, were forced to walk 60 miles in scorching heat without food or water. As many as 5,000 Americans died.

On April 18, 16 B-25 bombers from the aircraft carrier *Hornet* led by Lt. Col. James Doolittle bombed Tokyo to give the Americans a temporary morale boost. But by the end of the month the Japanese, having taken Singapore, moved into Burma. The Doolittle raid caused negligible damage in Japan, but represented a propaganda boost for the United States. It also may have prompted the Japanese to move up their plan to attack Midway Island, a 2.4 square mile atoll in the Pacific. It was a decision that would change the course of the war in the Pacific Theater.

Back in the United States, the next big tournament was the PGA Championship in late May. But May was also the month for all Hale America National Open entries to be filed—and early signs were discouraging. At the end of April, USGA President George Blossom said the organization would lose 60 percent of its income due to its decision to cancel the US Open. "On top of that," he added, "we will have to dip into our reserve fund to the extent of $20,000 or $25,000 to carry on our war programs."

In early May, six weeks before the Hale America was scheduled to be contested, PGA President Ed Dudley noted the tournament had received only 200 entries, about one-fifth the total for a normal US Open. And half of those, Dudley said, were from amateurs. Due to what he saw as a lack of interest, Dudley suggested that the tournament might have to be canceled.

Tournament chairman Francis Ouimet noted, "Of course we have been concerned with the number of entries. But as a rule, half the total entries do not reach us until the last two days before closing time. Such is human nature."

The call went out from Dudley to all PGA pros who had yet to enter. The USGA appealed to all eligible amateurs to enter as well. "This is a great cause," Ouimet said. "We are confident that the golfers of the nation will be found solidly behind it when the noses are finally counted on May 13."

The floodgates would soon open when the USGA announced that Hogan, Jones (who had committed in January but didn't formally enter at that time), Nelson, and Wood all had entered. Additional entries had already been received from Sarazen, Mangrum, Horton Smith, and other top players. A May 8 dispatch from the Associated Press in New York reported that "the Hale America National Open will not only positively be held, but it promises to be a glowing success."

On May 12, the USGA received 327 entries, raising the total number to nearly 800. Sensing a trend, the organization extended the deadline for an additional two days and what ensued was a veritable tsunami of applications. The USGA announced it had received a record 1,540 entries, shattering the previous high for a US Open of 1,402 set in 1937 at the Detroit Golf Club. Any fears the USGA, the PGA, or the CDGA might have had about support for the tournament were erased by the late flood of entries. The organizers had themselves a legitimate tournament, even if the USGA wasn't going to call it a legitimate US Open.

The record number of entries had to be whittled down to a manageable 100 or so, and that is what the local and sectional qualifying tournaments are meant to accomplish. Bobby Jones nonetheless dutifully reported to East Lake Country Club to try to shake off the accumulated rust from 12 years of basic inactivity.

Jones was still a huge name and attraction on the links. It hadn't been that long since he dominated golf in the 1920s. He was as dashing and handsome as he was talented, and truly represented the gentleman that the sport aspired to represent. He had an undergraduate degree from Georgia Tech and advanced degrees from both Harvard and Emory, which separated him from pretty much everyone else on the circuit. He was a practicing attorney in Atlanta.

Yes, Jones had been a hothead early in his career—Philadelphia-area sportswriters rebuked him for his behavior in the 1916 US Amateur at Merion—but he had calmed down to become the consummate sportsman as he accumulated title after title.

How dominant was he? He played in 31 major tournaments—for Jones, that meant the US and British Opens and the US and British Amateurs—and won 13. He finished in the top 10 in all but 4 of them. In addition to his 13 major titles, he also finished second in the US Open four times, losing two playoffs, and lost twice in the finals of the US Amateur.

Writers chronicled his every shot with one in particular, the *Atlanta Journal's* O. B. Keeler, emerging as Jones's Bosworth. Hollywood sought out Jones, and he accommodated them by appearing in some instructional films after his

Grand Slam season of 1930. He also authored several books and was the subject of many others.

Getting Bobby Jones to play in the Hale America was a huge step for the fledgling tournament. His name brought instant credibility to any golf tournament, and he was still active in the sport through his stewardship of Augusta National and the Masters. And he could still play. In his final practice round for the 1942 Masters, Jones shot a 31 on the back nine.

Jones was one of 38 players competing for 12 slots at East Lake. He had not played competitive, tournament, stroke-play golf at East Lake since 1927, when he won the Southern Open there by a stunning eight shots over a professional field that included Gene Sarazen, Johnny Farrell, Joe Turnesa, Craig Wood, and Tommy Armour. The qualifying was over two days, and Jones finished second overall, shooting even par over 36 holes.

While that was going on, the 25th PGA Championship was getting under way with a reduced field, much like the Masters. The tournament was being held at what was then an ultra-exclusive club in New Jersey, Seaview Country Club in Atlantic City.

Seaview was founded by Charles Geist, a wealthy industrialist. He owned the Philadelphia Suburban Water Company, along with franchises for several other utilities. He had grown tired of the crowds at the Atlantic City Country Club, so he built Seaview a few miles up the road.

According to Leo Fraser, the former owner of Atlantic City Country Club and a former president of the PGA, "There was nothing else like Seaview in the rest of the country." For a mere $100 initiation fee, Seaview members could swim in an indoor pool, eat meals prepared by French chefs, and be transported by a chauffeur-driven Rolls Royce or Pierce-Arrow. In addition to the aforementioned amenities, Seaview also had horses, squash courts, and a trap-shooting range. The food was excellent. "There was no dining room in Philadelphia or New York that could excel Seaview's," Fraser wrote.

The club also had a "beautifully manicured and great golf course." And that is where the top pros showed up at the end of May for the week-long grind of the PGA Championship. The qualifying field was reduced from 64 to 32, and all matches were 36 holes.

All the big names easily qualified after two rounds of stroke play. Jimmy Demaret ousted defending champ Vic Ghezzi in the first round. Ghezzi, on leave from the Army, "was sent back to the bugler," wrote the *New York Times*'s William Richardson.

Ben Hogan lost in the quarterfinals to Jim Turnesa while Demaret, Nelson, and Snead all advanced to the semifinals. There, Snead eliminated Demaret while Turnesa denied Nelson a fourth straight trip to the final round. Snead then defeated Turnesa 2 and 1 for the first of his seven major championships.

Jim Turnesa, who had been stationed at Fort Dix in New Jersey, was allowed to participate in the Hale America. Tournament organizers also requested that Sam Snead be allowed to participate and were under the impression the US Navy would grant him leave. But Snead never made it to Ridgemoor. He went into the Navy as a second-class seaman and was the only big name missing from the event.

The local qualifying for the Hale America generally went smoothly, with one notable exception. Seven golfers, six from the greater Chicago area, who had registered for the tournament showed up for their qualifier at Olympia Fields and were told that they could not use the club's facilities. The men were African American.

Most private country clubs were segregated well into the 1990s. Olympia Fields did not admit its first African American member until 1992, a half-century after the Hale America qualifier. Augusta National did not admit its first African American member until 1990. So when the Olympia Fields seven showed up to play after they had paid their entry fee and received a confirmation, they were told that their applications had been withdrawn.

This was a two-day qualifying event for a national tournament to raise money for the war effort. The seven weren't applying to be Olympia Fields members. The Hale America organizers had urged as many people as possible to enter. It didn't specify race.

African Americans had long been absent from the PGA Tour; the tour had a "Caucasian Only" policy from 1934 until 1961. And in 1961, Charlie Sifford became the first African American tour regular. The Masters did not invite an African American golfer until 1975, when Lee Elder joined the field after winning the Monsanto Open the year before. Elder received death threats and decided to rent two houses and move between them while he was in Augusta. He ended up missing the cut.

But the Olympia Fields seven could point back nearly a half-century to what now is regarded as the first instance of an African American in the US Open. It's complicated.

In 1896 a 17-year-old caddie named John Shippen, whose father was an African American Presbyterian minister and whose mother was Shinnecock Indian, played in the second US Open at Shinnecock Hills. But he made sure he registered as Indian.

Still, some of the professionals considered Shippen to be black and threatened a boycott. But the USGA intervened and did the right thing. According to a history of Shinnecock Hills, the president of the USGA, Theodore Haver-mayer, said he would hold the US Open with just Shippen and another caddy, also Indian, if the pros followed up with the boycott. The players backed down. Shippen ended up tied for sixth and played in five more US Opens.

In 1942, despite the fact that the Hale America was a fundraiser and that the setting was a local qualifier, the USGA did not intervene in the case of the Olympia Fields seven. A Chicago alderman, Benjamin Grant, called attention to the situation and fired off a telegram to the USGA, calling the Olympia Fields decision "undemocratic and unpatriotic." The players, Grant pointed out succinctly, "were denied the right to participate because of their color. The action definitely does not tend to bolster the morale of the colored citizen and is not conducive to the democratic way of life for which all Americans are now fighting."

USGA President George Blossom washed the organization's hands of the whole matter, saying, "The decision to keep Negro competitors out of the quali-fying round was made by officials at Olympia Fields Country Club. The USGA merely respected the rights of a member club."

According to the *Chicago Tribune*, the seven African Americans were identi-fied as Clyde Martin from Detroit, Andrew Hammond from Chicago Heights, and five more from Chicago: Pat Ball, Horace McDougall, Alvin James, Willie Haze, and Edward Jennings.

Just before the start of the sectional qualifying rounds, which were to be staged over two days at the end of the first week of June, word came down that the United States had crippled the Imperial Japanese Navy at the Battle of Mid-way. In one brief but devastating stretch, the United States reversed the course of the war in the Pacific.

Some naval historians see Midway as the second part of a two-part naval engagement in the Pacific. Part 1 was the Battle of the Coral Sea, a four-day air-sea battle in the south Pacific. The two battles were roughly a month apart. At the Coral Sea, both sides suffered losses; the United States lost the aircraft carrier *Lexington.* The carrier *Yorktown* was wounded and limped back to Pearl Harbor for repairs. The Japanese lost some light cruisers, but the main impact was that Japan had to call off a planned invasion of Port Moresby, New Guinea.

At both the Coral Sea and Midway, the United States had a significant advan-tage unbeknownst to the enemy—its codebreakers had advance warning of the Japanese plans. In each battle, the Japanese moved as if they had the element of surprise, as was the case at Pearl Harbor. In each case, they ended up walking into a trap. The Japanese managed to survive the Coral Sea. Midway, however, would be a vastly different story.

Midway, consisting of two atolls lying midway between the United States and the Far East, was home to a US Navy air facility. The Japanese planned to bomb the airstrips and then launch an amphibious invasion. The idea was to extend the Japanese defensive perimeter in the Pacific as well as remove a small, but important, airstrip for the United States. The Japanese also hoped to sink American aircraft carriers, which they had failed to do at Pearl Harbor because the ships had left the base.

So Japan planned a two-pronged approach. But the United States knew of the attack and hid its carriers. It launched wave after wave of torpedo planes against the Japanese strike force, which included four aircraft carriers. But the torpedo planes did no damage.

Then, as the Japanese were preparing their planes to search and destroy the American carriers, a wave of US dive bombers swooped in, having been launched from the aircraft carriers *Enterprise*, *Hornet*, and *Yorktown*. They had been undetected (the Japanese carriers had no radar) and, in less than 30 minutes, unleashed a barrage that critically damaged three of the four Japanese carriers. The fourth carrier was spotted and similarly damaged later in the day. The Japanese also lost a cruiser, and three other ships in the strike force were damaged.

There was no way for the Japanese to recover from such a loss. The Imperial Navy had been crippled beyond repair. The United States lost the *Yorktown*, which had been attacked on three different occasions during the battle, but no other carrier.

The Midway victory was the first undeniably bit of good news out of the Pacific Theater for the United States. Within two months, the United States launched its first amphibious assault in the theater as Marines invaded Guadalcanal and Tulagi in the Solomon Islands. That campaign began nearly three years of island hopping in the Pacific, culminating in June 1945 with the end of Japanese resistance on the island of Okinawa. Six weeks later, the first atomic bomb was dropped on Hiroshima.

The sectional qualifying for the Hale America took place in the first week of June, with three rounds over two days. Bobby Jones remained at East Lake, which conducted the second round as well, staging 18 holes on June 6 and 36 holes on June 7. Jones blistered his home course with rounds of 67, 71, and 67, prompting the Associated Press to note that his swing was "as smooth as Dixie molasses."

O. B. Keeler, writing in the *Atlanta Journal*, concurred. "He looked like the Jones boy of a dozen years ago," he wrote. "Mr. Jones is taking the competition as seriously as if he was playing for a place in the sun, instead of being a specially invited entrant."

Sportswriter Grantland Rice asked Jones about the 11-under total at East Lake and how it might affect his performance at the Hale America. "Don't hold that over my head. Chicago is a long way from Atlanta," Jones told Rice. "I've been playing better, but you know what these big tournaments are to an old fellow who has been so long away from the wars."

Jones's 205 total was not only good enough to lead the East Lake qualifiers by six shots, but it was also good enough to lead every other score in all the sectional qualifying rounds from around the country. While Jones's play may have been the top news event of the sectional qualifiers, it wasn't the most unusual. An amateur golfer named Charles (Babe) Lind played in the Denver sectional and shot a 214 total, 1 over par. In between the morning and afternoon rounds, however, Lind had been watching a billiards match when a ball careened off the table and knocked him unconscious for 15 minutes. He was quickly revived and not only qualified for the Hale America, but led the Denver sectional with his 214 total.

But on that particular weekend, all the golf world was marveling at the achievements of 40-year-old Bobby Jones. Among those whose scores did not match Jones's were regular touring pros Ky Laffoon, Sammy Byrd, Dick Metz, Abe Espinoza, Jim Ferrier, 1931 US Open champion Billy Burke, and Mike Turnesa, who would chase Hogan to the finish line at the Hale America. Two other Turnesa brothers—there were seven golfing brothers in the family—would also be in the Hale America field.

Other pros not involved in the qualifying followed the USGA's advice and played in war relief exhibitions prior to the start of the Hale America. Ben Hogan and Jimmy Demaret participated in a 36-hole fundraising event at the Charles River Country Club outside Boston while Craig Wood and Corporal Vic Ghezzi played in an exhibition in Bloomfield, New Jersey, along with Bob Hope and Babe Ruth.

Before leaving for Chicago, Jones reconfirmed a date with Uncle Sam to report to Mitchel Field on Long Island the day after the tournament ended to begin a stint in the Army Air Corps. He also agreed to play an exhibition with Bob Hope the day before the start of the Hale America. It promised to be an eventful week at Ridgemoor with all the big names participating and with other sideshows such as a long-drive contest, a trick-shot performance, and a golf clinic. The Chicago club had raised its profile significantly by agreeing to host the event. Now it would be front and center, hosting what *Chicago Tribune*'s Charles Bartlett called "the most important week in Chicago golf history."

II

FOUR DAYS

3

HALE AMERICA
ROUND 1, JUNE 18, 1942

Ridgemoor and Mr. Icicle

I don't know a single pro on the circuit who is nursing an ulcer.

—Lloyd Mangrum

As Ridgemoor Country Club was getting ready to host the biggest event in its 37-year history, an Associated Press report marveled at the preparations for the Hale America Tournament. "Ridgemoor has been lengthened and generally toughened up with bottleneck fairways and heavy thickets of trees," the report read. "Few observers believe the course record of 65 will be bettered or even approached."

The first part may have been correct. The second part was wildly off base, and therefore the USGA always insisted that the Hale America could not have been an "official" US Open because Ridgemoor had not offered a sufficient challenge for a typical US Open. But this was an after-the-fact assessment.

Ridgemoor had never hosted a USGA event before 1942, and it has never hosted one since. But it did host a USGA-sponsored event in 1942 that would conclude on Father's Day, which has generally been the case for the US Open since it went to four days in 1965. Hosting a single US Open is not common; the USGA has a list of about a dozen "usual suspects," courses it inevitably selects to host its prime championship. But since Ridgemoor moved in to fill the 1942 slot, there have been more than a half-dozen courses that hosted only one US Open.

So Ridgemoor wasn't an outlier in that regard. It just wasn't Medinah, Olympia Fields, or any of the other blue-blood courses in greater Chicago. The Ridgemoor membership wouldn't have it any other way.

Founded in 1905 as Irving Golf Club, the original 9-hole layout was expanded to 18 in 1909. At that point, the new real estate had expanded outside of the Irving Park section of Chicago. So another name was needed. Thanks to a ridge running through the course, the name Ridgemoor was adopted. The club was located in northwest Chicago, a short drive from what today is O'Hare International Airport. It raised its first pennant in the fall of 1909 and staged a 36-hole match with all four players dressed in kilts. Four years later, members pooled together $82,500 to purchase the land from the estate owner. His farmhouse was later developed into a clubhouse.

Ridgemoor liked to say that it was "a club without airs" due to its economically diverse membership. For every titan of industry or corporate lawyer, there was a policeman or fireman who was a member. Pulitzer Prize–winning columnist Mike Royko was a member. One member said Royko loved to hang around good golfers. "But he stunk," the member joked.

Other famous members included longtime Chicago broadcaster Jack Brickhouse and the founder/owner of the Chicago Bears, George Halas. During the 1932 Democratic National Convention in downtown Chicago, party bosses wanted a venue away from the convention site to work their smoke-filled-room magic. Ridgemoor was the selected site. From there, the operatives engineered the nominations of Franklin D. Roosevelt and James Nance Garner.

The signature logo of Ridgemoor is the so-called Indian Marking Tree. It was rooted in a special way so as to grow in a direction that would point to Lake Michigan along what was then called the Indian Trail. The tree greets visitors entering the fenced-in property.

Ridgemoor had one brief burst of acclaim in 1928, when it hosted the second of five exhibitions between Walter Hagen and Johnny Farrell. If Bobby Jones was the number 1 golf celebrity of the 1920s, the flamboyant Hagen was 1A. He was an international golf celebrity, winning five British Opens during a time when few American pros ventured across the pond to play in the tournament. He won four PGA championships and two US Opens, the first in 1914 at the age of 21.

Hagen and Jones staged a number of dramatic exhibition matches in the 1920s, expertly retold by Stephen Lowe in his book *Sir Walter and Mr. Jones*. The 36-hole, match-play event between Hagen and Farrell was scheduled for September 1; there would be 18 holes in the morning and 18 in the afternoon. Players were accustomed to such inconveniences in those days.

Farrell was an accomplished pro—he won six consecutive tournaments at one stretch in 1927–1928, and played on three Ryder Cup teams. But he had nowhere near the star power of the charismatic Hagen. What he did have was something only one other golfer could claim—a playoff victory over Bobby Jones in a US Open. That year, Jones was riding high per usual, winning a fourth US Amateur and captaining the American Walker Cup (the amateur version of the Ryder Cup) team to a blowout win at the Chicago Golf Club. At the US Open at Olympia Fields, Jones and Farrell tied at 294, 10 over par. The 36-hole playoff went to Farrell by a single shot.

Farrell would finish second in both the PGA Championship and the British Open the following year, but would never win another major. He did accumulate 22 PGA Tour victories. The only other player to defeat Jones in a US Open playoff was Scotsman Willie Macfarlane in 1925 at Worcester Country Club in Massachusetts.

Hagen outlasted Farrell 5 and 3 in the match. He also won the five-match exhibition series with Farrell, 3–2.

The man known as "The Haig" planned a return visit to Ridgemoor in 1942. Like Jones, he would come out of semiretirement to lend his cachet and celebrity to a worthy cause. The first-round pairing sheet had Hagen in a threesome with Bing Crosby and 58-year-old Jock Hutchinson, who had been invited to participate as the "defending champion" of sorts, having won the last canceled US Open substitute due to World War I at the Whitemarsh Valley Country Club outside Philadelphia in 1917.

Crosby never made it, and his name was no longer needed for publicity. The event itself provided plenty of anticipation and excitement. As for Hagen, he would turn 50 in December 1942 and was no longer a factor. But he was a dashing presence nonetheless, a certifiable "name," and the sport of professional golf owed him a great deal for elevating its stature at a time when amateurs, like Jones, were considered to be more legitimate golfers. (The same was true in England.)

Hagen had long developed and nurtured a custom of arriving at a tournament in a flashy car and going directly from the vehicle to the first tee. That was all part of his shtick. It had caused him to be disqualified from the 1940 US Open when he missed his tee time for the third round. Hagen was not the only one disqualified in that tournament. Ed (Porky) Oliver was disqualified for teeing off too early on the final day. His final tally of 287 tied him for first place with Lawson Little and Gene Sarazen. Oliver was inconsolable after his round, coming to tears as he described how he was given the go-ahead by the starter and that the group ahead of his had already teed off. "My heart is broken," he said. "Tying for the Open and getting a chance to win it in a playoff may come just once in a lifetime."

Little and Sarazen pleaded with the USGA to restore Oliver's score and let him participate in the playoff. The USGA stood firm. Rules are rules. Little won the playoff. And Oliver never won a major. He was eviscerated by Ben Hogan in the finals of the 1946 PGA Championship and finished second to Hogan in the 1953 Masters, five shots off the lead.

As for the swashbuckling Hagen, perhaps it was fitting that the 1940 US Open would be his last, given the way he was disqualified. He nonetheless was determined to make it to the Hale America two years later, but poor travel conditions delayed him and he was one of 11 no-shows when the first round began. Hagen did finally arrive at the site on Saturday to watch the final rounds.

The day before the tournament started, Jones and Bob Hope were the big attractions in an exhibition at Ridgemoor. The comedian was late to arrive, however, and the foursome did not begin play until after 4:00 p.m. Jones was paired with Gene Sarazen. The 40-somethings took on Hope and Ed Dudley, the PGA president who also happened to be an accomplished professional golfer. Bing Crosby was supposed to be in the group, but his travel arrangements fell through.

The match went 13 holes and ended all square when Jones won the final hole with a birdie. An estimated 1,500 followed the foursome around the course, with Hope interjecting wisecracks in between swings. Earlier that day, many of the golfers showed up for a lunch at the LaSalle Hotel in downtown Chicago hosted by the city's Chamber of Commerce.

The first pairing of the first round was scheduled to tee off at 9:30 a.m. on Thursday, June 18. Among the interesting names in the field was Harvey Penick, a professional out of Austin, Texas. At that stage of his career, Penick was into the second decade of what would be a 33-year stint as the head golf coach at the University of Texas. In those 33 years, the Longhorns won 21 conference titles. He coached Hall of Famers Ben Crenshaw, Tom Kite, Mickey Wright, Betsy Rawls, and Kathy Whitworth.

But Penick is perhaps better known as the coauthor of *The Little Red Book*, which contains anecdotes and teaching insights. It became the highest-selling golf book ever published. Crenshaw remained an ardent student and close friend and served as a pallbearer at Penick's funeral in April 1995. The following day, Crenshaw began the first round of the Masters and ended up winning the tournament, breaking down in tears as he holed his last putt. Crenshaw was 43, the second oldest Masters champion at the time. Jack Nicklaus was 46 when he won in 1986. Tiger Woods was 43 when he won his fifth Masters in 2019.

Nearly 90 minutes after the Hale America opening shots were fired, a marquee threesome took to the first tee. There was Jimmy Demaret, the 1940 Masters champion. There was Billy Burke, the 1931 US Open champion who, like Jones and Gene Sarazen, would turn 40 in 1942. The third member of the group was the man sometimes called Mr. Icicle, for he could be cool, calculating, sometimes standoffish, and was almost always smoking a cigarette. He also could play a bit. He was Lloyd Mangrum, and he was destined for big things.

In June 1956, the year Lloyd Mangrum won his fourth Los Angeles Open and the 36th and final PGA tournament victory of his career, he wrote a first-person account of his thoughts on professional golf for the *Saturday Evening Post.* By that time he was well worth reading. He had established himself as one of the great players of his time. One of those 36 victories had been the 1946 US Open. He was a member of four Ryder Cup teams. He was a two-time Vardon Trophy winner for the lowest scoring average, led the tour in earnings in 1951, and held or shared the Masters' scoring record for one round (64) for 46 years.

But Mangrum was never about titles, and individual accolades meant nothing to him. And in the *Post* piece, he laid bare his opinion on the pro game: "Pro golf simply isn't that tough." He criticized the USGA for publicizing its signature event, the US Open, as "a figment of the public's imagination. The USGA itself makes no claim to the title, National Open. Strictly speaking, there just is no such a tournament." (He would later admit to having many arguments with the USGA— and winning none of them.)

Mangrum went on to say that no title, "not even the National Open, can be this important in the life of a golf pro. Pro golf is a week-to-week proposition. As such, it has no more pressure attached to it than any other business. As a matter of fact, it probably has less. I don't know a single pro on the circuit who is nursing an ulcer."

This was vintage Mangrum. To him, golf was not a game or even a vocation. It was a job. It required work. And, in Mangrum's thinking, a professional golfer's success was measured not by victories and achievements, but by dollars and cents. He was in the business to make money. He never suggested otherwise. He estimated he traveled 40,000 miles a year by car and another 40,000 by plane, and deliberately charged exorbitant rates for lessons so that members at the club that sponsored him would leave him alone to concentrate on tournament golf.

Nowhere is this unending pursuit of the mighty dollar better exemplified than in the pages of *My Greatest Day in Golf*. Written in 1950, author Darsie L. Darsie asked 51 of the top players in the game, male and female, professional and amateur, to describe their greatest individual day. Mangrum did not pick the 1946 US Open championship or any of the four Los Angeles Opens he won, three of them at Riviera Country Club. He did not pick his first PGA victory or any of his Ryder Cup matches. He picked a day in August 1948 when he won what was called the All American Tournament, staged at Tam O'Shanter in Chicago, a club he represented at the time. "It is the richest event in golf and since we are in golf to make money, it always draws the top players in the world," he said.

To call Tam O'Shanter a country club may be a bit of an understatement. In 1955, *Sports Illustrated,* then just a year old, sent a writer to Tam O'Shanter, and the story revealed the club looked more like it belonged on the Las Vegas strip. Inside its opulent clubhouse one could play Keno or roulette. One could imbibe at more than a dozen bars.

In 1948, the All American Tournament was actually two events spread over several days. There was the 72-hole All American Open. And there was the 36-hole World Championship of Golf. The latter was limited to 12 players and a winner-take-all paycheck of $10,000.

Mangrum then went on to document how he outlasted Bobby Locke and secured the winner's check of $5,000 in the 72-hole event. But that was only the beginning. Mangrum was among the lucky dozen to play in the World Championship of Golf the following day. He rallied from six strokes back after 18 holes, shooting a 63 over the final 18 holes to tie two others, Sam Snead and Dutch Harrison. Mangrum then won the playoff for the $10,000 and another $2,500 for setting the course record with his 63. Finally, he received a $5,000 bonus from tournament promoter (and Tam O'Shanter owner) George May for being the top money winner for the first six months of 1948. May had hired Mangrum to be the Tam's head pro after Mangrum won the 1946 US Open.

So Mangrum collected an astonishing $22,500 for his week's work. To give some idea of just how astonishing, the leading money winner in 1947, Jimmy Demaret, officially earned almost $28,000 for the entire year. "In professional golf, where the money won tells the story, a win like that means a lot," said Mangrum.

Three years later, Mangrum was leading the St. Paul Open heading into the final round when he was informed by police that he was the subject of death threats. The threat makers were bookies who wanted him to tank the final round. The police wanted him to withdraw. He would neither tank nor withdraw, growling, "What do you think I'm playing for, tin cups?" Police followed him over the final round and Mangrum won the tournament, pocketed the check, and was none the worse for wear.

This in no way suggests that Mangrum was an outlier in his money *uber alles* approach. Ben Hogan came out of wrenching poverty and lived for a while on oranges. Hogan's father committed suicide when Ben was nine years old. (Mangrum's father deserted the family when Mangrum was eight.) Hogan appreciated the dollar as much as anyone.

But few, if any, were so nakedly honest about why they played the game. For Mangrum, golf was a Machiavellian pursuit. He never saw it any other way. He spent a great deal of the 1956 *Saturday Evening Post* article debunking the notion that a US Open victory was worth as much as $50,000, calling it "a lot of blue sky." And as an aside, he added that if they named the richest tournament the "Hot Dog Championship, it would be the one I'd most like to win."

Wrote Darsie, "To Mangrum, the playing of championship golf is a means of livelihood, a source of income, a profession—and he measures his success not by his low scoring and not by the titles he holds, but by the cash he is able to put in the bank by virtue of his fine play."

If Lloyd Mangrum could have made similar money singing in the opera or repairing water mains, he likely would have striven with a similar bent and determination. But he fell into golf at an early age and determined as a teenager that it would be his professional livelihood.

Mangrum was born in Trenton, Texas, on August 1, 1914, the same day Germany declared war on Russia and launched its invasion of Belgium and France, setting off Word War I. According to a *Golf World* profile, Mangrum grew up in a large family led by an itinerant father who eventually abandoned his brood and headed for California. Two of Mangrum's siblings died in infancy. The other children were left to fend for themselves. Lloyd was the youngest of three brothers.

Mangrum's oldest brother, Ray, turned to golf and was so proficient that he landed a job as a club professional at Cliff-Dale in Dallas. Ray had given Lloyd a 2-iron as a 12th birthday present, and soon the younger Mangrum started caddying at the Dallas club. But both Mangrums soon moved to Los Angeles, which is where Lloyd spent most of his life when he wasn't spanning the globe.

Lloyd Mangrum continued to caddy at Sunset Fields in Los Angeles (which has been replaced by a shopping center) and attended junior high school. He never made it out of high school—by design. Instead, he continued to zero in on golf, caddying and hustling on the side. He also did the odd jobs (driving taxis, parking cars) as Hogan did to make the extra dollar. This is where Mangrum developed the instinct of a survivor, which served him well throughout the years. He hustled at *everything*—because he had no other choice. It not only honed his survivor skills but also developed his intense competitive streak, a streak that was not limited to the golf course. He was as much a presence at the card table as he was on the first tee, and one of the nicknames he earned—Riverboat—was because of his penchant for gambling. It wasn't social. It was business. Money was at stake.

Fellow Texan Jack Burke Jr. said Mangrum was one of the few whom he admired and tried to emulate. "I modeled myself after (Clayton) Heafner and Mangrum and those kinds of guys," said Burke. "They were fierce competitors, bet their own money. They were gamblers and gamblers are the most perceptive people. . . . All these guys were hustlers. I knew that's where I was going to learn. I'd sit and watch them gamble at cards, watch them when the money was up."

Ray Mangrum had a similar affinity for the gambling life, and it detoured his golf career. While he did finish tied for fourth in the 1935 US Open and won four tournaments, "he spent most of his life in the hunt for full houses and royal flushes—among other things," according to the *Golf World* piece.

Lloyd hustled through his teenage years and then, at the age of 20, made a critical, life-altering decision. He married Eleta Hurst, who not only was 10 years older than Mangrum, but had three daughters, one of whom wasn't that much younger than Mangrum. (Hurst's first name is almost always spelled Eleta or Elita in various magazine and newspaper articles. But Mangrum's 1949 book, *Golf: A New Approach*, is dedicated to "my wife, Aleta, who has made my golfing career possible by her willingness to sacrifice the pleasures of home life in favor of a steady diet of indigestible food in strange restaurants, boardlike beds in unique hotels, and laundering facilities in bathroom wash basins." But that is the only time in the many stories about Mangrum—or, in this case, something written by Mangrum—that her name is spelled with an A.)

Eleta Hurst ran a beauty salon in Los Angeles, which instantly provided a source of income to the struggling Mangrum. It also provided a roof over his head. The two would have no children, but they had each other and remained married until Mangrum died in 1973.

Eleta was a constant presence on the tour in the 1940s and 1950s. At the end of her husband's golf career, Eleta had a memorable chat with the wife of an up-and-coming pro named Jack Nicklaus.

It was 1962. Mangrum was 47 and had not won a tournament in six years, but managed to finish tied for 33rd at the Masters that year. He was likely there due to a special invitation because of his relationship with Masters founder Bobby Jones and the fact that he still held the course record at the time. He was a yearly participant in the Masters, an event he loved, in the late 1950s and early 1960s.

Barbara Nicklaus, by then a first-time mother, was "bemoaning the fact that I missed my baby and this and that and the other thing." Sitting nearby, on the patio knitting, was Eleta Mangrum. As Barbara recalled, "She put her knitting down and had her finger in my face and she said, 'Listen little girl. You had Jack long before you had that baby and you hope to have Jack a long time after that baby's gone. Now you grow up and be a wife.'" Barbara Nicklaus said she was "taken aback" by the verbal upbraiding, but when the two saw each other 10 years later, she thanked Eleta. "You'll never know what you did for my marriage," she told her.

Eleta could be just as sharp and confrontational as her husband, who was known as Mr. Icicle because of his icy demeanor. While he played, Mangrum never connected with spectators or even those with whom he was paired. He had no use for the reporters who covered the events. "We've seen him crack about a dozen smiles in that many years," *Sport* magazine wrote in 1952.

But while Hogan's fierce inner drive and introversion was chalked up to his concentration and determination, Mangrum's dour mood was often seen as abrasive or even hostile. When Hogan won a tournament, he would crack a smile and talk to reporters. Mangrum always looked like he had just been told that his dog had died. His stepdaughter once remarked that she had no idea how Mangrum had fared in a particular event by the look on his face.

But that was his personality. Prickly? Aloof? Abrupt? Direct? All the above. But, as Darsie wrote, "Mangrum is a money player and when the chips are down, he is one of the greatest money players the game of golf has ever known."

It wasn't always that way. Thanks to the newfound stability at home, Mangrum set out to turn himself into a professional golfer in the mid-1930s. The early returns were not promising. He entered the 1936 Southern California Open and finished sixth, winning $45 (which quickly was reduced to $23 after he paid his entry and caddie fees). He tried the pro tour in 1937 but soon found his way back to Los Angeles with little left but his pride. No one, except perhaps Mangrum himself, could have envisioned that he would set the Masters scoring record in three years.

Nothing came easy for Mangrum. As the great *Los Angeles Times* columnist Jim Murray wrote in 1973, "Life always seemed to deal Lloyd Mangrum a lot of unplayable lies. He always had a blind shot to the green."

Thanks to his brother Ray's connections, Mangrum was able to caddy at some PGA Tour events, and he made sure he looped for the "name" players. He studied the players as much as he caddied, eventually developing his own game, which was an amalgam of several pros at the time. He had his own ideas about the game, especially putting, but he copied the games of several known pros and adapted their styles to form his own.

He modeled his swing after the smoothest one in golf, that belonging to Sam Snead. He copied the putting stroke of Horton Smith and the short irons of Johnny Revolta. George Fazio, who was in a three-way playoff with Mangrum and Hogan in the memorable 1950 US Open at Merion, recalled a time when an unfortunate reporter in Birmingham, Alabama, approached Mangrum on the putting green to ask him about his swing and his approach to golf. "Monkey see, monkey do," Mangrum replied. Pressed by the reporter to elaborate, Mangrum said, "That's it. That's how you learn to play golf." And Mangrum returned to practice his putting.

In 1937, Mangrum played in the Pennsylvania Open at Merion, passing himself off as a native. (Ray Mangrum had landed a summer job as a pro in a club near Pittsburgh.) He finished fifth. He qualified for the US Open that year but missed the cut and came home broke at the end of the season. He won the Pennsylvania Open the following year—his first victory as a pro—at Pittsburgh's Field Club. His brother finished second.

Lloyd Mangrum won a couple of smaller tournaments in 1938, and in 1939 had his first taste of true PGA competition, finishing second at the Western Open by one shot to Byron Nelson. In 1940, he took a job as an assistant pro at Oak Park Country Club outside Chicago. But by then, he was no longer an unknown.

His coming-out party was the 1940 Masters. He was a late invitee due to his play on the winter tour, which included his first tour victory, the 54-hole Thomasville Open in Georgia. Mangrum and Willie Goggin received the final two invitations to the coveted tournament.

On his first competitive round at Augusta National, Mangrum shot a 64, bettering Byron Nelson's course record by two strokes. And although the concept of a "major" golf tournament was still evolving, especially as to which tournaments qualified, the Masters was always near the top of any list. The 64, which featured nine birdies and a single bogey, also bettered by one the best 18-hole score in any major. It was a stunning achievement.

When Jimmy Demaret, who would go on to win the tournament (Mangrum finished second) saw the 64 posted, he said, "Oh my God. What am I doing out here?" Demaret rallied to shoot a 67.

Mangrum left the grounds before reporters could get him to talk about the round, so there was no breakdown of the historic 18 from the man who achieved it on his first crack at the celebrated course. But the fact that it stood unmatched until 1965 and unbroken until 1986 reflects just how superlative the round was.

By the time Mangrum rolled into Chicago in June 1942, he had established himself as one of the up-and-coming stars of the PGA Tour. He was approaching his 28th birthday and had won three tournaments that year.

Hogan and Snead also had three wins apiece, Snead's third coming in the PGA Championship three weeks prior. Mangrum had defeated Snead by one stroke in the New Orleans Open in February, and three weeks later won a 36-hole tournament in Florida by one stroke over Lawson Little. A week before the Hale America, Mangrum teamed with Little, the 1940 US Open champion and a back-to-back winner of both the US and British Amateurs in 1934–1935, to win the Inverness Four-Ball in Toledo, Ohio. Demaret and Hogan, who would win this tournament four times, including three straight from 1946 to 1948, finished fourth.

The Inverness tournament had its own unusual format, with eight, two-man teams playing seven rounds. The 16 players who participated were the cream of the PGA crop. They would all pack their bags to make the short journey west to Chicago to participate in the Hale America Tournament.

Mangrum had scorched the front nine at Ridgemoor in Round 1, firing a 30 and nearly a 29. But he cooled off on the back nine and ended with the 67, still good for second place along with four others. Demaret shot 68, while Jones had a 70 and Hogan a disappointing 72.

Decades later, in discussing the Hale America, Hogan recalled that it was the only time in his career that he won a tournament—and whiffed during it. And the whiff came on the first day, on the penultimate hole, a 403-yard par 4. "They had planted some trees in the rough and I hit my shot between the well and the tree," he said. "The only way out was to invert a nine-iron and try to get it back onto the fairway. But I hit behind it and jumped the ball, a real miss. Finally I hit it and made a six."

The big names were part of a 96-man field, which included 81 pros and 15 amateurs. USGA officials swooped in before the first ball was struck and determined that the grooves in the clubs of Sam Byrd did not conform to its specifications. Byrd was forced to scramble for another set of clubs. He ended up shooting a more-than-respectable 72, even par.

Byrd, Mangrum, and all the other big names were chasing two players who set the course record of 65, a score that also would have been a record for a US Open—if the USGA counted the tournament as a US Open. One of the two low shooters was well known. The other was one of those nondescript individuals who occasionally surface at the top of tournaments like these, get their moment in the spotlight, and then return to the life of anonymity from which they had come. This one's name was William Otey Crisman who, like William

Ben Hogan, went by his middle name. That is pretty much all the two had in common. Crisman was a 28-year-old pro from a daily-fee, nine-hole course in Selma, Alabama, the Riverside Golf Club. He had gone through both rounds of qualifying at East Lake, winning the right to move on to Ridgemoor due to a coin flip. He had tied for the last available slot, so officials used the coin flip to settle the matter.

Crisman had qualified for previous US Opens, but was not a regular on the PGA Tour primarily because he simply wasn't good enough. He told reporters after his round of 65 that he had just been "gallivanting around," which was also the name of a song from the 1936 musical *Show Boat* by Jerome Kern and Oscar Hammerstein Jr.

Crisman would, however, achieve a certain degree of notoriety in the sport later by launching a brand of putters that would be used by some of the top players in the game. "Otey quit the circuit because he couldn't putt and started making putters," Jack Burke Jr. recalled. "You always find the guys who are bad putters; they make putters. Guys who are good putters, they can putt with a shoehorn."

You can still acquire what is commonly known as the Otey Crisman Timeless Putter through collections, online auctions, or the company website (otey putters.com.) The history link on the website shows a picture of Crisman and Ben Hogan giving golf instruction to wounded vets during World War II. The website states that Jimmy Demaret used an "Otey," as they were called, when he won the 1947 Masters. Another satisfied "Otey" customer was Doug Ford, winner of the 1957 Masters.

The diminutive Crisman (listed at 5-feet-6, 150 pounds) did all his damage on Thursday on Ridgemoor's back nine, rattling off five consecutive birdies, which included a chip-in, and climaxed by a 40-foot birdie putt on the 15th hole. His nines of 34-31 put him atop the leaderboard until Mike Turnesa, one of the three Turnesas in the tournament, matched him almost hole for hole.

It is literally impossible to chronicle this period in professional golf without mentioning the name Turnesa more than once. That's because Mike was one of seven Turnesas, all of whom played golf, three of whom turned pro, and the last one—Willie—who won two US Amateurs and a British Amateur. He never turned pro.

The Turnesas (there were also two non-golf-playing daughters) were Italian immigrants who settled in New York City early in the twentieth century. The patriarch, Vitale, got a job as a greenskeeper at a now-demolished golf course in Westchester County, and one by one the boys picked up the game.

Mike, Jim, and Joe were the Turnesas who took turns excelling on the PGA Tour. Phil and Frank Turnesa, the two oldest brothers, and Doug, the third from last, all became club pros in the metropolitan New York area. In addition to his two US Amateurs in 1938 (at Oakmont) and 1948 (at Memphis Country Club), Willie Turnesa also won the British Amateur in 1947 at fabled Carnoustie.

Joe, the third oldest, won 14 PGA tournaments and played on two Ryder Cup teams. He finished second to Bobby Jones at the 1926 US Open at Scioto Country Club and lost in the finals of the 1927 PGA Championship 1-up to Walter Hagen.

Jim Turnesa won the family's own major tournament, the 1952 PGA Championship. It was the second of his two PGA tour wins, the other coming at the Reading Open in 1951. He also reached the finals of the 1942 PGA Championship, just prior to the Hale America, beating Ben Hogan and Byron Nelson along the way.

Mike Turnesa won six times on the PGA Tour. His best showing in a major tournament was in the 1948 PGA, when he lost to Hogan in the finals.

Joe, Jim, and Mike Turnesa all were in the field at the Hale America, but it was Mike who had top billing on the first day. Like Crisman, he also went 34-31 while making five straight birdies on the back nine. Unlike Crisman, however, Turnesa at least was a known quantity (although it was sometimes hard to tell one from the other.)

The twin 65s would have horrified the USGA had they been shot at one of the doughtier clubs which usually hosts the US Open. The fact that they came at Ridgemoor only underscored the belief that this would never seriously be considered as the *de facto* US Open of 1942.

The assault on par produced 63 rounds of either 72 or better. The gallery, estimated at 6,500, gravitated to Jones toward the end of the day, as he was playing in the penultimate threesome with Ed Dudley and reigning US Open champion Craig Wood. After shooting his 70, Jones said, "It was as good as I hoped to do."

Jones would be a member of the Army Air Corps in less than a week. Hogan and Demaret would soon follow in the Army and Navy, respectively. Mangrum was the last to go, but he was one of the few professional golfers who actually saw combat in World War II.

On January 18, 1944, Lloyd Mangrum tied for third in the San Francisco Open at Harding Park, eight shots behind the winner, Byron Nelson, and two shots behind runner-up Harold (Jug) McSpaden. He received $1,062.50 in war bonds. The following day, he was officially inducted into the US Army.

Mangrum's personnel record shows December 27, 1943, as his enlistment date, but he received permission from Uncle Sam to play in the San Francisco tournament. It would be two years before he rejoined the PGA tour.

Much has been written about Mangrum's service career—and much of it is contradictory. Although most of his military personnel files were destroyed in a 1973 fire at the St. Louis National Personnel Records Center, enough material is available to get a reasonably accurate and realistic account of his time in the European Theater of Operations (ETO).

His short biography in the World Golf Hall of Fame, into which he was rightfully inducted in 1999, says he served his country with distinction—which he certainly did—as a staff sergeant in the 3rd Army. There is no record to show he was a sergeant; he was promoted from private to corporal in April 1945 and his discharge paper shows he was still a corporal.

The short Hall of Fame biography also noted Mangrum broke his arm in two places when his Jeep overturned during the invasion of Normandy. That is technically true, but he was not involved in D-Day, according to the records. The biography also notes he suffered shrapnel wounds to his chin and knee during the Battle of the Bulge. Mangrum was in England recovering from his Jeep accident during that mammoth engagement in December 1944 and January 1945.

Finally, the biography states that Mangrum returned home with four battle stars and two Purple Hearts. One of those Purple Hearts is on display at Mangrum's "locker" in the World Golf Hall of Fame. In a number of articles, Mangrum describes wounds that he received—wounds that would merit a Purple Heart. His preliminary discharge report—the final, more detailed one is not available—lists only the World War II Victory Medal and the World War II Service Lapel Button under the category Awards and Decorations.

Mangrum reported to Fort McArthur in California and then underwent much of his basic training at Camp Wheeler in Georgia. In March 1944, while still in Georgia, he talked to the Associated Press about his early Army days. "To think that I used to gripe about having to walk 36 holes of golf a day," he said. "If I had carried my caddie on my back, I might not find this field equipment and tin hat such a burden. But it's getting lighter every day."

He likely underwent additional training at Fort Meade in Maryland before deployment, and numerous articles say Mangrum turned down a chance to be the base's golf pro and remain in the United States. It is not clear when he was shipped overseas, but once arriving in England, he was assigned to the 48th Replacement Battalion.

On June 6, 1944, around 160,000 men landed in Normandy in what at the time was the greatest amphibious assault in history. Mangrum, records show, did not touch down in France until the end of July. His was one of 57 names on a personnel roster headed for Cherbourg, south of the D-Day beaches, and a port unavailable to the Allies and general shipping for most of July. The Allies had deemed by this to be critical to the campaign in Western Europe for the arrival of its troops.

The original plan had been to capture Cherbourg a week after D-Day and to reopen the harbor three days later. Instead, the city did not fall until June 26, and it took the Allies another three weeks just to make the port remotely operational. The Germans had done such a thorough job of destroying the port and harbor that Adolf Hitler awarded the Knight's Cross to the man responsible for the demolition—Rear Admiral Walter Hennecke. (The German general in command of Cherbourg, Friedrich Dollman, was not so fortunate. Hitler called for him to be court martialed and relieved him of his command. Dollman died three days after Cherbourg fell under still unknown circumstances. He may have taken poison. Hennecke died in 1984 at the age of 95.)

One American serviceman looked at the carnage in Cherbourg and called it "a masterful job, beyond a doubt the most complete, intensive and best-planned demolition in history." Author Rick Atkinson, in his book *The Guns at Last Light*, detailed the destruction that the Allies encountered after capturing the city. "Electrical and heating plants were demolished, along with the port rail station and every bridge, every building, every submarine pen. Each ship basin and dry dock was blocked with toppled cranes and more than a hundred scuttled vessels," he wrote.

Private Mangrum disembarked into this sea of debris on August 2, 1944, as a mortar crewman. Nine days later, his name appears as one of 71 men assigned to the 90th Infantry Division, the so-called Tough Ombres. He joined a reconnaissance unit on August 15. The division had been activated in March 1942 and entered combat on June 9 in Normandy. It spent 308 days in combat, suffering 19,000 casualties in campaigns in France, the Rhineland, the Ardennes and, finally, central Europe. The nickname for the division dates back to its formation in World War I. Most of the draftees were either from Texas or Oklahoma, so the division insignia incorporates the letters T and O. That led to the term Tough Ombres.

Mangrum's initial stint with the 90th didn't last long. A morning report dated August 31 details the Jeep accident, which occurred on August 21. Mangrum and Sergeant Duke Victor were injured and "dropped from assignment."

Mangrum talked about the accident after the war, telling reporters in 1946 that he broke his upper left arm and shoulder blade in the accident.

Mangrum was injured during the Allies' successful drive to close the Falaise Gap, a critical bottleneck south of Caen (one of the D-Day target cities which took a month to capture) that they had to clear to be able to fan out across northern France. They did, defeating the German 7th Army in the process and capturing tens of thousands of prisoners.

It's not clear if Mangrum was driving, but according to the report, he was given pain medication at the site and then transported seven hours by ambulance. He spent the next six months recovering, much of it at a hospital in England. It was there that Mangrum said he was told by doctors that he'd be lucky to ever play golf again.

When he was finally able to raise his arm, he later said that it gave him a greater thrill than when he won the US Open. He said he was able to play golf four times while recuperating in England.

The morning report from February 28, 1945, shows Mangrum returning to the 90th Infantry, which was by now engaged in western Germany. A month before the war in Europe ended, Mangrum was promoted to corporal. It was still a dangerous time, as almost as many servicemen died in April 1945—the last full month of hostilities—as in June 1944. Mangrum served out the war with the 90th, which was en route to Prague when hostilities ended in early May. The division helped liberate the Flossenbürg concentration camp near the Germany-Czechoslovakia border, which still held some 1,500 prisoners. The Germans evacuated the camp three days before the 90th arrived. It's not known if Mangrum was part of the liberation, but Sam Snead said later of Mangrum that "some of us weren't sure he was quite right mentally because of what he went through in the war."

In April 1945, Mangrum wrote a heartfelt letter to Fred Corcoran, then the PGA tournament manager. The letter was timed to coincide with the Masters, which was not being held that year. "We wonder what these people are fighting for. The German people are now seeing what war is like," he wrote. "Some of the places that were towns are now broken up rocks, etc. After our artillery and air corps pay them a visit, there isn't much left." He added, "When shells are breaking all around you, if you have time, you wonder if the next one will land where you are. I cheated death many times and have been quite lucky."

He went on to wish the other PGA players well—there had been tournaments throughout 1944 and 1945—and ended with "may God guide us to a speedy victory." He signed it, THE HACKER, LLOYD.

In June, with the 90th stationed in Weiden, Germany, Mangrum's name comes up again on two morning reports. Both of these detail changes in work assignments. There is no mention of any Purple Hearts. He does mention in a number of stories that he had been shot in the chin and leg in separate incidents. In a *Morning Golf News* article, Mangrum said that "one of our little buddies clipped me in the leg from about 300 yards while we were on reconnaissance. He must have been a lousy shot. Imagine only nicking a guy from that distance."

In reading a trove of stories about Mangrum, there are countless errors and inaccuracies that makes it more difficult to piece together his actual service record. In 1953, an article on Mangrum in *Time* magazine said he was the recipient of three Purple Hearts. A 2014 article in *Golf News* said he landed on Omaha Beach and helped win the Battle of the Bulge, getting two Purple Hearts. A section of the book *When War Played Through* by John Strege details Mangrum's Jeep accident as occurring on D-Day. Virtually all the articles that mention Mangrum receiving a Purple Heart (or two) state it as a matter of fact. There is nothing direct from Mangrum. In a *Golf Digest* article from 1974, Mangrum is said to detest talking about his war experiences, which was typical of his generation. The article does, however, quote Mangrum telling another, unidentified golfer, "Don't ever say I won a Purple Heart. You don't win it. You just get it. You're in the wrong place at the wrong time and you just get it. Winning is something that's happy and I never saw any happiness over getting your tail shot off."

Historians from the 90th Infantry Division have yet to find any mention in the morning reports or special orders of Mangrum being awarded a Purple Heart. Yet there is one with his name engraved on the back sitting at the World Golf Hall of Fame. (In most cases, Purple Hearts were not engraved unless the recipient had died.) His name is not listed as a recipient at the Purple Heart Museum in New York, but that could be because no one forwarded the information. And when he resumed playing golf in a military tournament in France in August 1945, he was not identified as a Purple Heart recipient in a story by the author, the sports editor of *Stars and Stripes*.

The ever-needling Jimmy Demaret quipped, "I'm tired of reading about Purple Heart Veteran Lloyd Mangrum in the newspapers. I know how you got one of your Purple Hearts, Lloyd. You stepped on a broken beer bottle running out of a Paris whorehouse!"

Also in Mangrum's locker at the World Golf Hall of Fame is a dollar bill torn in half. As told by former HOF curator Tony Parker, Mangrum and another soldier tore it in half on their way to France, agreeing to put it back together at the end of the war. The other soldier didn't make it back. Mangrum carried the torn bill with him for the rest of his life.

In late July 1945, a year after he landed in Cherbourg, Mangrum played in the four-day, 72-hole ETO Golf Championship outside Paris. (*Stars and Stripes* noted the first threesome to tee off would do so at "0900 hours.") His only real competition was a Philadelphia area pro named Matt Kowal. Mangrum shot 9 under par over the four rounds to comfortably win the tournament. The course played to a par 75.

In September, after getting his release from the 90th Infantry, Mangrum finished in a tie for fifth at what was called the "British PGA golf tournament" in St. Andrews. A third-round 79 took Mangrum out of contention, but he still left with $120 after four rounds over the Old Course. In October, he won the Army's Inter-Theater golf tournament in Biarritz, France.

Mangrum was officially discharged from the Army on February 12, 1946, 10 days after arriving back in the United States. His final payment sheet shows he left with $341.23, including $50 in cash.

Ten years later, after the publication of the *Saturday Evening Post* article, Mangrum received a letter from James Kincheloe of Stewartsville, Indiana. Kincheloe was discharged from the Army in December 1945 and had served in the same regiment as Mangrum. He recalled a golf exhibition Mangrum put on in Amberg, Germany, and was one of the men who shagged the golf balls that Mangrum hit. "Ever since that day, the name Lloyd Mangrum always catches my eye," Kincheloe wrote. "We can't all become famous in life and since I never will be, I can at least pull for someone that is most deserving as you."

Mangrum wrote back, thanking Kincheloe for the note and added, "I am enclosing a magazine which I thought you might enjoy reading. Yours truly, Lloyd Mangrum."

It's not known which magazine Mangrum enclosed.

HALE AMERICA
ROUND 2, JUNE 19, 1942
Mr. 62

*The worryin' days are over—for Ben. And they're just starting
for the rest of us.*

—Jimmy Demaret, 1940

Forty-eight golfers had broken par 72 at Ridgemoor on the first day of the Hale America Tournament, and Ben Hogan, still stung by his double bogey on 17, was not at all happy that he was not one of them. The scoring had been historically low on the first day and it would continue on the second. This time, Hogan put his unmistakable stamp on the course in a spectacular round of precision excellence.

Hogan had shown up two hours before his 10:10 a.m. tee time for his usual practice session, determined to work out the kinks from his disappointing opening round. Normally, even par is a goal in a US Open. But not this time. Describing the scoring conditions at Ridgemoor, Charles Bartlett of the *Chicago Tribune* wrote that "officials did nothing in the direction of toughening up the course in the way of back tees or pin placements, and it just sat there and took the lashing for the second straight day."

And no one lashed it more, or better, than Ben Hogan.

He walked off the 18th green having shot a 62, only the fourth time that had ever been done in a tour event. Hogan himself had done it the year before in the third round of the Oakland Open in 1941. He finished second in that event. Walter Hagen and Lawson Little also had shot 62s, Hagen's coming 19 years earlier.

But this was a first for a tournament purporting to be a US Open substitute and shattered the 24-hour course record of 65 that had been set by Mike Turnesa and Otey Crisman. Mike Turnesa added a 66 to his opening-round 65, a round which included back-to-back eagles, and led the field by three shots. The 131, two-round total, had eyes popping. He was 13 under par. Hogan was next at 10 under. Crisman found his new notoriety a bit too much and shot what one writer called a "scandalous" 72. Only at Ridgemoor in 1942 could par be called scandalous. But if you shot par, you were looking up at a lot of names.

To those who insist that the Hale America be counted as an official US Open, the second round 62 would go down as the lowest in the history of the tournament. It would be the lowest score ever fashioned in a major tournament until Branden Grace of South Africa shot a 62 in the 2017 British Open at Royal Birkdale.

As ripe for the plucking as Ridgemoor was, no one else came close to Hogan's 62 over the four days of the Hale America.

Hogan's scorecard was one for the ages. It featured nine 3s, one 2, and only one 5. Overall, he had eight birdies, nine pars, and one eagle. He carved up the front nine in 30, starting birdie, birdie, eagle. He played the back nine in 32. Through 11 holes, he was 8 under par on his round. It was a round that, considering the field, would resonate for decades.

Hogan's playing partners that day were Tommy Armour and Jock Hutchinson, both late invitees. The tournament committee initially had Vic Ghezzi in the threesome instead of Hutchinson. But Ghezzi couldn't get out of his military commitment, while Hutchinson's original pairing had him grouped with two players who didn't show—Bing Crosby and Walter Hagen. So Hutchinson joined Armour and Hogan for the first two days.

It really didn't matter to Hogan who played with him. His ability to focus on the task ahead—the next shot—was so legendary that his partners eventually came to grips with the fact that the most you *might* get out of him was "nice shot." Gary Player recalled playing 36 holes with Hogan, and Hogan saying only five words to him: "Morning, fella" at the first tee on the first day, and "Well played, son" after the conclusion of their two rounds.

There are stories galore of Hogan's surreal tunnel vision, none better than Claude Harmon's account of his own hole-in-one on the 12th hole at Augusta during the 1947 Masters. As the two walked off the green to thunderous applause—there had been only three aces at the hole in Masters competition through 2018—Harmon could only shake his head as Hogan turned to him and said, "That's the first time I ever birdied that hole."

Close friend Jimmy Demaret would constantly needle Hogan about his lack of chattiness but, as Hogan's playing partner in a number of match-play competitions, he also understood it perhaps better than anyone. In his book, *My Partner, Ben Hogan*, Demaret wrote, "Ben has the kind of will that makes the rest of us look like carefree schoolboys. He doesn't ignore people. He just doesn't see them. He divorces himself from the rest of the world when playing in a tournament. He is completely and absolutely detached from everything but that golf game of his."

Sam Snead, who beat Hogan in their three head-to-head competitions, including the 1954 Masters playoff, said he loved playing with Hogan "because I knew he wouldn't say anything to me. That was good, because it helped me concentrate."

George Fazio, who played with Hogan and Lloyd Mangrum in a three-way playoff at the 1950 US Open, called Hogan "the most perfect gentleman on the golf course that I ever played with. He's not going to do anything *for* you but he's not going to do anything against you. You play your game. He plays his. There's nobody better than that to play with."

Jack Burke Jr. recalled a time playing with Hogan at a slower-than-usual clip. With any other golfer, Burke would have gone up and asked the individual to pick up the pace. "Except maybe if it's Hogan," Burke wrote. "We were playing at Augusta one year and we were a couple holes behind. An official asked me to go over and talk to Ben and I said, '*you* go over and talk to him. Hell, Ben Hogan's *wife* doesn't talk to him too much.'"

Burke said he eventually told Hogan that they might be hearing from a Masters official and possibly be penalized two strokes for slow play, but Hogan just snapped, "Let 'em come out and do it then." Burke added, "He wasn't going to change his timing for any group of officials or anybody.'"

But as Hogan's playing partners for the Hale America, Hutchinson and Armour knew one thing—they were witnessing one of the finest rounds of golf in *any* competition. Soon, the gallery of around 5,000 was doing the same thing as word circulated around Ridgemoor that something special was happening in the 10:10 grouping.

Hogan was laser-like off the tee, hitting the fairway in 13 of 14 holes. He said he missed three birdie putts he expected to make, given the way he was playing. But it was the putter, not always the most trustworthy club in Hogan's bag, that helped him the most on his way to that 62. Only two of his eight birdies were 10 feet or shorter, and the birdies and eagle combined totaled 133 feet of putts, or an average of 14.8 feet.

Hogan being Hogan, he wasn't going to wax poetic about a second-round score, regardless of the number. He didn't wax poetic about anything, except perhaps the golf swing. The news coverage of the tournament in those days rarely included quotes from players about their rounds. That didn't come until much later.

But sportswriter Grantland Rice managed to coax out an almost Gettysburg Address–like quote from Hogan about the round. Only Hogan could have looked at a 62 and found it wanting. And he did: "The tough part of it all was this—I missed my three easiest putts for a 59."

Hogan later had the sportswriters rolling on the floor laughing with another gem, saying, "Think I can get in the money if I shoot two more 62s?"

Armour had shot a 72 to go with a first-round 75 and was well down the leaderboard. Hutchinson was even worse, at 153, and would drop out of the tournament. But both players knew they had been part of something special on that Friday afternoon. While Hogan wouldn't go there, it was Armour, the 45-year-old, three-time major champion who was left to sum up one of the most remarkable displays of shot-making he had ever seen. "It was," Armour said, "the closest thing possible to a perfect round."

It also remains the single greatest forgotten round of championship golf in any national tournament, official or otherwise. It is almost as if every golf writer and golf organization excised it from memory. It is almost never mentioned when low-scoring rounds in majors—or any tournament, for that matter—become the topic of discussion or dissertation.

For years, it was almost an article of faith that the single greatest round of golf in a US Open was Johnny Miller's 63 in the final round at rain-soaked but still demanding Oakmont in 1973. The round was good enough for Miller to leapfrog from 13th place to win his only US Open title. His was one of only four sub-70 rounds shot that day, and it literally was a shot heard round the golfing world.

A 63? At Oakmont? On the final day? Until that day, the best scoring round in a US Open had been 64, accomplished by three golfers. The first was Lee Mackey, an unemployed club pro from Alabama who had grown up in the same Birmingham neighborhood as Sam Byrd. He became the first to shoot a 64 when he did so in the first round of the 1950 US Open at Merion. Fourteen years later, at Congressional, Tommy Jacobs shot a 64 in the second round and, in 1966 at the Olympic Club, Rives McBee shot a 64 in the second round.

Of the three who shot 64, only Jacobs contended, finishing second to Ken Venturi by four shots. Mackey followed up his 64 with an 81 and ended up tied for 25th. McBee finished tied for 13th, which was the best finish of his career in a major tournament.

Johnny Miller was already establishing himself as a top professional when the 1973 US Open began, but what he did during the fourth round was other-worldly. It was the golfing equivalent of Bob Beamon's astounding long jump in the 1968 Summer Olympics at Mexico City. Beamon set a world record, break-ing the old record by almost 2 feet. No one else came close to that until 1991, but it is still an Olympic record.

In reading the many stories of Miller's 63, there are no references to what Hogan did at Ridgemoor 31 years earlier. Not even as an aside, let alone that the 63 might be considered only the second-lowest round in an event sponsored by the USGA. Hogan's round of 62 was 10 under par. Miller's 63 was 8 under par. This in no way is to diminish what Miller did, but to suggest that one might at least *mention* Hogan's round when discussing great US Open rounds. Even if it wasn't part of an official US Open. (Dan Jenkins' article in *Sports Illustrated* on Miller's 63 contained no references to Hogan's 62.)

Miller had nine birdies in his round. Hogan had eight. Miller had one bogey. Hogan had none. Miller had no eagles; Hogan had one. While Ridgemoor could in no way compare in difficulty to stately Oakmont, no one else at the Hale Amer-ica shot a 62. Or a 63. Or a 64. The only two 65s were the two posted by Mike Turnesa and Otey Crisman on the first day, and the only two 66s were posted by Mike Turnesa on the second day and Jimmy Thompson on the final day.

The 62 tends to get overlooked even by many Hogan aficionados looking at the bigger picture—whether the Hale America was an official US Open. If it wasn't, shouldn't the scoring from the Hale America be considered in that it was still an event organized and sponsored by the USGA?

There have been a handful of 62s since then in USGA events, but all have come in the US Senior Open. Miller's 63 is still the benchmark. It had been matched five times since then in a US Open through 2020, but the first time is the one everyone remembers. Vijay Singh shot a 63 in the second round of the 2003 US Open at Olympia Fields, which included a 29 on the back nine. Does anyone but Singh remember that round?

If the USGA had decided to include Hogan's 62, then it would also have had to include two more record scores. Hogan's four-round total of 271 easily eclipsed the record at the time, Ralph Guldahl's 281 from five years earlier at the Detroit Club. (Hogan would nonetheless own the US Open scoring record of 276 for 19 years.) And Hogan's three-round total of 203, which he shared with Mike Turnesa, also would have been a record.

Hogan's 62 was still unmatched in US Open competition through 2020. Justin Thomas looked as though he might catch Hogan's mark in 2017, but he ended up with a 63. Singh (2003), Nicklaus (1980), Tom Weiskopf (1980), and Tommy Fleetwood (2018) also have shot 63s in a US Open.

Miller and Nicklaus went on to win the tournaments in which they shot 63. Thomas shot his 63 in the third round and then blew up in the fourth round with a 75, tying for ninth. Singh was tied for third after three rounds but ended up tied for 20th after shooting a 78 in the fourth round. Weiskopf came completely undone after his 63. He didn't shoot any lower than 75 in each of the next three rounds and finished tied for 37th. Fleetwood's 63 came in the final round, like Miller's, but he ended up one shot behind winner Brooks Koepka.

Prior to the final round of the Hale America, sportswriter Grantland Rice asked Jimmy Demaret how he felt about his chances. Demaret was in third place, two strokes behind the leaders, Hogan and Mike Turnesa. "This doesn't go," Demaret told Rice, "if Hogan shoots another 62. Which he might do."

Miller might have come the closest to matching Hogan's 62. He lipped a putt on 18, and Miller's playing partner at the 1973 US Open, Miller Barber, said the round could easily have been a 60 had a couple more putts dropped. That mirrors what Hogan told Rice after his 62—save for a few putts, he could have shot a 59. Both players were precision instruments in their respective rounds. Miller's iron play was spectacular. Hogan's putting was just as superb.

You will find no references to Hogan's 62 in any of the USGA Media Guides. Not even with an asterisk attached to it. The greatest round Hogan ever shot in a competitive national tournament (apologies to the Oakland Open) is nowhere to be seen. While Branden Grace's 62 at Royal Birkdale in 2017 is now in the books—there had also been 12 rounds of 63 in British Open history through 2020—the magical "63" still stands as the lowest round in the other three majors through 2019.

Only two players, Nick Price and Greg Norman, have shot 63 at Augusta National (Price's came more than four decades after Lloyd Mangrum's 64 in 1940, while Norman's came in 1996). Neither player ended up winning the tournament. The PGA had yielded 17 rounds of 63, two of them by Brooks Keopka in 2018 (Bellerive Country Club in St. Louis) and 2019 (Bethpage Black in Farmingdale, New York). Koepka won both tournaments and was one of three players to have more than one 63 in a major through 2020. Norman also had a 63 in the British Open in 1986 at Turnberry, which he won, and Singh's first 63 came a decade before his round at Olympia Fields in the 1993 PGA Championship at Inverness Club in Toledo, Ohio, where he finished fourth.

Hogan's 62 might have been completely forgotten by now had he not won the Hale America. Or maybe it's not being recognized as it should be because he didn't shoot it on the final day to rally from behind, as Miller did. But a 62 is a 62 is a 62 and, until 2017, no one had done that—officially—in any of the four majors.

Grace, meanwhile, shot his 62 in the third round—par is 70 at Royal Birkdale—and finished tied for sixth, eight shots behind the champion, Jordan Spieth. He could only match par on the final day. Hogan followed up his 62 with rounds of 69 and 68 to win the USGA's signature event of 1942 by three shots. But in the minds of golf's gatekeepers and numbers men, that round has been consigned to the dustbin of history. It deserves better.

So after two rounds, Mike Turnesa led by three shots over Hogan. Others were lurking. Horton Smith and Lawson Little were at 135, one shot behind Hogan, while Herman Barron and Jimmy Demaret were two shots behind Hogan and five off the lead. Otey Crisman was one of three in at 137.

Bobby Jones, encouraged by his opening-round 70, stumbled to a 75. He told Rice, "I was all right except I couldn't drive, approach or putt. Especially putt. I might as well have used a whisk broom for every shot."

Lloyd Mangrum slipped back to even par and was at 139 while his older brother, Ray, was at 140. Sam Byrd recovered from the opening-round inconvenience of replacing his illegally grooved clubs and fashioned a 68 to also stand at 140. Gene Sarazen was at 142, while Joe and Jim Turnesa were both at 143. Harvey Penick was in at 147.

The leading scores were distinctly un-Open-like. When Tommy Armour won the 1927 US Open at Oakmont Country Club outside Pittsburgh, he had done so with a four-round total of 301, or 13 *over* par. (Oakmont played to a par 72 in 1927 and a par 71 in 1973.) Byron Nelson won the 1939 US Open at Philadelphia Country Club with a total of 284, which was 8 *over* par. (It played to a par 69.) Craig Wood had won at Colonial in 1941 with an aggregate total of 284, 4 *over* par.

But Mike Turnesa was already 13 under par, and the tournament was only half completed. Players applauded Ridgemoor's pristine conditions, if not its demanding layout. Half of the field was under par for the first two rounds. This looked more like the Greater Hartford Open than anything like a US Open.

And things looked like they could get even easier for the field late on Friday, when it started to rain as a cold front approached. If all those players had broken par in dry conditions, what on earth was going to happen with the greens softened up by Mother Nature?

There would be no more 62s, however. That round will remain as one of the finest in championship golf—and the best for Hogan in tournament conditions. But he did have one better.

In May 2020, the auction website Golden Age Golf Auctions offered some-thing quite enticing to the legion of Ben Hogan fans—a scorecard that purported to be his lowest round ever. The round was shot at Seminole Golf Club in Juno Beach, Florida, where Hogan used to encamp in the spring to prepare for the Masters. It revealed he shot a 61.

The 11-under round consisted of an eagle, nine birdies, and eight pars. While the card is not dated, it came from the estate of Robert Sweeny, a friend of Hogan and a Seminole member. Sweeny was an accomplished player in his own right, having won the 1937 British Amateur at Royal St. George while also, at the age of 43, advancing to the finals of the 1954 US Amateur at the Country Club of Detroit. Sweeny was 3 up in that final at one point, but lost, 1 up, to a swashbuckling 24-year-old named Arnold Palmer. The Hogan scorecard was found with others from the period of 1954–1955, so that is when it was likely played.

Hogan, Sweeny, George Fazio, and 1948 Masters champion Claude Har-mon comprised the foursome that day. No one shot worse than 72. At the bot-tom of the card, in Hogan's printing, is written "23 putts" with the word "putts" underlined. Directly under Hogan's unmistakable signature, all in capital let-ters, are the words LOWEST ROUND EVER PLAYED.

Thirty-six bids came in for the scorecard from May 7 to May 23. The item sold for $28,096. (In the same auction, an autographed pair of Michael Jordan's FootJoy golf shoes sold for $9,286.)

While the 61 at Seminole may be Ben Hogan's lowest round, the 62 at Ridgemoor during the Hale America National Open in June 1942, along with the 62 at the 1941 Oakland Open, remain his lowest competitive rounds in the 294 tournaments he played in from 1932 until 1970. He played 705 rounds over those 38 years, and it would be hard to find one finer than his second round at Ridgemoor.

Jimmy Demaret recalled a time when Hogan had shot a 64 in the opening round of a tournament and celebrated by going back to the practice tee while Demaret and his friends enjoyed "a little libation." When Demaret asked Hogan why he was still out there, given his excellent play, Hogan told Demaret that he didn't see why there was any reason a player couldn't birdie all 18 holes. Hogan really believed that.

He had birdied or eagled half of the Ridgemoor Country Club course in the second round. It's noteworthy that the round, and the 62 in Oakland, still represent the best of Ben Hogan. This speaks volumes because he had rounds that he thought were better, more fulfilling and, in one case, career-saving. None was a 62.

Countless trees have died for the sole purpose of bringing Ben Hogan's compelling life story to print. He also was the subject of a movie, *Follow the Sun*, which starred Glenn Ford and Anne Baxter. He was one of two golfers to receive a ticker tape parade in New York City. Hogan started his own golf company and is memorialized at two Fort Worth country clubs, Colonial and Shady Oaks. He has his own room at the United States Golf Association Museum in Far Hills, New Jersey.

But as much as the Hogan story is one of success, it is more so a story and study in resilience and perseverance. Ben Hogan never forgot where he came from or how he managed to get from where he came from. That made his improbable life journey even more remarkable and, for him, that much more satisfying.

The phrase "humble beginnings" does not begin to accurately describe Hogan's early years in small-town North Texas. To hear it from the man himself, "We were very poor." He was born on August 13, 1912, in Stephenville, Texas, but the family lived in Dublin, now the home of the Ben Hogan Museum. They subsequently relocated to Fort Worth, where Ben was introduced to the sport that defined his life.

Hogan's father, Chester, was a blacksmith, a useful trade at one point but decidedly less so by 1912. Ben (who was born William Ben Hogan) was nine years old when his father committed suicide. There are various stories as to whether he witnessed his father's suicide, but he was in the house when it happened. And Chester Hogan's death put the family on even more shaky financial footing. Ben's mother, Clara, went to work as a seamstress at a dress store in Fort Worth.

In a 1953 *Sport* magazine article, Hogan reflected on his introverted personality and how it had been forged by what he had gone through as a child. "I know a lot of people don't like me," Hogan said. "They say I'm selfish and hard and that I think only about golf. Maybe I do. But there's a reason.

"I know what it means to be hungry," Hogan continued. "I never intend to be hungry again."

Hogan sold newspapers at the train station in town and then discovered there was additional money to be made by caddying at Glen Garden Country Club. He knew next to nothing about golf, and it was almost seven miles from his home to the club. But Hogan dutifully made the trek as often as he could. There, he would sometimes camp out overnight, using one of his unsold newspapers as a pillow or covering while nestling in one of Glen Garden's sand traps. That way, he was assured of being in line early the following day to make sure he got a bag to carry.

Caddying introduced Hogan to the game, and it wasn't long before he was off hitting balls by himself, a sign of things to come. He loved the solitary nature of the game; you didn't need a partner or an opponent. You could just play. He collected wooden shaft clubs which, years later, he admitted "weren't very good clubs. But they were my clubs."

Byron Nelson also caddied at Glen Garden, and the two 15-year-olds paired off in the Christmas Caddy Tournament in 1927 that Nelson won on the final hole, earning Glen Garden's only junior membership the following year. Hogan had to find other clubs for work; Glen Garden did not allow caddies 16 years or older, and he would turn 16 in 1928.

That was just one of many obstacles and disappointments that shaped Hogan. Writer Dan Jenkins believed the Glen Garden snub scarred Hogan and drove him even harder. Hogan often talked about how those hardscrabble years made him not only tough, but also more appreciative of the journey he had to endure. "I feel sorry for the rich kids now," he said in 1983. "I really do. They're never going to have the opportunity I had. Because I knew tough things. And I can handle tough things. And they can't."

Two years after the caddy tournament at Glen Garden, Ben Hogan dropped out of high school and turned pro. He was 17 and more than a decade away from doing anything meaningful as a professional golfer.

That was really the only route available for the pros in those days. Mangrum did it. Demaret did it. Hogan did it. There were no elite college programs offering golf scholarships back then, and the country clubs generally supported amateur golf. The three didn't come from privilege, as Bobby Jones did, so the country club life and prestigious amateur tournaments in which to compete were beyond their reach.

To make it even harder for Hogan, Mangrum, and Demaret, they all started to make their way in the challenging world of professional golf in the middle of the Great Depression. The prize money wasn't great. There was little to no travel other than by car or train. Players looked for the cheapest hotel. It all led to a lifestyle unthinkable for today's PGA touring pro.

The nonmarried players would bunk three or four to a room, and fruit was a subsistence food group. Demaret recalled a tournament in California where the players would deliberately take an out-of-bounds penalty to rummage through an adjacent orange grove and stuff their bags with oranges while supposedly trying to find their errant shots.

It was a wild, unpredictable, chaotic, and sometimes rewarding existence. It bred companionship and camaraderie. Occasionally, players in a playoff would agree in advance to split the winnings, regardless of the official outcome. It may not have been the Wild West, but at times it sure seemed like it. "The players of today might make more money than we did," recalled Demaret. "But we had more fun."

It would be wrong to view Hogan in that context, as he struggled mightily to make a living as a professional golfer. While he did announce he was turning pro at 17, he waited another three years to try his luck on the tournament circuit. Then he really found out what life was like on the tour. "I was a terrible player. And I was broke," he said. "I wasn't a good player at all. It wasn't until I turned pro that I realized I didn't belong out there at all."

His early record backs him up. In his first four years as a professional, Ben Hogan earned a total of $362 over 10 tournaments. Two of those tournaments were the US Open, where he failed to make the cut in 1934 and 1935. He fared marginally better in 1938, when he won more money in one tournament ($375 for a third-place finish at the Lake Placid Open) than he won in the previous four years combined.

But he still hadn't *won* anything. From 1932 to 1940, he won just once, and that was in a four-ball tournament in Hershey, Pennsylvania, in 1938 with a partner (Vic Ghezzi.) He was battling more than just financial woes; he had a bad hook and kept saying to himself, "You can't play this way."

He eventually got rid of the hook, thanks in part to golfer Henry Picard, who won the 1938 Masters and the 1939 PGA Championship and was the head pro at the Hershey Country Club. According to Picard, Hogan came to him and asked, "Why don't I win?" After Hogan revealed his tendency to hook the ball, Picard said he could fix the problem in five minutes.

"So I did," Picard said. He rearranged Hogan's grip so that it was not so dominated by the left hand and told Hogan, "If you can hook it then, I'd eat the golf ball." Hogan reported back that he was no longer hooking the ball. "That settles it," Picard said. Hogan thought so much of the advice that he dedicated his first instruction book to Picard.

Picard said that Hogan had asked him about getting rid of the hook in early 1940, before Hogan had won on his own. The two met at Pinehurst and soon they were on the course, where Picard told Hogan, "On the left is the railroad tracks. You've been over there a lot, haven't you?"

Hogan answered in the affirmative. Picard then told Hogan there was shrubbery on the right and that it was time for Hogan "to wheel it as hard as you can." And, Picard said, Hogan "went out and won that tournament." It was the first of three straight tournaments Hogan would win in 1940, heading up to the Masters.

It was also Picard who made sure that Hogan got invited to play at the Hershey Four-Ball in 1938 as a late fill-in. Picard, who sort of oversaw the event from his perch as the head pro, said he had to convince tournament officials that the then winless Hogan was good enough to join the field. That turned out to be the tournament that Hogan ended up winning with Ghezzi. It was the first time

Ben Hogan cashed a winner's check. Afterward, Ghezzi remarked that "if we had lost, I am quite certain he would have jumped out of a window."

Picard may be guilty of a little hyperbole, for Hogan has always maintained he came upon the grip change on his own, tested it on the practice tee (where else of course?), and then tried it in competition. Eventually, it worked.

Picard soon left Hershey to take the head pro job at Canterbury Country Club outside Cleveland. Hershey club officials wanted Sam Snead to replace Picard, but Picard convinced them to hire Hogan instead. And that is how the tried-and-true Texan ended up in Pennsylvania.

There are a number of landmark moments in Hogan's brilliant career. There's the near-fatal car accident in 1949 and the spectacular comeback the next year to win the US Open at Merion. There's the so-called Triple Crown in 1953 when Hogan became the first (and as of 2020, the only) player to win the Masters, US Open, and British Open in the same year.

There was the victory with Ghezzi in 1938, and then Hogan's first tournament victory on his own in 1940. There were dozens of other tournament victories along the way. But for Ben Hogan, there was no bigger tournament than the 1938 Oakland Open. He didn't even finish in the top five, but for him, it changed everything. He has told the story of that life-changing event many times.

Hogan was nearing the conclusion of his first venture on the California part of the PGA Tour, having already played in Los Angeles and Pasadena and with the Sacramento stop the following week. Oakland and Sacramento are not that far apart, but Hogan wasn't sure he could continue beyond Oakland. He and his wife, Valerie, started the trip with $1,400 and were down to their last $86 when they arrived in Oakland in late January.

He needed a decent finish to continue on to Sacramento and replenish some of the $1,314 they had spent. On the morning of his first round, he went to retrieve his maroon Buick from a parking lot across the street from his hotel and saw that the rear tires had been stolen. The car had been jacked up and the wheels were on rocks. The jack had been pilfered as well.

He made his way to Sequoyah Country Club—which was hosting the tournament for the first time—barely making his tee time. He had no time to practice, which was, for Hogan, akin to a violation of the Eighth Amendment. But he opened with a 70 and concluded the final round with a 67, winding up in a tie for sixth. Better yet, he earned $285, which was enough to continue on to Sacramento. He would finish third there and pocket another $350.

"This wasn't a terrific day in golf, but it was an important day in my golf life," Hogan was quoted in Darsie's *My Greatest Day in Golf.* "The money I won in the Oakland Open in 1938 was the turning point in my golf life. And, for that reason, I consider it my greatest day in golf, although few persons aside from Valerie and I knew what it meant to us."

Hogan earned nearly $4,800 in 1938. The figure illustrates just how hard it was to make a decent living on the PGA Tour at that time. Most of the players supplemented their tour winnings with two important revenue streams—a salary from a club at which you were the head pro, and exhibitions.

The club attachment was a two-way street, for if the player was any good, he brought notoriety to the club. That is also why you see born-and-bred Texans like Hogan (Hershey, Pennsylvania), Mangrum (Tam O'Shanter in Chicago), Demaret (Wee Burn in Connecticut, Plum Hollow in Detroit, and Ojai in California), and Nelson (Inverness in Toledo) listed from these locales. The clubs wanted the name pros. The name pros wanted the money, the attachment, and, most important of all, the club's blessing to continue on the tour.

The exhibitions were also where the top players earned extra cash. Hogan, who led the tour in earnings five times, said the tournament purses were so minimal that one had to play in exhibitions. A 1949 *Time* magazine profile reported that Hogan charged $500 for weekday exhibitions and $700 on weekends. Both of those figures were generally more than second- or third-place winnings in many of the tournaments in those days.

"I never made a cent from winning a tournament," Hogan said, an exaggeration for sure, but also an honest take on the amount of money offered. "You had to make your money in exhibitions. I'd book, oh, 25 exhibitions for myself after winning an Open. That was the only way you could make any money."

Hogan kept getting closer to winning a tournament in 1939, finishing second on three occasions. He also boosted his national recognition when he was one of four medalists in the PGA Championship at the now defunct Pomonock Country Club in Flushing, New York. (The tournament that year was being held in conjunction with the 1939 World's Fair.) All contestants in the PGA had to qualify for the match-play portion by being one of the top 64 qualifiers after two rounds of stroke play. Hogan shot 138 to advance to the match-play portion for the first time. He lost in the third round to Paul Runyan, the defending champion.

Hogan closed the year with a fourth-place finish at the Miami Open, giving him nearly $5,500 in earnings. The world would soon see the fruits of Hogan's labors pay off in a big way. All those top five finishes and hours of hitting practice balls finally turned Hogan into what he never thought he could be—a champion and a money-making machine.

An old adage about the military from World War II states that the "American Army does not solve its problems. It overwhelms them." That's how any PGA player not named Ben Hogan must have felt in the first three years of the 1940s.

Hogan led the tour in earnings all three years. He led the tour in scoring average in 1940 and 1941. He won four times in 1940, five times in 1941, and six times in 1942. But what is just as impressive as the victories is the mind-boggling consistency. He was almost always in the hunt. In those three years, he played in 72 tournaments and was in the top five in 57 of them. In 1941 alone, he played in 28 tournaments and finished in the top five in 26 of them.

As Jimmy Demaret recalled early in 1940, "I don't think there are many golfers who are going to beat Hogan from now on. He is just about ready to take charge. The worryin' days are over—for Ben. And they're just starting for the rest of us."

One of Hogan's victories that year was the first of his many collaborations with Demaret, at the Inverness Four-Ball. The two were polar opposites in terms of personality, what the Irish liked to call "chalk and cheese." But their partnership worked. They won four Inverness Four-Balls and four Miami International Four-Balls. They went undefeated in team play at the 1947 and 1951 Ryder Cup matches. They played in some faux Ryder Cup matches during the war for war bonds and won those as well.

As he rose in the ranks, but before he hit the big time, Hogan's practice sessions were legendary for length of time and dedication to purpose. How many players could learn something from their 30th consecutive 8-iron? Hogan could. "I had to practice and play well all the time," he said. "The only way I was going to win was to outwork these fellows. They might work two hours a day. I'd work eight."

He added, "I always got great satisfaction from practicing. It gave me a chance to go out on the tee and forget about everything else but what I was working on that day. And there is no greater pleasure than improving."

Did he ever get bored? "Never."

In his 1974 book, *The Golf Swing*, Cary Middlecoff wrote about Hogan's shot-making in the 1967 Colonial Invitational. Hogan was 54 and had long since retired from serious competitive golf. The Colonial was one of just four events he played in 1967, the others being the Masters, the US Open, and what was then called the Houston Championship Invitational. A shot-tracker examined 141 shots over four rounds (no putts), and 139 were judged to be superbly executed to near perfection. The other two were a drive and a 5-iron from the fairway, each deemed to be off by 5 yards. Hogan finished tied for third.

His practice sessions at Colonial or Shady Oaks prompted stories of near-disbelief from the individuals charged with collecting his shots. Lindy Miller, a former Tour player who shagged balls for Hogan, called the sessions "indescribable: "I never moved 15 yards one way or the other off the shag bag," he told the podcast *No Laying Up*. "And that was with [Hogan using] a driver. It would land by the bag, bounce up to you and you had to wipe it off and put it back in the bag. I never saw him miss a shot. They were all within a yard or two of the bag."

The only problem with Hogan's surge to the top was the timing. While he was stringing together three straight victories in North Carolina, the Nazis were preparing to launch Operation Weser-Exercise, the invasions of Denmark and Norway. By the time Hogan won his fourth and final tournament in 1940, the Nazis had just invaded France after overpowering the Low Countries.

Japan was into its second decade of occupying significant portions of China while expanding its imprint and influence along the Pacific Rim. Later that year, the Japanese would invade and conquer French Indochina, or what Americans came to know as Vietnam.

War was raging in Europe, Africa, and Asia. As Demaret put it, "Just as Ben was to reach the golfing heights for which he had worked so hard for so many years, his immediate future was being decided by a few people unacquainted with Hogan in Berlin and Tokyo."

By now, however, the issue for Hogan wasn't winning. As Demaret noted, if Hogan had ever asked "'When do you think I'll ever win a tournament,' I would have answered, 'Tomorrow.'" The issue was winning the so-called majors, although there was no official calculation in those days of what constituted a major and what did not. But for the professionals, three tournaments generally stood out: the Masters, the US Open, and the PGA Championship.

Hogan had 16 victories by the time the Allies, which now included a raw US Army, launched Operation Torch, the invasion of French North Africa in November 1942. He had come close at Augusta earlier that year, blowing a three-stroke lead and losing a playoff to Nelson. He had never gotten past the quarterfinal round of the PGA, losing there in 1940, 1941, and 1942. He had come close when Colonial hosted the 1941 US Open, finishing in a tie for third—five shots behind the winner, Craig Wood. It was a tournament he wanted to win not just because it was the US Open, but because Colonial owner and longtime Hogan friend and benefactor Marvin Leonard had convinced the USGA to come to Texas. Leonard also made sure the course had bent greens, more common in US Open–style courses.

Hogan did win the Colonial Invitation, a regular tour stop, on five occasions. He would have to wait until hostilities ended in Europe and the Pacific to make his claim for an *official* major. But in his mind, and in the minds of many of his friends and supporters, he already had that first major well before Germany and Japan surrendered. The only problem was that the people who mattered did not agree.

Lloyd Mangrum was the exception. Many active, big-name golfers entered the service in World War II, including Hogan, Demaret, Snead, and Jim Turnesa. The 1960 PGA champion, Jay Hebert, served in the Marines and was wounded at the 1945 Battle of Iwo Jima. Jack Burke Jr. also served in the Marines. Vic Ghezzi, the 1941 PGA champion who also was part of the three-way US Open playoff in 1946 with Mangrum and Byron Nelson, enlisted in the Army in January 1942 and rose to the rank of sergeant.

Among other sports celebrities, boxer Jack Dempsey, who was criticized for not enlisting in World War I, served in the Navy in World War II and was on an attack transport ship for the invasion of Okinawa in 1945. He turned 50 just after US Marine and Army forces secured the island after 82 days of fighting the Japanese defenders. Joe DiMaggio enlisted in the Army Air Corps in 1943, but never left the United States and spent much of his time playing baseball. He requested a combat assignment but was turned down.

Hogan played out the 1942 PGA season, participating in several more tournaments following his victory in the Hale America. He won once, at the Rochester Open in August. He received his draft notice in March 1943, but his official induction as a special services officer came in November 1943. Of the 16 million who served during World War II, roughly half of them enlisted.

The PGA Tour all but closed down in 1943 as players joined the service. Hogan, who did not return to competitive golf until June 1944, reported to the Fort Worth Army Air Field to begin his Army career. He told a local reporter that he was "eager to see what flying is all about."

Shortly before entering the service, Hogan had dinner with his wife, Valerie, and Bob Bumbry, a writer for *Sport* magazine. He confessed to a little anxiety as to when, or even if, he would be able to play tournament golf again. He had just started to peak when war broke out. "You know," he told Bumbry, "I don't mind going into the Army. It's something that has to be done and something anyone should be proud to do. But I'd gladly give everything I've got, gladly start all over again, if this hadn't happened."

While Hogan was serving his country, he undoubtedly had moments of despondency as Byron Nelson and Harold (Jug) McSpaden dominated professional golf when it was played during the War. Both men received medical deferments.

Despite having no high school diploma, Hogan was assigned to Officers Candidate School in Miami in the summer of 1943. Before he left, he told a Fort Worth reporter that he didn't expect to be playing a lot of golf, adding "I'm eager and willing to do what the Army tells me to do." After OCS, in November, he was promoted to second lieutenant.

He joined the newly minted Civilian Pilot Training Program, whose mission was to train flight instructors. Over the next several months his unit would spend time in Shreveport, Louisiana; Kilgore, Texas; and Tulsa, Oklahoma. Hogan would squeeze in a charity round of golf now and then and actually learned how to fly an airplane while on duty in Oklahoma.

His stay in Tulsa was cut short as experienced pilots were returning to the United States to assume the job that Hogan had. The Army sent Hogan back to Fort Worth in early 1944, where he was permitted to live at home and wear civilian clothes, earning $225 a month. During that year he was given leave to participate in two "Victory" Opens in Chicago and Dallas. He finished second in Chicago and tied for third in Dallas. He also played in the Minneapolis Four-Ball, finishing eighth.

Most of his remaining days in the service were spent playing golf, either in matches at Colonial Country Club in Fort Worth or the occasional exhibition with Bob Hope and Bing Crosby. He was promoted to captain just before receiving an honorable discharge in September 1945. His service to Uncle Sam had lasted 1 year, 9 months, and 23 days.

While his official release was in September 1945, Hogan somehow found the time to compete in 17 tournaments that year, winning five times. His first victory that year, at the Nashville Invitational, came two days before his official discharge date. Six weeks earlier, he had participated in the lucrative Tam O'Shanter Open in Chicago, a tournament he tended to avoid because he wasn't crazy about the promoter, the flashy, flamboyant George May. Hogan tied for second and pocketed $5,667, by far the largest paycheck of his career to that point.

Germany had surrendered in May 1945, so the only fighting still going on for American troops in the summer of 1945 was in the Pacific Theater. Eleven days after Hogan picked up his check for his second-place finish at the Tam O'Shanter, the *Enola Gay* dropped an atomic bomb on Hiroshima. Three days later, a second atomic bomb was dropped on Nagasaki, and the Japanese finally capitulated. The official surrender ceremony was held on September 2, the day before Hogan cruised to a four-shot win in Nashville over Johnny Bulla and Byron Nelson.

The gifted Nelson won 19 times in 1945, including 11 straight. And while the field may have been weakened by the war, Snead competed in 26 tournaments and won 6, including the first event of the season, the Los Angeles Open.

Hogan biographer James Dodson recounted a conversation Hogan had with his wife after all the hostilities had ended, clearing the way for a full PGA season in 1946. "I'm damn glad it's over," he told Valerie. Two years earlier, as he was about to be inducted into the Army Air Corps, he had given Valerie a sapphire ring, which she wore for the rest of her life.

5

HALE AMERICA ROUND 3, JUNE 20, 1942

Good Times Jimmy

Thus I was saved at the last moment from the terrible fate of a Bing Crosby.

—Jimmy Demaret

A sense of scoring normalcy—or what would pass as scoring normalcy at Ridgemoor—made an appearance on Saturday during the third round of the Hale America National Open. The rains came and remained, making the course soggy and vision difficult. And the scores looked a little bit more like scores you might see at an official US Open.

Whereas 48 players broke par on Thursday and Friday, only 19 could better 72 on Saturday. Only six more could equal par. Six players dropped out, reducing the no-cut field to ninety, and there were more scores in the 80s (nine) than in the 60s (six.) One of the six to equal par was Bobby Jones, who was listed in the *Chicago Tribune* as "Capt. Robert T. Jones of Mitchel Field." He wasn't there yet, but would be soon.

Another oddity was that the USGA had decided before the tournament took place that the most celebrated amateur golfer in the history of the sport was no longer an amateur. After retiring from golf, Jones had made money from a movie deal he signed with Warner Brothers for instructional videos. In the eyes of the ever-vigilant USGA—but not in the eyes of Jones—that was a no-no for an amateur.

The leaderboards published in those days usually had an asterisk affixed to an amateur. There was never one attached to Capt. Robert T. Jones over the four rounds he played at Ridgemoor. So the last competitive medal tournament in which he competed—aside from his yearly appearances at the Masters—Bobby Jones, consummate and evergreen amateur, was deemed to be competing as a professional.

Jones and Ben Hogan were paired together for the last two rounds, as tournament officials had gallery size in mind when doing the pairings. Jones was still one of the most recognizable and important figures in the sport. It would be another 20 years before television insisted on having the lowest scorers in the final groupings.

Jones more than held his own off the tee with the longer-hitting Hogan, as Grantland Rice recounted in his story about the round. Later, Jones told Rice that he had made a change in his stance which had resulted in the improvement. "It felt like old times," Jones said. The pairing had a distinct "changing of the guard" feel to it, even if Jones was no longer the dominant force in golf and Hogan had yet to become it. Rice wrote that "Hogan, struggling desperately to win his first major, will be hard to beat." He was correct on the "hard to beat" part. The part about the "first major" would be the source of debate for decades.

The weather not only held down scores, it also held down visitors. No official crowd estimates were listed by the major papers; the *New York Times* simply referred to the galleries as "small." The rain didn't last all day and that proved to benefit Hogan, who went out in the afternoon after the course had started to dry out. Mike Turnesa, the halfway leader by three shots, caught the full brunt of the inclement weather in the morning.

Turnesa bogeyed two of the first four holes. He then played the final 14 holes in 2 under par, getting a birdie on the 5th hole and then draining a 20-foot birdie putt on the 18th hole to avoid going over par for the day. He was still playing steady golf—14 pars in 18 holes in bad weather is evidence of that. But this also was the same player who had traversed Ridgemoor in an astounding 13 under par over the first two rounds. After all the rain and pars, he was right back where he started, at 13 under par.

Mike Turnesa was not accustomed to such rarified company on the PGA Tour, though in this tournament, he would turn out to be the runaway winner for Best Performance by a Turnesa Brother. Little brother Jim and big brother Joe were both 13 shots behind the leaders.

Ben Hogan ended up tying Turnesa for the 54-hole lead. He would have held the lead by himself had he not bogeyed the 18th hole, the first time he had gone over par since making the double bogey on the 17th hole in the first round. He still finished with a 69 to also stand at 13 under par.

Hogan did the bulk of his damage on the front nine, with consecutive birdies on the two par 5s, the second and third holes, and a third birdie at the par 4 ninth hole after a superlative shot from one of the many Ridgemoor bushes. He was 1 under par on the back nine heading to the 18th tee, but an errant 3-iron found the back bunker on the 175-yard hole.

Hogan faced a difficult up-and-down as the 18th was fronted by a pond, the sand was still wet, the green sloped away from him, and if he caught the ball too clean in the trap, the shot might well skip across the green and into the water. Hogan ignored going for the hole, opting simply to get his sand explosion on the putting surface. He succeeded, as the ball came to rest about 25 feet from the hole. He two-putted from there for his bogey. He had played the last two rounds at 13 under par after his disappointing first-round 72.

Lloyd Mangrum had a more-than-respectable 71 to stand at 210, 6 under par. He would pay for his inability to put a low number on the board during the second round, when he posted a 72. And first-round co-leader Otey Crisman continued his predictable descent down the leaderboard, fashioning a 76. He was still among the top 20, however, and those who finished in the top 30 would be compensated for their performance. Austin's Harvey Penick, meanwhile, got a dose of Mother Nature and had one of the 80s. He wasn't in bad company, as three-time major winner Denny Shute also shot an 80. Shute also had finished second to Craig Wood in the US Open at Colonial the previous year.

Joe and Jim Turnesa were at even par 216. Shute and Jones were at 217. Joe Kirkwood, a trick-shot artist who was scheduled to demonstrate his shot-making ability after the round in an exhibition, was also at 217. Previous major champions Henry Picard, Billy Burke, Tommy Armour, and Ralph Guldahl were all above par after three rounds. So while the scoring was still absurdly low for a US Open, the majority of the 90 players still competing were over par after 54 holes.

The leaderboard after the third round delighted everyone—the fans, the players, and the three sponsors who, weather permitting, were sure to get a large crowd for the final day. It was a veritable who's who of the leading luminaries in the game. Two strokes behind Hogan and Mike Turnesa was Jimmy Demaret. Lawson Little and Horton Smith were one further behind, and Byron Nelson and qualifier Jim Ferrier were five strokes back. Harold (Jug) McSpaden was at 209 while Lloyd Mangrum led a group of three at 210.

While Hogan, Mike Turnesa, Demaret, Little, Smith, and Nelson were all familiar names to even the casual golf fan of the early 1940s, the same could not be said for Ferrier. Unless, that is, you were referring to the golf fans in Australia whose source of information was the *Sydney Morning Herald.*

Ferrier learned the game from his father, who was of Scottish descent with family in Carnoustie. He was a low handicapper and soon took a job as secretary at the Manly Golf Club, where young Jim started to play golf at age four. By his teens, Jim was a scratch golfer and started piling up amateur titles in Australia. At the age of 16, he was the runner-up in the Australian Open, making a 6 on the final hole to lose by one shot.

In 1940, with a slew of successes Down Under, Ferrier moved to the United States where he worked as a golf journalist. The USGA prohibited him from its US Amateur because Ferrier had made money from his golf writings in Australia. But he got an invitation to the 1940 Masters, where he finished alone in 26th place and was the third lowest amateur. He won an amateur tournament in Chicago that same year. He turned professional in March 1941, taking a job as the head pro at Elmhurst Country Club outside Chicago.

Ferrier showed he was ready for the Hale America by leading the sectional qualifying at demanding Medinah, also outside Chicago. His career, too, would be sidetracked by World War II; he and his Australian-born wife worked in defense industry jobs in the Chicago area as a condition of citizenship. He later served in the Army, but stayed stateside, and even scored his first PGA Tour win, the 1944 Oakland Open, while stationed at nearby Camp Roberts.

Ferrier also became the first Australian to win a major tournament when he triumphed at the 1947 PGA Championship. He nearly won the 1950 Masters, blowing a three-shot lead with six holes to play, finishing alone in second place, two shots behind Jimmy Demaret. He finished fifth in the 1950 US Open, just two shots behind the trio tied for first: Hogan, Mangrum, and George Fazio. Ferrier won 18 times on the PGA Tour and is widely viewed as the most influential and successful non-American professional golfer before the arrival of Gary Player two decades later.

The Hale America top five were cumulatively 57 under par over the three rounds, "one of the greatest scoring sprees in the history of the ancient game," according to Rice. He continued, "There has been nothing like it in any major tournament and there is no sign that there will be any letup" for the fourth and final round.

The most formidable challenge to the leaders, however, stood two shots off the pace. It had been more than two years since Jimmy Demaret had won his first Masters and rattled off a slew of victories to signal his arrival as a force to be mentioned in the same company as Snead, Nelson, and Hogan. The fashionista, now playing out of Plum Hollow in Detroit, wore a green knitted tam o'shanter and finished with a 69. The *Chicago Tribune* referred to Demaret as "the gay Texan whose labors in the recent PGA and in the current event are evidence of his aim to return to the Demaret form of 1940, when he won six championships, including the Masters and the Western."

Among the leaders, Demaret had been the steadiest, with rounds of 67 and 69 to go with his third-round 69. He was making a name for himself as both a successful player and a buoyant, fun-loving personality on the PGA Tour. He was fun to watch, both as a golfer and as a clotheshorse—and he was worth watching because he was very good at what he did.

The career arc of Jimmy Demaret was more or less the same as that of Hogan and Mangrum. All three were Texans, born four years apart early in the twentieth century. All three got into golf through caddying. All three had impoverished upbringings.

Golf writer/historian Al Barkow recalled that later in life, Demaret could still "recite the name of every street he crossed as he walked the couple of miles to the course. . . . He may have been a three-time winner of the Masters, the winner of over 20 other events on the pro tour, but his caddy days were good times, too."

Demaret loved to regale his friends. He loved to sing. From a personality standpoint, he was like a rose between two thorns when in the company of the taciturn Mangrum and Hogan. A 1947 *Time* feature was headlined "Good Time Jimmy" for a reason. He enjoyed golf and life, sometimes the latter more than the former. He was the logical successor to Walter Hagen and the equally logical predecessor to Lee Trevino.

He dressed outlandishly for the times. While Hogan, Mangrum, and most of the pros wore varying shades of gray and brown, Demaret preferred colors. Lots of them. Mix and match. He was described as a "sartorial sunset" by Grantland Rice, while another writer said looking at Demaret on the golf course was like watching "lightning strike a paint factory."

Demaret came honestly to his love of colors. His father was, among other things, a house painter, trying to raise a family of nine in Houston. Demaret dressed like everyone else on the tour when he started out, but then one day in New York City he stopped to check out a store where movie stars' clothes were made. "There, he saw bolts and bolts of lightweight material in many bright shades," Barkow wrote.

Demaret was told that the material was for ladies' clothing. He said that didn't bother him in the slightest and asked if he could be fitted. So the clothier measured him and made shirts and slacks in a number of different hues, "and a sartorial revolution in golf got under way."

For Demaret, it was a no-brainer. Not only did he like the way he looked, he also liked the fact that the new clothes were lighter, which made it easier for him to swing the golf club. "I learned early that color puts life into things," he wrote in his book, *My Partner, Ben Hogan*, which is equal parts Demaret autobiography and Hogan hagiography. At that time (1954), Demaret claimed that he owned 43 hats, 71 pairs of slacks, 20 sweaters, 55 shirts, and 39 sports jackets. "I'm partial to brick-red, mulberry, royal crimson, pale pink, purple, hunter green, Nile green, heather green and flaming scarlet," he wrote. Not a brown, black, gray, or white in the bunch.

The fashion plate that Demaret became was wholly in keeping with his outsized and outgoing personality. But he also falls into the category of being one of the most underappreciated great golfers of his time, despite the three Masters championships and a spot in the World Golf Hall of Fame. He briefly held the scoring record for the US Open until a man named Hogan came in later the same day and posted an even better score.

In that respect, Demaret falls more into line with Mangrum, golf's so-called Forgotten Man. It wasn't that Demaret couldn't play as well as the others. He most definitely could. Hogan called him "the most underrated golfer in history," while another close friend, Jack Burke Jr., said "his career meant nothing to him. He enjoyed the people in it."

Or maybe it was just Jimmy being Jimmy, and understanding that it was all part of one, big, vibrant, occasionally successful, always entertaining package.

Demaret was born in Houston in 1910, two years ahead of Hogan and four ahead of Mangrum. There were five boys in the nine children. Jimmy and his brothers Milton and Al would all become exceptional golfers. But early on, Demaret was strictly a baseball and football guy. He was hoping for a career in baseball until he was told he could earn 65 cents a bag caddying for soldiers at nearby Camp Logan.

He never gave baseball another thought. He won his first tournament, an all-caddy event at Camp Logan, when he was 11. Five years later he had his first golf job—an assistant at the ultra-exclusive River Oaks Country Club in Houston. Jack Burke Sr. gave him the job. Part of the responsibility was watching over Jack Burke Jr., who was 13 years younger than Demaret. Thus, Demaret became "one of Texas' most celebrated high school dropouts," in the words of the Texas Sports Hall of Fame.

Jack Burke Sr. was a player in his own right, in addition to running things at River Oaks. He finished second in the 1920 US Open, a stroke astern of Englishman Ted Ray. Demaret said he never had a lesson before he started watching, following, and listening to Burke. He never had one after that, either.

In that respect, he had the ideal apprenticeship. He dedicated his 1954 book on Hogan to Jack Burke Sr., "who made a professional golfer of me. You can't repay a man for that."

Later in life, Demaret and Jack Burke Jr. would found Champions Golf Club in Houston. But in the mid- to late 1920s, Demaret performed all the thankless tasks of a country club assistant pro while also being the requisite sponge to absorb all the important lessons of the sport.

Demaret moved to Galveston Country Club in 1932 to become the head pro. It was there, along the windswept course, that he developed the game for which he was known and at which he excelled. Many pro golfers will tell you that their biggest fear is the wind. Not rain. Not cold. The wind. Demaret honed his game playing on gusty Galveston in the mornings, learning how to play in the wind.

It was in Galveston that Demaret not only learned to play—and excel—in the wind. He also scratched the other major itch of his—the yearning to sing and perform. You could no more imagine Hogan or Mangrum performing at a club than you could imagine Demaret dressing in browns and whites. But it was classic Demaret.

The man responsible for all of this was Sam Maceo. He owned a dinner club in Galveston, became friends with Demaret, and one thing led to another. Soon, Demaret was joining orchestras to belt out a tune. One of the bandleaders thought so much of Demaret's smooth baritone that he suggested Demaret give up golf. But Maceo and another local businessman thought otherwise, offering to sponsor Demaret on the professional tour. "Thus I was saved at the last moment from the terrible fate of a Bing Crosby," Demaret wrote.

The "tour" in question at this point in time was in California, which staged a number of tournaments. Demaret earned $385 for finishing third in Sacramento in 1935 and picked up another $750 with a third-place finish at Agua Caliente. Hogan played in some of these tournaments as well. He didn't win a dime.

The money was enough to convince Demaret that he might have a future in the game. He won four straight Texas PGA titles and took the job as head pro at Brae Burn Country Club in Houston, where he worked from 1936 to 1941. An article in the *Houston Post* announcing the appointment referred to Demaret as "one of the finest shotmakers in the Southwest." That would soon turn out to be more than just hyperbole.

Demaret slowly but surely established himself as one of the players to watch as the 1930s ended and the 1940s began. In 1937, he tied for fourth in the Houston Open, his only top 10 showing of the season. But also that year he was a guest on the Sammy Kaye radio show and was so impressive that it led to an endorsement deal with MacGregor clubs. He became MacGregor's first contract golfer and was still playing MacGregor clubs when he won his third Masters in 1950.

The following year, Demaret broke through with six top-10 finishes and his first official PGA Tour victory, the San Francisco Match Play tournament. He defeated Sam Snead, 4 and 3 in the final, which the *New York Times* reported was contested in "rain, wind and spongy turf." "It really gave me my golfing start," Demaret was quoted in Darsie's *My Greatest Day in Golf*. "Sam Snead was the biggest name in golf in 1938." Demaret said he matched Snead shot for shot, adding, "I played that round without a single mistake."

Snead never won a hole in the 15 that were played that day. Demaret recalled that "after that kind of victory, I felt I could hold my own with anyone in golf. It gave me just the lift and just the confidence I needed." He had another fourth-place finish at the Houston Open and came in sixth at the Inverness Invitational. The following year, he claimed his second PGA Tour victory at the Los Angeles Open, then one of the signature events on the PGA Tour. He missed tying the tournament record by one shot, finishing seven strokes ahead of Harold (Jug) McSpaden.

In late March 1939, Demaret reported to Augusta National Golf Club to participate in his first Masters. It was the sixth Masters overall, and Demaret finished in a tie for 33rd with Bobby Jones, Walter Hagen, and Englishman Harry Cooper. In those days there was no cut, and in 1939 the total purse was $4,950. Only the top 12 and ties received money—and Demaret's 304 was 11 strokes out of 12th place. He remedied that situation the following year.

Demaret not only won at Augusta in 1940 by what was then the largest margin of victory in tournament history (four strokes), he also dominated the tour leading into that April weekend. In the months leading up to the Masters, Demaret won five events, including three in succession. One of those victories was the Western Open in February, held in Texas for the first time at Demaret's former stomping grounds, River Oaks Country Club. The Western at the time was considered one of the most important tournaments of the year, a major in the minds of those who were competing.

Demaret finished fourth on the money earnings list in 1940 with more than $8,600, not far behind Hogan's $10,343, which marked the first time Hogan led the tour in winnings. He would do so four more times, all in the 1940s.

While Demaret had played all across the country, and would soon include South America among his favorite places to play, he had remained a tried-and-true Texan in terms of club employment. That ended in 1941 when he left Houston for Wee Burn Country Club in Darien, Connecticut.

Demaret described Wee Burn's offer as too attractive to pass up. He was given more time to play in tournaments and did not have to be on site for six months of the year. (Winters in Connecticut generally militated against playing golf.) While at Wee Burn, Demaret reverted briefly to his first love by playing with the Noroton Knights softball team. A history of Wee Burn described Demaret as the "sparkplug" of the team. While at the course, he would often play more than 18 holes a day to acclimate himself to the New England greens. He stayed there for only one year.

Hogan and Demaret teamed to win the Inverness Four-Ball in 1941, his only victory of the season. (He tied for 12th in his defense at Augusta.) He finished ninth in earnings, but spent a considerable amount of time that year playing in South America. He won the Argentine Open (he referred to Argentina as the Texas of South America) with what was then a record score of 279. He would not grace the winner's circle again until after World War II, but he did get to the semifinals of the 1942 PGA championship, one of three times he advanced to the final four players while the tournament was still a match-play event. He also finished sixth at the Masters.

Demaret and Hogan partnered again in the Inverness Four-Ball in 1942, finishing tied for fourth. That was the last tournament before the Hale America, where Demaret came close to winning the same gold medal that Hogan always said looked a lot like the four other US Open medals he won.

Unbeknownst to the players, fans, and sponsors in Chicago for the Hale America Tournament, the US government was soon to announce an astounding development in its war with Germany. The FBI had, with the help of one of the saboteurs, cracked a Nazi spy ring inside the United States. Eight men, two of whom were US citizens, had been recruited and trained by the Third Reich to sneak into the country and perform various acts of sabotage. Two had ended up in Chicago.

The Germans had landed two squads of saboteurs in the United States, taking one squad to Florida and the other to Long Island via submarine from occupied France. They came with explosives and plans to destroy bridges and water lines, with an attendant spread of panic thrown in. One of the Long Island crew's targets was the Hell Gate Bridge in New York City, a four-rail structure that carried passengers and freight across the East River. Other targets included Penn Station and the New York water supply.

German espionage in the United States was not uncommon; in 1941 the FBI had infiltrated a spy ring in New York City led by a South African who had lived in the United States for 30 years. The 1942 "invaders" had one benefit that the 1941 group did not—law enforcement was mostly looking to the West Coast after the Japanese attack on Pearl Harbor in December 1941.

That was due in part to the February 1942 shelling of the Ellwood Oil Field in Santa Barbara, California, by a Japanese submarine. There were no casualties and the damage was minimal, but the attack raised the panic level on the West Coast, just as the Japanese had desired. The very next day, antiaircraft batteries in Los Angeles opened fire against what were suspected to be Japanese aircraft. There were none. And shortly after the Ellwood attack, President Roosevelt authorized the internment of what would be more than 120,000 Japanese American citizens.

The 1942 group of German spies and saboteurs consisted of longtime US residents, led by George Dasch. The eight were recruited by Walter Kappe, a German army lieutenant who had lived in Chicago and New York before moving back to Germany in the 1930s. The men underwent rigorous training in Germany for the operation, code-named Pastorius in honor of Francis Pastorius, founder of the first permanent German settlement in the United States.

Nine days before Ben Hogan teed off in the final round of the Hale America, the German spies landed on Long Island for what was expected to be a two-year reign of terror in the United States. Their arrival did not go unnoticed; a coastline spotter confronted the men, who were in German military uniforms so that they would be treated as POWs and not spies if they were captured. Dasch gave the coastline spotter a wad of cash and told him to forget what he had seen. The Germans then dug holes to bury their uniforms, explosives, and other armaments and quickly got a train into New York City. The four split up, but intended to come back for their cache.

The spotter immediately notified the Coast Guard. Officials toured the beach the following morning and found what the Germans had buried. Less than two weeks later, Bobby Jones would report for active duty at Long Island's Mitchel Field, 85 miles west of the saboteur's landing area.

The Florida saboteurs landed just off the coast of Jacksonville two days before the Hale America began. They landed without incident, buried their cache, and took a bus into Jacksonville. Their targets were primarily in the Midwest, as two went on to Chicago—they were there while the Hale America was underway—and the other two to Cincinnati.

Operation Pastorius was unfolding as planned, and on schedule, when the 96 golfers began play at Ridgemoor. And there's little evidence that the plotters would have not succeeded, as the FBI did not so much crack the case as it was handed to them on a silver platter. (FBI Director J. Edgar Hoover would long claim that the bureau had indeed cracked the case. It simply wasn't true.)

Shortly after Dasch checked into his hotel in New York City, he began to have second thoughts. The Nazis had provided the plotters with bundles of US currency. The German government also promised the eight ripe, postwar job opportunities. In short, they would get the heroes' treatment. Dasch expressed his misgivings to Ernst Peter Burger, who had been in the Long Island landing party. Burger did nothing to deter Dasch.

Dasch had been born in Germany, as had the other seven, and served as a 14-year-old clerk for the Germans during World War I. But he had come to the United States as a stowaway in the early 1920s and even served a stint in the US Army, receiving an honorable discharge. Dasch settled in New York, where he became a waiter. He had no desire to live in Germany, regardless of what status he might attain. His wife was an American. The United States was home. So he went rogue and notified the FBI. Dasch told the bureau's New York office that he would soon be in Washington, DC, and would call the FBI again.

The agency at first dismissed what looked to be a preposterous claim. The FBI was accustomed to receiving all kinds of calls about suspicious people and activities. This, while outlandish and potentially grave, seemed like all the others.

Then came the call from Long Island, alerting the FBI to what was on the beach at Amagansett, near where the saboteurs had landed. Dasch told the FBI's New York office about the plot and insisted on being put through to speak to Hoover. That did not happen.

Undeterred, Dasch took a train to Washington, DC, and once again called the FBI, just as the second round of the Hale America was being played. He told them he was the same person who had called a few days earlier, and that he was at the Mayflower Hotel. FBI agents then spent the next two days interrogating Dasch, and he gave them the soup-to-nuts version. He told them how they were trained outside Berlin. He gave them the name of contacts in the United States. He gave them the cash he had brought over, about $82,000. The following day, Dasch's three New York accomplices were arrested.

Two days after the Hale America concluded, two of the Florida saboteurs were arrested. The other two were taken into custody on June 27, two weeks after Dasch and his party had landed on Long Island. Within two weeks, or shortly after the tournament concluded, the FBI had arrested all eight plotters. They quickly changed their stories to say they only took on the assignment so that they could return to the United States which, they reminded their interrogators, was where they lived. That did not wash.

The eight were tried before a military tribunal, and all were convicted and sentenced to death. In the end, Dasch had his sentence reduced to 30 years, and Burger's was reduced to life. The other six were electrocuted. Dasch and Burger served six years in prison and then were deported to Germany. Hoover spoke to the nation after the arrests, just a short time after the Hale America, and took full credit for the capture of the saboteurs, turning it into a publicity coup for the FBI. Hoover also persuaded President Harry Truman to deny repeated requests by Dasch for a pardon.

Sixty-four years later, a group of power company workers in southwest Washington stumbled on a granite slab in a thicket. It was a memorial plaque for the six Nazi spies who had been electrocuted in 1942, on US government property, and was believed to have been placed there by a group of white supremacists. That's because after the names of the men, on the very bottom of the plaque were the initials NSWPP, which stood for National Socialist White People's Party. Until the mid-1960s, that group had been known as the American Nazi Party. Four years later, the granite slab was removed and placed in an unidentified location in Maryland.

Things were heating up in other war theaters around the globe. The Japanese, still licking their wounds from their staggering losses earlier in the month at the Battle of Midway, were busy reassessing their goals in the Pacific. That tends to happen when most of your operational navy gets wiped out.

On the final day of the Hale America Tournament, well before Ben Hogan, Bobby Jones, and Denny Shute teed off at 1:36 p.m., Allied forces surrendered the North African port of Tobruk to the Germans, under the command of General Erwin Rommel. The city was a strategic one; it had a deep-water port and was surrounded by steep hills, making it easy to defend. The British had ruled the port after defeating an Italian garrison two years earlier, but were sent back to Egypt by Rommel's Afrika Korps.

With more than 30,000 troops captured, this ranked as one of Britain's worst defeats of the war, second only to the humiliating fall of Singapore to the Japanese, when 80,000 British and other Allies were forced to surrender to a Japanese force of around 20,000. Tobruk would remain in German hands until the Allies pushed them out of North Africa entirely in 1943.

While Jimmy Demaret never left the United States while serving in the US Navy during World War II, neither did he ever come close to something so potentially dangerous as Operation Pastorius. He basically played a lot of golf. As only Demaret could, he described his time in the service thusly: "Every war has its slogan. There's Remember the Alamo. Remember the Maine. Remember Pearl Harbor. Mine was 'That'll play, Admiral.'"

Demaret won a pair of tournaments in 1943, when the PGA Tour essentially shut down, one of them being the Golden Valley Four-Ball with Craig Wood. He played in two events in the Chicago area and then, in November 1943, he was hired to be the head professional at River Oaks, succeeding his mentor, Jack

Burke Sr., who had died earlier that year. He was on the new job for less than a month when he enlisted in the Navy.

The closest Demaret got to joining Lloyd Mangrum in the ETO was Bainbridge, Maryland, where he was stationed for nearly a year at the Naval Training Station on the shores of the Susquehanna River. He was one of nearly 25,000 sailors who passed through while getting trained for noncombat duty; Demaret was taught to be a physical training instructor. He earned $85 a week at the outset. He entered the Navy as an apprentice seaman in late November 1943 and served two years and eight days, discharged as a seaman, second class. These were not "lost years" in terms of professional golf for Demaret. On the contrary, he played quite a bit while stationed at Bainbridge, San Diego, and Corpus Christi, Texas.

While serving Uncle Sam, Demaret nonetheless found time to play in several war relief matches as well as PGA tournaments, with the blessing of his supervisor. He wasn't "tournament ready" and would not be so again until 1946. But he could still compete.

In January 1945, he took what was called "special leave" from his Corpus Christi posting to book a room at the St. Anthony Hotel in San Antonio. The hotel was the site of one of Demaret's famous and frequent pranks, this one coming at the expense of singer Don Cherry, who was a solid golfer and friend to Demaret and many of the touring pros.

As Cherry told the story in a 2000 *Golf Digest* article, he was about to sing the song "Band of Gold," which he planned to dedicate to Demaret, who was in the audience along with several other pros. As the song began, the pros, at Demaret's command, threw golf balls onto the stage, which forced the band—and Cherry—to stop. Demaret was laughing uncontrollably in his seat.

When the show ended, Demaret received the check for the accompanying meal. Not just his meal. All the meals for all the pros. Demaret told the headwaiter that the players were Cherry's guests and that he, the headwaiter, should instead send the check to Cherry. The headwaiter obliged.

Demaret still wasn't through. As the players prepared for a practice round the following day, Cherry was among those slated to join them. Demaret came onto the tee and said he had an announcement to make—that Don Cherry's show the previous night had not gone well and that the golfers had taken up a collection to help. Demaret unrolled a wad of $20 bills he had collected the night before and gave the money to Cherry, more than enough to cover the dinners. Said Cherry, "He'd fly places just to needle me. When I yelled at him at the St. Anthony that night, I had just started wearing a hairpiece. He told me to shut up or he'd hit me in the hair."

That was vintage Demaret. Bing Crosby called him the funniest man without a script. He once helped organize a charity event with Gene Sarazen and boxers Gene Tunney and Jack Dempsey. The round was contested as Fred Waring's orchestra played on the course. Golf, set to the Big Band sound. Demaret still shot 70, even with all the music in his ears.

"You know, people think Demaret would have won more tournaments if he'd been serious," said George Fazio. "But if you got Jimmy mad enough to say 'I'll beat him,' if you backed him into a corner, he'd beat Nicklaus, Hogan, Palmer, anybody. I saw him beat Hogan in a playoff.

"Everybody says he was a coward, that he didn't want to be up there. No. I think he was just lazy. If Jimmy concentrated and wanted to go, he could be a tiger. But he didn't want to be a tiger. He wanted to be a pussy cat. He wanted to have some fun. I liked his style because he did both. He played and he had fun," Fazio said.

The "special leave" to San Antonio in 1945 resulted in a tie for 20th at the Texas Open, which was won by Sam Byrd. It was the fifth of six official PGA Tour victories for Byrd, who may well have been the best overall athlete on the PGA Tour. He also was pretty efficient on the golf course using his or someone else's clubs, as he displayed in the Hale America and in at least one other notable case. He also played with borrowed clubs one day in Atlanta as the guest of Bobby Jones, who had heard about Byrd's golfing prowess. Playing with the unfamiliar clubs on a course he had never seen, East Lake in Atlanta, Byrd shot 1 under par and earned this accolade from Jones: "He's the best man off the tee I ever saw. Not one of the best. The very best man with a driver I ever saw."

And this was while Byrd was playing not on the PGA Tour, but as a member of the New York Yankees. The team had been in the Atlanta area for an exhibition game, and Byrd had earlier captured the baseball players' golf championship by 14 shots. New York manager Joe McCarthy gave Byrd his blessing to join Jones. While Jones would soon retire, Byrd would soon leave baseball for a second, successful life as a professional golfer.

Samuel Dewey Byrd is the answer to the following trivia question: Name the only individual to play in the Masters and the World Series. He is another of the colorful characters who populated the PGA Tour in the era of Hogan, Demaret, Nelson, and Mangrum.

Raised in Birmingham, Alabama, he was drafted by the minor-league Birmingham Barons as a 20-year-old and embarked on a career in baseball, despite showing ability on the links as well. Like so many players of that era, Byrd had been introduced to the game while caddying at a local club. Three years after signing with Birmingham, Byrd joined the Yankees, mainly as a reserve. For the longest time he was known as "Babe Ruth's Legs" in that he would frequently pinch-run for the Bambino. He also would be used in the outfield in late-game situations, which is how he got his name into a World Series box score with a cameo appearance in the ninth inning of Game 4 of the 1932 World Series. He replaced Ruth in the outfield, and was on the field when the Yankees completed their four-game sweep of the Chicago Cubs. While that was Byrd's first World Series, it turned out to be Ruth's tenth—and last. The Yankees appeared in just the 1932 World Series during Byrd's six years with the team.

While Byrd was known largely as a utility or substitute, he was hardly a cipher on the diamond. He was with the Yankees from 1929 to 1934, and then spent two more years in the major leagues with the Cincinnati Reds. He appeared in 745 major league games and left baseball for good in 1936, taking his talents to the PGA. Over those 745 games, Byrd had a batting average of .274 with 38 home runs, 220 RBIs, and a .412 slugging percentage. He also was very adept in the outfield as evidenced by his .975 career fielding percentage.

In 1936, Byrd turned 30. He was constantly battling malaria. The Reds had lost interest in him and he ended up being assigned to a minor league team in Rochester—the St. Louis Cardinals' farm team at the time. The Cards gave Byrd his release after the 1936 season, and that was when he made the decision to try his hand in golf. "I feel much happier now that I've finally made up my mind on a subject that has had me somewhat up in the air for months," Byrd told his local paper, the *Birmingham News*. "If I could get rid of that malaria, I believe I could stay in big league baseball. But I think I'm doing the best thing."

The following spring, he snagged a job as an assistant to Ed Dudley, the PGA pro at Augusta National in the mid-1930s who also headed the pro shop at the Philadelphia Country Club in the summer. Dudley was also one of the PGA Tour's tournament chairmen and an influential voice in the organization. He was instrumental in getting Byrd out on the tour.

Like most other golfers of the day, Byrd had to wait his time to crack the winner's circle, finally triumphing in the 1942 Greater Greensboro Open, where he pocketed $1,000 for his two-stroke victory over Ben Hogan and Lloyd Mangrum. Two weeks later, he finished fourth in the Masters, five shots behind Hogan and Nelson. He had made his Augusta debut in 1940 where he tied for 14th, then came close in 1941, finishing in third place, five shots behind the winner, Craig Wood, and one shot ahead of Ben Hogan. Overall, he played in five Masters.

The closest Byrd came to winning one of the majors of that era was in 1945. But he happened to run into the red-hot buzz saw Byron Nelson in the finals of the 1945 PGA Championship outside Dayton, Ohio. En route to the finals,

Byrd beat a couple of club pros as well as established stars Johnny Revolta and 1941 PGA champion Vic Ghezzi to reach the finals. He even erased an early Nelson lead in the 36-hole final and stood 2-up after the morning 18-hole round.

But this was 1945 and this was Nelson, who was in the process of reeling off 11 consecutive victories. In the afternoon session, Byrd got to 3-up and was still ahead through 7 holes. But the relentless Nelson gradually evened things out and took the lead for good on the 11th hole. That was the first of four straight holes Nelson would win, and he closed Byrd out, 4 and 3, after the 15th hole.

There certainly was no shame in losing to Byron Nelson in 1945. Everyone did. In addition to the Texas Open victory in January, which Byrd won by one shot over Nelson, Byrd added the Azalea Open (also called the Mobile Open) in November 1945, beating Dutch Harrison in a playoff. That was the last of his six PGA tour victories. He had five other unofficial victories.

Byrd's effectiveness waned after the war. He placed 40th and 47th in his last two Masters' appearances, the finale being in 1948, the same year Bobby Jones finished competing in his own event. He lost in the first round in his final three appearances in the PGA Championship and ended his US Open career with a tie for 49th place in the 1951 tournament at Oakland Hills.

Jimmy Demaret always figured he would be like Byrd and become a professional baseball player. But he found golf at an early age and played baseball or softball only for enjoyment through the years. After Byrd won the 1945 Texas Open in January, Demaret returned to his Texas naval base until his next tournament appearance a month later at the Pensacola Open. He finished in 11th place, well behind the winner, Sam Snead, who was no longer in the Navy.

That was the year Nelson and Snead dominated the tour in the early stages, Snead having been discharged from the Navy in September 1944 due to a back injury. Hogan would not win a tournament until September. That year saw most of the established pros gradually work their way back to the tour, the primary exception being Mangrum, who went into the Army in 1944 and thus did not get out in time to play any of the 1945 season.

Demaret next surfaced at the Atlanta Iron Lung Open in April (the same week that would have been slotted for the Masters had it not been canceled) and placed 10th. In July, he again received "special leave" and checked into the posh McAlpin Hotel in New York City, not too far from Toots Shor's, one of his favorite watering holes. He then made his way to Chicago to play in the lucrative Tam O'Shanter Open, but was one of three players who withdrew after the first round in deference to a US Navy directive concerning playing off base. He had shot a 73.

Still, he played well enough in 1945, and often enough, to record six top-25 finishes. In addition to his finishes in Atlanta, Pensacola, and San Antonio, he was sixth in the Corpus Christi Open, seventh in the Tulsa Open, and second in the Glen Garden Invitational. On November 27, 1945, he received an honorable discharge from the Navy along with a check for $256.93, covering his back pay.

Over the course of four rounds at Ridgemoor, Jimmy Demaret did what no player had ever done in an official US Open—he had shot four consecutive rounds in the 60s. But, as the Hale America wasn't deemed an official US Open, Demaret's performance went unrecognized—if not unnoticed. It would be 26 years before someone finally did break 70 in all four rounds of an official US Open; Lee Trevino did it at challenging Oak Hill outside Rochester to win his first major in 1968.

Through 2020, four others accomplished the feat—champions Lee Janzen (1993), Rory McIlroy (2011), and Gary Woodland (2019), along with 2019 runner-up Brooks Koepka. So Demaret shares with Koepka the distinction of being the only players to shoot four rounds in the 60s in a US Open—or the wartime substitute for a US Open—and not win the tournament. In 2020, Cameron Smith became the first player in the history of the Masters to shoot four rounds in the 60s, but still finished five shots behind winner Dustin Johnson.

Demaret also had a brief brush with US Open fame in 1948. He finished four rounds at Riviera at 278, or 6 under par, and was the leader in the clubhouse. His 278 also bettered by three shots the existing US Open scoring record of 281 set by Ralph Guldahl in 1937.

Demaret didn't hold the record for long. Along came his good friend, Ben Hogan, who was finishing off a 69 after a morning 68 and ended up at 276, two ahead of Demaret and five strokes better than Guldahl's record. Jim Turnesa also bettered Guldahl's 281 by one shot. Sam Snead, who had led the tournament after two rounds, shot 3 over par over the final two rounds on Saturday to finish in fifth place. Snead, who never won a US Open, said that he would have won *nine* of them had he merely been able to shoot a 69 on his final round. It wouldn't have mattered in this case. He would have needed a 65 to tie Hogan.

Demaret's second-place finish in 1948 at Riviera was his best in a US Open. He had a third-place finish at the age of 47 in the 1957 US Open at Inverness, where he led the field after the first and third rounds. He finished one shot behind co-leaders Dick Mayer and the defending champion, Cary Middlecoff. Mayer prevailed in a playoff the following day. Demaret also tied for fourth in the 1953 US Open, 11 shots behind the champion, Hogan, who won the title by 6 strokes over Sam Snead.

6

HALE AMERICA
ROUND 4, JUNE 21, 1942

Ben and Bobby, One Last Time

The right man won. He had it coming.

—Grantland Rice, on Ben Hogan's
victory at the Hale America

The Sunday galleries were huge. The weather cooperated, and the three-some of Ben Hogan, Bobby Jones, and Denny Shute drew a sizable lot of the estimated 12,000 in attendance. Jones was still a draw, even if he trailed Hogan by 14 shots and had no chance of winning.

It had been a dozen years since Jones pulled off the almost unfathomable: winning what was then called the Grand Slam—the US Open, the British Open, the US Amateur, and the British Amateur—in one calendar year. He then abruptly retired at the age of 28.

You can count on one hand the elite performers who retire, still healthy, in their prime. Football's Jim Brown probably comes closest to Jones. Baseball's Sandy Koufax wanted to save his arm for future use. Hockey's Bobby Orr had badly injured knees. Jones was 28 and at the absolute peak of his sport when he went from the course to his law office in Atlanta. In one respect, you could understand his reasoning. He had nowhere to go but down.

Jones's privileged upbringing—his father was a lawyer as well—and his access to a terrific golf course—East Lake—gave him a huge advantage over the quartet of Texans who, along with Sam Snead, would dominate the sport after he left. Ben Hogan, Byron Nelson, and Jimmy Demaret were basically self-made golfers and got into the sport via caddying. Lloyd Mangrum, a Texan by birth, developed his game in California and had an older brother to lead the way. The Texans all came from humble beginnings and turned pro at an early age to make a living. Jones had no such concerns. In his mind, he never did turn pro, even if he was considered to be one at the Hale America Tournament. He never had to resort to subsisting on oranges or staying in fleabag hotels.

In that respect, he wasn't unlike many of the fine amateur players at the time. They were, like him, mostly country-club types to whom golf was an avocation rather than a lifestyle. He honed his game at East Lake, occasionally under the watchful eye of pro Stewart Maiden, whose game Jones attempted to emulate. ("Monkey see, monkey do," as Mangrum would say.) Jones never had any formal golf lessons so, in that one respect, his golf education mirrored that of the Texans.

Hogan, Mangrum, and Demaret never finished high school. Jones graduated from high school at the age of 16 and from Georgia Tech at the age of 20. By that time he was already well known, especially in the South. His Georgia Tech yearbook entry notes, "Yes, this is none other than the famous Bob, of golfing fame. We can't tell you much about him that you don't already know, unless that he's a darn good student as well as golfer, not to mention that he is exceedingly popular with his fellow students."

He really did seem to have it all. He was skilled. He was educated. He was handsome. He was born on St. Patrick's Day. By the time he graduated from Georgia Tech with a degree in mechanical engineering, Jones had already competed in eight of the majors—the two Opens and the two Amateurs. At the age of 20, he had tied for second in the 1922 US Open, a stroke behind Gene Sarazen. He had twice reached the semifinals of the US Amateur and, as a precocious 17-year-old, lost in the 1919 US Amateur final to Davey Herron, or, as the USGA referred to the champion, S. Davidson Herron.

Jonesologists refer to this time span as the Seven Lean Years, from 1916 when he made his US Amateur debut through 1922 with close calls in both the US Open and the US Amateur. All those high finishes had yet to produce a victory. Hogan had gone through a similar "dry" spell, but the difference was that Hogan was a professional and needed to win. Jones did not.

Jones had come close in the US Amateur. In addition to the near miss in 1919, he had reached the semifinals in 1920 and 1922 and the quarterfinals in 1921. He tied for fifth in the 1921 US Open at age 19. After that tournament, Walter Hagen told Jones's chronicler, O. B. Keeler, that Jones had "everything he needs to win any championship except experience and maybe philosophy. He's still a bit impetuous."

Those who played with and against Jones in that time frame marveled at his game as well as his more-than-occasional flashes of temper. The fact that Jones's comportment and reputation today is widely considered to be beyond reproach does not belie the truth: he was a teenage hothead. During one of his World War I exhibition matches outside Boston, he had startled the gallery by breaking a club, tossing it, and then picking up his golf ball.

But he was followed and written about more for his talent than his temper. And the talent was considerable. He won a slew of tournaments, including the Georgia state championship at the age of 14, beating fields of adult men. His first US Amateur appearance was in the same year, 1916, where he reached the quarterfinals.

Jones wrote in his book, *Golf Is My Game*, that not winning in 1916 might have been a blessing in disguise: "Had I won that championship, I should have been amateur champion for not only the next twelve months, but, because of the suspension of play (1917 and 1918) for three whole years. I shudder to think what these years might have done to me, not so much to my golf, but in a vastly more important respect, to me as a human being."

But as he entered his 20s, the big wins eluded him. That would change, and in a hurry. From 1923 to 1930, Jones won four US Opens and finished second three other times. He played in three British Opens in that time frame and won them all. He won four US Amateurs in the space of five years, finishing runner-up in the one year (1926) that he did not win. He added a fifth in 1930. He competed in two British Amateurs and won one, reaching the quarterfinals in the other. In all, he won those 13 "majors" in 21 attempts.

These are the names to remember when chronicling Jones's exploits in match-play events in that period: Max Marston, George Von Elm, Johnny Goodman, and Andrew Jamieson. All could eventually tell their grandchildren that they defeated Bobby Jones in head-to-head competition when Jones was in his absolute prime. Marston would go on to win the 1923 US Amateur after beating Jones 2 and 1 in the round of 16. Von Elm had denied Jones a third-straight US Amateur title in 1926, defeating him 2 and 1 in the final.

Goodman stunned Jones in the first round of the 1929 US Amateur at Pebble Beach, where Jones, fresh off his US Open victory at Winged Foot, had set the course record and been co-medalist with Eugene Homans after the two qualifying rounds of stroke play. Goodman's upbringing was a lot like that of Hogan and Mangrum, one of poverty and need. He was, however, widely seen as the best golfer from the state of Nebraska and he upset Jones, 1-up. "Shock waves reverberated from the stunned galleries at Pebble Beach to sports pages and radio reports across the country and around the world," wrote Mark Frost in his

Jones biography, *Grand Slam*. Goodman fell in the second round but enjoyed success in the next decade, winning the 1933 US Open—the last amateur to do so—and the 1937 US Amateur.

Jamieson was the unlikeliest of all Jones's conquerors in this time period. He rode his bike to Muirfield, site of the 1926 British Amateur and, by the time he met Jones in the quarterfinals, was regarded as the weakest of the eight remaining players. Jamieson was only 20 and was making his British Amateur debut.

The British Amateur matches were 18 holes, and Jones always preferred the 36-hole format used in the US Amateur. The second 18 gave him time to overcome a slow start or, had he played well in the morning 18, to go for the jugular in the afternoon 18. But on this day, something remarkable happened. The match lasted 15 holes with Jamieson eliminating the prohibitive favorite, 4 and 3. Jones did not win a single hole.

Jones had already decided at that point to return to the United States and forgo the British Open, being contested at Royal Lytham and St. Anne's. He was tired. He was bothered by a sore neck. He was homesick. Plus, he didn't like his chances at a tournament that had not been won by an amateur since 1897, which was the case with the British Open.

But he also didn't want to look like he was returning to the United States with his tail between his legs and his ego bruised. So he had a change of heart and decided he would stay in Great Britain and try his luck at the British Open. Before that, however, were the Walker Cup matches at St. Andrews. Jones won both of his matches, getting revenge against Jamieson in one of them, and the US team edged the British team by one point.

The golfers who defeated Jones in match play at either the US Amateur or British Amateur from 1923 to 1930 have another thing in common: they never did so again. Von Elm, who counted the 1926 US Amateur as his only "major," may have been the most accomplished of the lot. He won the deciding match at the 1926 Walker Cup and then finished third at the 1926 British Open. He also had a second-place finish in the 1931 US Open.

While his match-play losses between 1923 and 1930 were few and far between, what really spoke to Jones's greatness and championship motivation was the way he played when he reached the finals of either the US Amateur or British Amateur. In winning the six combined titles, his *closest* final was his next-to-last, the 1930 British Amateur, which was the first leg of his Grand Slam that year. He won at St. Andrews, 7 and 6.

His five US Amateur titles were won by margins of 9 and 8, 8 and 7 (three times), and 10 and 8. He shares the USGA record for largest margin of victory with a 14 and 13 drubbing of the unfortunate John Beck in the third round of the 1928 Amateur at Brae Burn Country Club in West Newton, Massachusetts. He also was sole medalist in four US Amateurs, and shared medalist honors two other times.

In the 1929 US Open at Winged Foot, Jones and Al Espinosa were tied at the end of 72 holes after Jones had made a difficult, sidehill 14-foot putt to force a 36-hole playoff. (He had been six shots ahead with six holes to play.) Twenty-five years later, Jones sat in a golf cart and watched four players—Tommy Armour, Craig Wood, Gene Sarazen, and Johnny Farrell—re-enact the famous putt on the same green at Winged Foot. None made it.

Jones went on to beat Espinosa in the playoff by the still-astounding total of 23 shots, as Espinosa failed to break 80 in either of the two 18-hole rounds.

In 1926, Jones overcame deficits of two shots (British) and three shots (US) to win both Opens. That year marked the first time Jones competed in—and finished—all four so-called majors of the day. The world's most celebrated and decorated amateur golfer of his time won both professional tournaments that year while losing out in both amateurs. He had entered and competed in all four events in 1921, but a disastrous third round at the British Open at St. Andrews prompted Jones to pick up his ball on the 11th hole, tear up his scorecard, and be disqualified. This was the fifth of the Seven Lean Years.

The only other time Jones competed in all four events in the same year was, of course, 1930, the year that he won them all. He had pretty much decided he was going to retire even before destroying the field at the US Amateur at Merion. Joe Dey reported on the tournament for the *Philadelphia Bulletin* and recalled that Jones's dominance was such that he counted 13 times that Jones three-putted and still easily won all his matches.

Jones had begun his career as a raw, hot-tempered 14-year-old at the US Amateur at Merion, and he had concluded his career as a distinguished, commanding presence as a Grand Slam champion at Merion in 1930. It is hallowed ground for the USGA. No other golf course in the country has hosted as many USGA events.

So much had happened between the bookend Merion visits. Jones had gone on to earn a degree in English literature from Harvard, where he worked as an assistant manager on the golf team. He couldn't compete in matches, having exhausted his eligibility while at Georgia Tech. Jones then moved on to Emory Law School in Atlanta. He passed the bar exam after one year at Emory and joined his father's law firm in Atlanta.

He also had married and started a family, which would eventually grow to three children, the only boy being named Robert Tyre Jones III. (Bobby Jones was named for his paternal grandfather, not his father, whose full name was

Robert Purmedus Jones.) He was one of the most famous athletes on the planet, an icon who easily rivaled the likes of Jack Dempsey, Babe Ruth, or Bill Tilden. Jones had received a ticker tape parade in 1926 following his British Open victory, and another in 1930. What makes his success even more remarkable is that he was not a tournament hound. He played no more than three months of competitive golf in any given year. Jones was the anti-Hogan, going days without practice or touching a club. Then again, his life and lifestyle was not predicated on him winning golf tournaments.

But now, having stepped away from competition at age 28, Jones wanted to pursue other adventures. He continued to work in the law. He made a series of instructional films with Hollywood celebrities for Warner Brothers. And he would very soon embark on a challenge that would define the rest of his life—the design of a majestically beautiful golf course in Augusta, Georgia, and the staging of an invitational tournament at that same venue, year after year.

The Masters had staged nine tournaments by the time Jones reported to Chicago to play in the Hale America Tournament. It had taken four years from the date of Jones's retirement to the inaugural Masters in 1934. For years, the Masters would represent Jones's only public golf appearance.

Augusta National Golf Club came to be several years after Jones first met Clifford Roberts, an investment partner at Reynolds & Company in New York. Roberts was a golf fan and suggested to Jones that Augusta would be the perfect location where Jones could build his "ideal golf club," as Jones described it in a September 1931 letter to Crawford Johnson of Birmingham, Alabama. The Fruitland Nurseries proved to have the necessary acreage (365 acres) and location, and it was purchased for $70,000 in 1930.

Jones set about designing his dream course with help from Alister MacKenzie, a golf course architect who in 1928 designed Cypress Point on California's Monterey Peninsula. Augusta was completed in December 1932, and the first group of members, by invitation only, were the predictable captains of industry from across the country. Jones and Roberts called the club Augusta National in part because they viewed it as a national course with a national membership.

The first several Masters events were called the Augusta Annual Invitational Tournament. By 1938, Roberts had suggested calling the tournament the Masters, which Jones at first thought was presumptuous. But he eventually relented, reasoning that "the tournament is quite well entitled to be called the Masters because it has continued to assemble those who are entitled to be called the masters of the game."

The tournament, like the club membership, was at first by invitation only. The first Masters of 1934 had only 45 entrants, including three Turnesa brothers—Mike, Joe, and William. Jones ended his four years of competitive golf abstinence and shot 294, 6 over par, to finish in a three-way tie for 13th with Walter Hagen and Denny Shute. In that tournament the winner, Horton Smith, received $1,500. Only the top 11 finishers were compensated, and it would stay that way until the Masters resumed in 1946 following a three-year break due to World War II.

Jones continued to play in the Masters until no longer physically able to do so. His first Masters was his best. He was still just 32. He would play in every Masters through 1942, with the exception of 1940, when he withdrew after shooting 11 over par for the first two rounds. After the war, he returned to play in three more Masters, his final being a 50th-place finish in 1948. He did finish in the top 25 in three of the Masters in which he played.

By June 1942, Jones had two immediate goals in mind: to serve his country by raising money in a golf tournament in Chicago, and to serve his country as an officer in the US Army Air Corps. He had shown that he could still play, leading the country in the sectional qualifying for the Hale America. He had no illusions, however, about competing against the likes of Ben Hogan, Byron Nelson, Jimmy Demaret, or Lloyd Mangrum over the course of 72 holes. He had competed against the very best a dozen years earlier, had beaten them all, and wanted to play four rounds of golf to raise money and not embarrass himself. He succeeded on all fronts.

A day after his finish at the Hale America, Bobby Jones left Chicago for Mitchel Field on Long Island to officially enlist in the US Army. It was something he had wanted to do during World War I, but he was too young and instead raised money playing golf exhibitions.

Jones had burst into the amateur golf scene as a teenager, too young for the service but not for winning golf tournaments. His burgeoning celebrity—he won the Southern Amateur in 1917—earned him the nickname "Dixie Whiz Kid" and caught the attention of those scheduling exhibitions with the proceeds going to war relief. The charity matches were about the only vehicles for the top amateur players, as the USGA had canceled its tournaments following the United States' entry into World War I.

In the first series of exhibitions, Jones and fellow East Lake amateur (and roommate in Philadelphia for the 1916 Amateur) Perry Adair played with two women: the reigning US Women's Amateur champion, Alexa Stirling, and a teenager from Chicago named Elaine Rosenthal. Stirling also won the 1919 and 1920 US Women's Amateur, giving her three in a row, as there were no tournaments in 1917 and 1918. Rosenthal's mother chaperoned the group as they toured New England resorts in 1917, where they were given the celebrity treatment.

Additional tours through the South and Midwest enabled the foursome to raise more than $150,000 for the war relief effort and the American Red Cross.

It was such a success that Jones and Adair were invited to Chicago by reigning Men's Amateur and US Open champ Chick Evans to play in more charity events. The fourth member of their group was Bob Gardner, the man who had eliminated Jones in the quarterfinals of the 1916 US Amateur before losing to Evans in the final. The group also played in New York, where Jones would meet writer Grantland Rice for the first time, forging a lifelong friendship. Later, Jones played in a War Relief Fund Tournament that would be the marquee event of the year. In a weird, match-play format, Jones won all three of his single matches against professional golfers. In the summer of 1918, Jones resumed his matches with Adair, Stirling, and Rosenthal. He would then enter Georgia Tech as a 16-year-old freshman.

But things were different when the United States entered World War II. Jones was 39 when Pearl Harbor was bombed, and he was determined to enter the service, preferably abroad in the European Theater of Operations. A year later, he was readying to enter the Army Air Corps following his appearance at the Hale America National Open in Chicago.

The final day of the Hale America again featured the star grouping of Jones and Hogan. Denny Shute was the third wheel. With the improved weather, the huge gallery followed the two icons over Ridgemoor's 6,500 yards. Those gallery estimates were huge numbers for the time, hearkening back to when similar crowds followed Jones in his Grand Slam year of 1930.

The tournament had surpassed even the modest expectations of the sponsors, who had considered canceling it a month earlier due to a perceived lack of interest. But over 54 holes, the top names in the sport took their accustomed spots on the leaderboard while leading an all-out assault on defenseless Ridgemoor. What was not to like? Tournament chairman Francis Ouimet had said before the first ball was struck that his main objectives were "to raise funds for a most worthy cause and, as a starter, we wanted a field of proven quality." He got both.

The three names to watch—Ben Hogan, Jimmy Demaret, and Mike Turnesa—went out in three different groups. Demaret, two shots astern of Hogan and Mike Turnesa, went off first, at 12:56 p.m. His partners were Lawson Little, three shots behind the leaders, and Ed Dudley, who was 10 strokes back. Hogan, Jones, and Shute went off at 1:36 p.m.

Mike Turnesa was in an interesting threesome, paired with first-round co-leader Otey Crisman and Ray Mangrum. Crisman had followed up his second-round 72 with a 76 and trailed the leaders by 10 shots. Ray Mangrum was 8 shots off the pace, while little brother Lloyd was 7 behind the leaders.

Byron Nelson, 5 shots off the lead, was in the final pairing of the day, going off at 2:38 p.m.

While Hogan and Jones commanded much of the attention—understandably—it soon became clear that the man to watch as Day 4 unfolded was the man who loved to be seen—Demaret. He played the course and he played the crowd. "To me, the faces of spectators in a golf gallery are the most interesting in the world," he told the magazine *Professional Golfer of America,* which was distributed to golf pro shops across the country. "They express the inward feelings of the player himself. Chagrin or joy can be registered in a moment, all depending on how the shot goes." Demaret said he was "gallery bit," describing the sensation as a "burning desire to entertain the gallery and, incidentally, give them something that may help their own game."

He wasted no time on the final day delighting those who had come out to see him. Wearing a red, white, and blue tam o'shanter, Demaret birdied the first two holes and moved to 13 under par, tying Hogan and Mike Turnesa, before either of the leaders had teed off. He then birdied the ninth hole to stand at 14 under par with nine holes remaining.

Both Hogan and Mike Turnesa, meanwhile, were not matching Demaret's blistering pace. Each birdied the first hole and finished with 1-under 35s on the front. Hogan's steely concentration was broken briefly as he stood on the second tee, preparing to drive, when he stepped away. A rabbit was skirting down the fairway, trying to find a way through the crowds. Hogan would later say that the incident "relaxed" him, adding, "it came at the right time and did me a lot of good."

It may have helped his nerves, but the rabbit incident did not help Hogan's scoring. He played the next eight holes in even par, making a birdie on the third hole and a bogey on the eighth. But as he and Mike Turnesa made the turn at 14 under par, Demaret was pushing the envelope even more, to the point where it looked to one and all that he would emerge as the Hale America champion.

Demaret barely mentions the tournament in his book, *My Partner, Ben Hogan,* and there is next to nothing on it in a 2004 biography, *Jimmy Demaret, The Swing's the Thing* by John Companiotte. So we can only surmise how he felt as he took the lead and gave it back. But knowing what we know about the carefree Texan, it's unlikely he spent a great deal of time ruminating about it. That wasn't who he was.

Things got really interesting on the 13th hole. Demaret had parred the first three holes on the back nine and was looking at a 125-yard approach shot to the 13th green. The ball landed about 5 feet from the hole and rolled in for an eagle two. That got everyone's attention, including the other golfers, for the Chicago

District Golf Association had made sure there were updated scoreboards at various points on the course.

The eagle moved Demaret to 16 under par. Hogan was still at 14 under through 12 holes, while Mike Turnesa had bogeyed the 10th to fall back to 13 under. Demaret then nearly matched his eagle from 13 with another on 14, hitting the par-5 hole in two and narrowly missing the putt, settling instead for a birdie 4. He was now at 17 under, leading the tournament by three shots with four holes to play. It was his tournament to win or lose. What could possibly go wrong?

As it turned out, a lot could—and did—go wrong. On the 15th hole, another par 5, Demaret drove it poorly into the right woods and had to play a left-handed shot with his putter just to get the ball back onto the fairway. It had come to lie near the base of a tree. It was not all that dissimilar to what Hogan had faced in the first round, when he whiffed on a shot. He then missed the green with his third shot and could not get it up and down for a par. The bogey 6 dropped him back to 16 under.

Demaret then hit another poor drive on 16, hooking it left. He hit a spectator on the chest with his second shot, the ball coming to rest in the rough around the green. A poor chip led to a missed 15-footer for par, dropping Demaret to 15 under.

Hogan, meanwhile, would register consecutive birdies on the two par 5s, 14 and 15, to move to 16 under. As his group was roughly 40 minutes behind Demaret's, by the time of those back-to-back birdies, Demaret's self-immolation was complete.

On the par 4 17th hole, Demaret again missed the fairway off the tee. But he got his second shot near the green and then executed a beautiful chip shot to within 2 feet of the hole. He then proceeded to miss the putt, giving him three straight bogeys and dropping him back to where he had been before his eagle, at 14 under. That's where he remained after a routine par on the 18th hole. All he could do was wait for Hogan to finish.

Hogan still had not been able to close out a major national tournament such as the US Open, the Masters, or the PGA. But at this particular event at this particular point in time, he closed like it was a matter of course. After his two birdies, he made three straight pars and was still at 16 under when he went to the 18th hole, the 175-yard par 3 across the water. Mike Turnesa, still a few holes behind Hogan, got as low as 15 under par after a birdie on the 15th. But he gave one back on the 16th.

Hogan drilled his tee shot on the 18th, then dropped a 30-foot birdie putt for a 68 and a four-round total of 271, 17 under par. Those were numbers unseen at a US Open, and Charles Bartlett of the *Chicago Tribune* would characterize Hogan's four-day performance as "a ruthless 17 under." Grantland Rice would write, "The 62 and the 271 constitute two of the finest chapters in the history of American golf."

Mike Turnesa was three shots back after his bogey on 16, and that is where he ended up after pars on 17 and 18. He had tied Demaret for second place. But one felt like a legitimate runner-up, and the other felt as if he had blown a chance to win a national tournament.

Jimmy Corcoran, a writer for the *Chicago American*, wrote that as well as Hogan had played—and Corcoran used words like "meticulous" and "precise" to describe the champion's round—"it wasn't so much that Hogan won the Hale America. It was that Jimmy Demaret laid the title right in his lap."

New York Times writer William Richardson focused on Demaret's demise in his story on the final round. He said Demaret's name could be added to those of Sam Snead and Roland Hancock "and others who have tossed major golf honors over their left shoulders."

Snead's inability to win a US Open ranged from comical to diabolical as he finished second in the event on four different occasions. The most painful runner-up finish for Snead was in 1939, when he came to the 18th tee needing a par to claim the title at Philadelphia Country Club. He thought he needed a birdie and aggressively went for it. He ended up in two bunkers and made a triple bogey eight on the hole, finishing two shots behind eventual winner Byron Nelson. Snead also lost a playoff with Lew Worsham in the 1947 US Open despite holding a two-shot lead with three holes to play.

Hancock was another story altogether, an unknown club pro from North Carolina. He had a two-shot lead with two holes remaining in the 1928 US Open at Olympia Fields and was charitably dubbed a "dark horse" by the sportswriters. He double-bogeyed the 17th and bogeyed the 18th to fall a shot behind Bobby Jones and Johnny Farrell. Farrell won the playoff, and Hancock retreated back into obscurity in North Carolina.

Hogan's three-stroke victory at the Hale America earned him $1,000. Craig Wood had received $1,000 for winning the 1941 US Open. By 1946, the top prize had been raised to $1,500. Richardson, in the *New York Times*, noted that Hogan "scored his first victory in a tournament designated as National, as the Hale America was golf's No. 1 event of the year. His feat will duly be recorded in the annual yearbook of the United States Golf Association which, its own conducted events canceled for the duration, lists Ralph Guldahl's 281 at Detroit as the National Open record."

Grantland Rice didn't mince words, or his opinion, in his lead in the Monday *Atlanta Constitution*: "The right man won. He had it coming. Ben Hogan ... finally won his first major championship by taking over the Hale America war fund tournament at Ridgemoor by one of the record all-time scores at 271, just 17 under par."

It was a stunning number. But over four days, only 22 players ended up under par. The USGA noted that there were 50 rounds in the 60s, which was more than had been shot in the previous eight US Opens combined. Hogan's 271 was 10 shots better than the existing US Open scoring record.

When the final group had finished, representatives from the three sponsoring organizations gathered with Hogan. George Blossom presented Hogan with the winner's gold medal, which had already been crafted in anticipation of an official US Open in 1942. The front looked nearly identical to the one awarded to Wood in 1941 and to the four Hogan would receive in 1948, 1950, 1951, and 1953. On the back, however, was a different inscription, with the names of the tournament sponsors, not just the USGA. The 18-inch USGA trophy awarded to the winner of the US Open remained with the 1941 champion.

Asked by reporters if he considered the victory to be that of a major championship, Hogan said, "Yes. Given the quality of the field, it's a major championship. At least I feel that way. Don't know about you boys." He added, "If this wasn't an Open competition, I don't know what it could be. I'm glad to win it, whatever they call it."

The tournament had been a smashing success not only in producing a worthy champion, but also in raising money. That had been the sole purpose of the Hale America, and by the time the money was counted, the tournament had raised more than $22,500 for the USO and the Naval Relief fund. An auction after the final round netted $2,450, with Hogan's putter and golf ball going for $1,650. A jacket worn by Demaret fetched $500, while one worn by Mike Turnesa went for $300.

Byron Nelson finished in a three-way tie for fourth place with Horton Smith and Jimmy Thompson, whose 66 was the low round of the day. Lloyd Mangrum and Jim Ferrier were in at 281. Sam Byrd, Craig Wood, and Jug McSpaden all finished at 283.

Johnny Dawson finished as the low amateur at 287, 1 under par. Otey Crisman closed with a 76 to finish at 289 and a tie for 29th with Gene Sarazen, among others. Joe Turnesa finished at 290, while his brother Jim returned to Fort Dix after shooting a 76 for a total of 292.

Ray Mangrum finished at even par 288, seven shots behind his little brother. Harvey Penick returned to his teaching duties at the University of Texas after carding a final round 75, to finish at 302. And Charles Lind, the Denver qualifier who had been knocked unconscious by the billiard ball in the sectionals, was in at 299 after a final-round 80.

Then there was Capt. Robert T. Jones Jr., about to enter the Army Air Corps. He finished in a five-way tie for 35th place at 2 over par after bogeying the last two holes. Hogan told Grantland Rice that he thought Jones was paying more attention to his (Hogan's) game than to his own. The purse doled out money to the top 30 professionals. Thirty-four players ended up tied for 29th or better, and Otey Crisman was one of five who tied for 29th. He walked away with a check for $16.66.

We can reasonably assume that Jones, had he finished in the money, would have declined to accept any remuneration, even though the USGA thought of him as a professional and thus he would have been entitled to it. While Jones had been a smashing success as a draw, his mediocre (at best) scoring made him a distant sidebar to the play of the leaders, especially his partner of the last two days, Ben Hogan. Jones had told Grantland Rice before the tournament that the field at the Hale America would be vastly more talented than anything he had personally encountered in a dozen years. He was spot on.

"What can you do, when you go out and shoot par golf and still find yourself eight strokes behind," Jones said afterward. His math was a little shaky, as he did not shoot par golf, nor was he 8 strokes behind. Had he shot par golf, he would have finished 17 shots behind. As it was, he ended up 19 shots behind Hogan. "They were," he concluded, "just too good for me at Chicago."

For the next two years, Jones would get in occasional rounds of leisurely golf, but his allegiance would be to Uncle Sam. That is how he wanted it.

Before Jones had left for Chicago to participate in the Hale America, he allowed himself to be photographed in his Atlanta law office by Hixon Kinsella. It's an iconic photograph of Jones, who is wearing an Army helmet and smoking a pipe. It's also unusual because Jones was hardly ever seen smoking a pipe; cigarettes were a different story. And he hadn't officially reported for duty yet, although he had received his acceptance notice.

Still, given his age (40), family situation (three children), and celebrity, he was not the ideal candidate for military service. It would be the equivalent today of Tiger Woods enlisting. "There is no better man to size up the distance, get the range and advise whether a bazooka or a mashie is needed on the next shot," wrote H. I. Phillips of the *New York Sun*. That was written just after Jones arrived in England in 1944. After the Hale America, he would spend nearly 18 months in the United States, doing everything in his power to wrangle an appointment in the ETO. And like pretty much everything Jones set his sights on, he succeeded.

Soon after Jones retired following his 1930 Grand Slam, he was in the Officer Reserve Corps. In his desire to enter the Army Air Corps (there was no US Air Force at the time), he went back and forth with the Army in early 1942 as to whether his reserve status was still intact. He received contradictory responses until told in late March that his commission had, in fact, expired. He was invited to re-enlist, which he did, targeting the AAC "about the possibility of making application for assignment to this service." His Selective Service card noted he was 5-foot-7 and 1/2 inches tall, weighed 170 pounds, had blue eyes, brown hair, and a ruddy complexion. (The other complexion options were sallow, light, dark, freckled, light brown, dark brown, and black. His race was listed as "white." The other possibilities were Negro, Oriental, Indian, and Filipino. It was 1942.)

He then proceeded to line up an A-list of Atlanta movers and shakers for references in his effort to join the Army Air Corps. His privileged life allowed him certain advantages that grunts like Lloyd Mangrum never experienced. Jones had golf in common with Mangrum, Hogan, and Demaret, but that was about it. He had the luxury of picking and choosing his preferred branch of service, when he could join, and, early on, where he would be stationed.

Among those championing Jones's cause were Jackson P. Dick, vice president of the Georgia Power Company; C. A. Stair, vice president and treasurer of Southern Bell Telephone and Telegraph Company; Robert B. Troutman, associate general counsel of the Coca-Cola Company; and Carl Wolf, president of the Atlanta Gas Light Company. All enthusiastically endorsed Jones as the ideal candidate for a commission.

On Memorial Day 1942, Jones got the news he was hoping for—an eight-page communiqué from the adjutant general's office in the War Department telling him "without delay" to complete the oath of office form and have it notarized. There was news on what to expect in the short term, from his uniform allowance as a captain ($150) to the preferred list of clothes (among them two overcoats; six pairs of socks in khaki, rayon, or cotton; and a necktie.)

Ten days later, Jones was notified by telegram from the US Signal Corps to report to Mitchel Field to join the First Fighter Command. On that day he prepared a memo to himself: to send a confirmation telegram by his appointment date from the site of the Hale America, Ridgemoor Country Club. He did. The Army confirmed

The unit Jones was joining was tasked with defending the Atlantic Seaboard from possible German attack. While Germany did not declare war against the

United States until December 1941, President Franklin D. Roosevelt had ordered the Navy to track the Atlantic Coast and West Indies for possible hostile forces as far back as September 1939, four days after Germany invaded Poland. These were called Neutrality Patrols.

The threat was deemed to be real—and it was. A German U-boat fired torpedoes at an American destroyer southwest of Iceland in September 1941, and later that month the Navy started to escort eastbound trans-Atlantic convoys to England. The following month, the American destroyer *Reuben James* became the first US ship lost in the Atlantic in World War II. It was torpedoed off of Iceland and 100 servicemen were killed.

There still was no state of war existing between Germany and the United States when the *Reuben James* went down. In November 1941 Roosevelt ordered the Navy to extend its patrols from the 300 miles it had been patrolling since September 1939 all the way to the 25th meridian, which cuts through the Azores Islands off the coast of Africa. The thinking was that this would free up the British Navy to worry about U-boats closer to home.

The following year, 1942, marked even more attacks. From January to June, U-boats sank 226 Allied merchant ships along the East Coast. The month of June alone proved to be the worst month of the war for Allied and neutral shipping. More than 170 ships were sunk and 60 percent of those were in the Caribbean and the Gulf of Mexico. It had gotten so bad that Mexico, then neutral, itself declared war on Germany, Italy, and Japan on May 22, 1942, after losing two large oil tankers in the Gulf of Mexico. A weekly magazine, the *American Mercury,* told its readers that the United States was convinced the Germans would attack the East Coast. It read, "They'll come over. Make no mistake about it."

Against that chilling backdrop, Jones threw himself into his position with Fighter Command as an aircraft service warning officer based in Jacksonville, Florida. "Tis Better To Be Bored than Bombed" was the unit's motto, and Jones told his civilian volunteers, most of whom were women, that "in modern warfare, a country's first line of defense is its aircraft warning service. Fighter planes afford the best real defense against enemy bombers. Yet the best fighter is at a considerable disadvantage if the surprise of the raid is complete. The advance warning must come in time to allow the defending planes to gain altitude for an advantageous attack."

In March 1943, Jones was promoted to major and prepared for a new challenge—Army intelligence. Before leaving, however, he received a letter of commendation from Brigadier General Willis Taylor of the First Fighter Command for his work with the civilian volunteers.

The Army Air Forces Air Intelligence School held an eight-week course in the summer of 1943 in Harrisburg, Pennsylvania. Its goal was to train its students "for the purpose of pursuing the combat intelligence course." Jones received training as both a POW interrogator and as a teletype operator and, while there, studied maps of the straits of Dover while also learning aerial reconnaissance and techniques of bombing. But he still was no closer to his ultimate goal—getting shipped overseas—than he had been when he enlisted 13 months earlier.

He bounced around the East Coast in late summer 1943 but got his big break in November, when he was assigned to the 84th Fighter Wing of the Ninth Tactical Command. By Christmas, he received orders to report to New York for "eventual movement overseas." The order stated that "this is a permanent change of station." Jones was told to bring "winter clothing only" and was examined by a doctor on December 27. The next day he left LaGuardia Field bound for London. He was permitted to fly because it was deemed "necessary for the accomplishment of an emergency war mission." He was given a baggage allowance of 62 pounds and was paid $7 per diem.

"I was tired of fighting the battle of the Atlantic Seaboard," he told a reporter for the *Atlanta Journal* shortly after arriving in London. "When I entered the Army, it was in hope of seeing really active duty. That's why I am glad to be here."

In a 1966 interview for a dissertation by Richard Gordin of The Ohio State University, Jones said when he decided to enter the Army, the last thing he wanted was to go in as some "hoopty-da officer of some camp." He was now in England, helping to plan Operation Overlord—the invasion of France, better known as D-Day. That was anything but hoopty-da.

There isn't a lot of concrete information on what exactly Jones did in his stint overseas, which lasted about seven months. He rarely talked about it, which was not uncommon among World War II servicemen. His grandson, Robert Tyre Jones IV, recalled finding his grandfather's Army uniform folded neatly in the attic of their house at Atlanta. "Yes, I served in the war," he told his grandson. Then he changed the subject.

In England, Jones worked with other intelligence officers planning the Normandy invasion. A major in the 84th Fighter Wing reported receiving top-secret documents from Jones in May that listed, among other things, battery targets and German gun positions in France. Jones's separation qualification record notes that as an air combat intelligence officer, he "directed the collection, interpretation and distribution of information concerning location, strength and activity of enemy forces."

In February 1944 Jones was photographed leaving his hotel in London where he was "attached to the USAAF as an intelligence officer." The following month, he was promoted to Lieutenant Colonel and paid £3 to join the local officers' club, £1 for the initiation fee and £2 for the assessment.

Still in London 10 days before D-Day, Jones took time to write a letter to a Regent Street tailor, a fascinating representation of the attention to detail that served him so well throughout his life. The letter pertained to Jones's purchase of a service jacket and two pairs of trousers. He wrote that the trousers were "two inches too long in waist measurement, but I am having them altered at my own expense." He enclosed a check for £10, 11 shillings, and sixpence and returned the service jacket as it was "of no possible use without alterations." He closed by saying that he had no idea when he'd be back in London, but "if you have not otherwise disposed of the garment, I shall be glad to have you try again to give me a satisfactory fitting." He soon would be across the English Channel.

Virtually every story or article on Jones's war service states that he landed in Normandy on June 7, the day after the first wave of Allied troops stormed five beaches on the French coast. While you can look long and far to try to get Jones to confirm that, his grandson had no such hesitation, saying, "He landed in Normandy on D-Day plus one." There are photographs of Jones in Normandy with other soldiers.

His unit came under artillery attack, but even by the second day, things had started to calm down as the Allies established beachheads. British Prime Minister Winston Churchill, who had to be talked out of witnessing the invasion firsthand from a British destroyer in the Channel, did land in Normandy on June 12. (The Allies' breakout through Normandy would prove to be much more difficult than anticipated. Paris was not liberated until August 24, more than two and a half months after D-Day.)

Jones's grandson said he had heard from his grandfather's law partners that the senior Jones may have interrogated German POWs. "But," he said, "it's probably more like he walked into an interrogation room, popped a pack of cigarettes on the table and introduced himself. His fame was an interrogation weapon of his own."

What is known is that six weeks later, Jones wrote a memo to the commanding officer of the 84th Fighter Wing titled, "Relief from Active Duty of Officers for whom No Suitable Assignment Exists." He requested to be relieved from active duty, pointing out his age (42), and stating that to keep him on "is no longer essential to the war effort [because] the section to which I was assigned is now completely organized, adequately and capably staffed." He also noted his father was in ill health, and that he had 39 days of accrued leave time.

Jones's request was granted the next day. He was told to begin planning for his trip back to the United States. He was given a packet telling him he was allowed to bring home "small items of enemy equipment excepting nameplates removed from captured equipment" or personnel. It was also noted that Jones attended lectures for the newly arrived troops on "sex hygiene and sex morality."

Jones had one final stop in England before returning home to Atlanta in late August 1944: the Royal Lytham and St. Anne's Golf Club, the site of his 1926 victory in the British Open. It was a short drive from the American air base in Lancashire from which he would be departing.

During the 1926 tournament, Jones executed a breathtaking recovery shot out of the sand on the 71st hole, which helped him secure the championship by two strokes over American Al Watrous. When he returned to the course in 1944, he discovered that Henry Cotton, then a two-time British Open champion (he would win a third in 1948), had suggested that a landmark be placed at the site of the celebrated shot. Jones dutifully identified the spot and then played a Red Cross exhibition match with a club member, using borrowed clubs.

Jones returned to Atlanta in the final week of August, where he was met by his wife and three children at the Peachtree Brookwood Station. He is described in an article as "tanned and trim" but refused to talk about his exploits overseas. "Can't talk about those things, you know," he told reporters. But the article went on to suggest that due to Jones's trim figure, "it was clear that he had been where the going was rugged."

His son, Robert Tyre Jones III, also served overseas as a teletype operator in the Mediterranean Theater of Operations. He was honorably discharged in 1947 while receiving both the World War II Victory Medal and the Army of Occupation Medal. Documents show that while father and son were both in the Army, they were not overseas at the same time during the war.

Six months after arriving back in Atlanta, Bobby Jones was notified that he was entitled to wear the Bronze Star to indicate "battle participation" in "Air Offensive Europe" while a member of the 84th Fighter Wing. On the occasion of his 43rd birthday, March 17, he told an Associated Press reporter that he viewed himself as a "former golfer" and had little time for the law or the links while he served as the chairman of the Red Cross war drive in Georgia.

"Don't you believe that Bob is a former golfer," his wife said. "He plays every time he gets the chance. He just doesn't get many chances." Once the war was over, however, Jones showed he was anything but a "former" golfer when he shot a 29 on the front nine of East Lake.

1942

hale

AMERICA

NATIONAL OPEN
GOLF TOURNAMENT

June 18 · 19 · 20 · 21

25c

Ridgemoor
Country Club CHICAGO

| UNITED STATES U.S.G.A. GOLF ASS'N | CHICAGO DISTRICT C.D.G.A. GOLF ASS'N | PROFESSIONAL GOLFERS P.G.A. of A. ASS'N OF AMERICA | SPONSORS |

Benefit: NAVY RELIEF SOCIETY
UNITED SERVICE ORGANIZATIONS

The United States Golf Association, the Professional Golf Association, and the Chicago District Golf Association teamed to sponsor the wartime version of the US Open at the Ridgemoor Country Club in Chicago. The 1942 tournament, won by Ben Hogan, set a record for entries and raised thousands for war relief. *Courtesy of John Seidenstein*

Bobby Jones came out of retirement to lend his name and talents to the 1942 Hale America National Open. He was still a huge draw, as seen by all the servicemen watching him practice. Tournament sponsors allowed in military personnel for free. *Sidney L Matthew ARCHIVE*

Mike Turnesa (right), one of seven Turnesa brothers who played golf, is congratulated by his brother, Jim, after a first-round 65 at the Hale America National Open. Mike Turnesa ended up tied for second with Jimmy Demaret behind the champion, Ben Hogan. Jim Turnesa won the 1952 PGA Championship, while another brother, Willie, won two US Amateurs and the British Amateur. *From the author's collection*

Craig Wood (far left) joins Bobby Jones (center) and Ed Dudley in early action at the Hale America National Open. Wood won the 1941 Masters and 1941 US Open, but is almost as well known for being the first person to lose in a playoff in all four of today's major tournaments. Greg Norman duplicated that dubious feat decades later. Wood won 19 other PGA tournaments and was a member of three Ryder Cup teams in the 1930s. *PGA of America/Getty Images*

Ben Hogan finishing up a course-record 62 in the second round of the Hale America National Open. The score was the lowest recorded in any major competition until matched in 2017. The round featured nine pars, eight birdies, and one eagle. *Bettmann/Getty Images*

Hall of Famers Ben Hogan (left) and Bobby Jones, two of the icons of golf in the first half of the twentieth century, played two rounds together at the Hale America National Open. Jones, 12 years retired, was still a huge draw at the tournament. *Bettmann/Getty Images*

Hale America champion Ben Hogan receives the $1,000 winner's purse from the tournament sponsors. PGA President Ed Dudley (far left) played in the tournament and tied for 20th. George Blossom, president of the USGA, and Thomas McMahon (far right), president of the CDGA, offer Hogan their congratulations. *Bettmann/Getty Images*

Hall of Famer Jimmy Demaret (right) was noted for his sartorial flair, which even included the occasional bizarre-looking hat. But he could play. He was the first man to win three Masters championships, won 31 times on the PGA Tour, was undefeated in three Ryder Cups, and won the money title in 1947. *Bettmann/Getty Images*

Masters rookie Lloyd Mangrum (center) set a course record of 64 in the first round in the 1940 Masters. But Jimmy Demaret (left) eventually caught and passed Mangrum, winning the first of his three Masters by four strokes, the largest margin of victory in the 7-year history of the tournament. The golfers are seen here with Bobby Jones, who built Augusta National and started the Masters in 1934. *Augusta National/Masters Historic Imagery/Getty Images*

Lloyd Mangrum made his Masters debut a memorable one in 1940, setting the course record of 64 in his first competitive round at Augusta National. The record stood for 46 years. Mangrum finished second in 1940 and tied for second in 1949. *Augusta National/Masters Historic Imagery/ Getty Images*

Sam Byrd is the only person to have played in a World Series (1932, with the New York Yankees) and the Masters (five times). He was a World Series champion with the Yankees, replacing Babe Ruth in the ninth inning of Game 4. He also won 11 times on the PGA Tour after leaving professional baseball. He is seen here in an undated photograph from the 1930s. *PGA of America/Getty Images*

Jug McSpaden and Byron Nelson (putting) were called the Gold Dust Twins. Together they played more than 100 charity matches during World War II. Nelson retired in 1946 after a Hall of Fame career, which featured 52 PGA wins, including 11 straight in 1945. McSpaden holds the record for most second-place finishes, most of them to Nelson. *Bettmann/Getty Images*

At the age of 40, Bobby Jones wrangled an overseas assignment in World War II with the US Army Air Corps, landing in France shortly after D-Day, 1944. He doubled as a teletype operator and intelligence officer. He is seen here in Normandy, dining with the troops on Army haute cuisine. *Sidney L Matthew ARCHIVE*

After spending two years in the Army during World War II, serving in Europe with the 90th Infantry Division, Lloyd Mangrum returned to win the first official US Open after the war. He defeated By-ron Nelson and Vic Ghezzi in a 36-hole playoff. It was his only major title. *AP Images*

Jimmy Demaret picked up his second Masters championship in 1947, becoming the first Masters champion to shoot four consecutive rounds under par. It was his second Masters win in five tournaments, as the tournament shut down from 1943 to 1945. *Augusta National/Masters Historic Imagery/Getty Images*

The four finalists in the Miami Four-Ball from 1947. Can you guess which two won? Ben Hogan (far right) and Jimmy Demaret (second from left) defeated Lawson Little (far left) and Lloyd Mangrum. Hogan and Demaret were a formidable team in match play, both on the PGA Tour and in the Ryder Cup. *Bettmann/Getty Images*

Bobby Jones and Dwight Eisenhower became friends after World War II. The golf-crazy Eisenhower vacationed at Augusta National, became a club member, and donated a personal painting of Jones to the subject and the club in 1953. *Bettmann/Getty Images*

Bobby Jones and Ben Hogan, who played two rounds together at the 1942 Hale America National Open, are reunited at a dinner in New York to honor Hogan for his three major victories in 1953. The program from the dinner, sponsored by the USGA, lists the Hale America National Open as a major victory. Hogan and Jones are the only two golfers to receive ticker tape parades in New York City; Jones received two. *Sidney L Matthew ARCHIVE*

```
* BEN HOGAN *

MAJOR TOURNAMENT WINS

(THROUGH 1989)


* MASTERS *

1951, 1953

* U. S. OPEN *

1942 - 1948, 1950, 1951, 1953

* BRITISH *

1953

* PGA CHAMPIONSHIP *

1946, 1948
```

Ben Hogan

As if there was any doubt that Ben Hogan considered the 1942 Hale America to be an official US Open, he wrote it down in black and white, inserting "1942" as one of the years he won the USGA's signature event. He then signed the list at the bottom with his unmistakable signature.
Courtesy of John Seidenstein

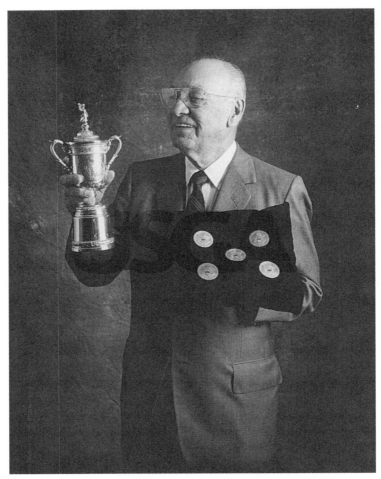

Ben Hogan always believed he won five US Opens. He pointed to the medal he received for winning the 1942 Hale America National Open as being identical to the other four official ones from 1948, 1950, 1951, and 1953. The USGA does not count the Hale America as an official US Open even though it conducted the tournament in almost exactly the same format. *USGA Museum*

III

CONTROVERSY
AND AFTERMATH

7

CONTROVERSY

When Is a US Open Not a US Open?

With this historical context for the tournament, as well as the USGA's clear cancellation of their official championships for 1942, the Hale America Open cannot be considered a U.S. Open.

—Official statement by the USGA in 2020

I already have five medals, and the president of the USGA has presented each one to me.

—Ben Hogan, 1983

The Hale America National Open Golf Tournament happened only once. Even though there would be no official US Open until 1946, there was no star-studded wartime replacement tournament in 1943, 1944, or 1945.

It was a singular event with a terrific field, won by arguably the best golfer of the day. There would be something called the Chicago Victory Open which ran from 1943 to 1948 with Sam Byrd, Byron Nelson, and Jug McSpaden winning in 1943, 1944, and 1945 respectively. There is no controversy today surrounding those tournaments in terms of prestige, or even as a possible US Open.

From 1937 to 1941, there was a regular stop in Chicago for the Chicago Open. Ben Hogan won it in 1941 and he is credited with winning it in 1942, as the Chicago District Golf Association deemed that whoever won the Hale America would also be crowned as the 1942 Chicago Open champion.

The USGA did not get involved with any of the Chicago Victory Opens. The organization's involvement with the Hale America is one of the many facts pointed out by those who believe the Hale America should be, at best, a fifth US Open for Ben Hogan or, failing that, be recognized as an official major. That would give Hogan 10 majors, trailing only Jack Nicklaus, Tiger Woods, Bobby Jones, and Walter Hagen.

The late Dan Jenkins, who spent much of his golf-writing career championing the Hale America as an official US Open, posed the question to USGA Executive Secretary Joe Dey in the 1960s. Why, Jenkins wondered, wouldn't the USGA award a fifth Open to Hogan?

"I would love to give Ben a fifth Open," Dey told Jenkins. "However, the lack of suitable course preparation at Ridgemoor prevents it from being official." Dey said there wasn't sufficient manpower to transform Ridgemoor into a USGA-approved venue. The rough wasn't thick enough. The greens weren't slick enough. He said the "length and design of Ridgemoor" was acceptable and then added, "but I do count it as a major for Ben."

So it wasn't an official US Open, but it should count as a major? That sounded a bit like a distinction without a difference. And while today the majors in golf are identifiable and unchanging—the Masters, the US Open, the PGA Championship, and the British Open—that wasn't always the case.

Bobby Jones's Grand Slam in 1930 did not include the PGA (as an amateur, he could not participate) or the Masters (which didn't start until 1934.) So the four "majors" in those days were the US Open, the British Open, the US Amateur, and the British Amateur. No one really kept track in those days, and to settle on those four tournaments precluded established professionals like Walter Hagen from participating in half of them. Jones played in all four events three times—in 1921, 1926, and 1930. The last two were years in which the Walker Cup was being contested in Great Britain. In 1921, there was an unofficial Walker Cup at Royal Liverpool Golf Club. Jones played in that as a member of the eight-man American team. The first official Walker Cup was in 1922 in the United States.

As a member of the unofficial Walker Cup team in 1921 and as a member of the official Walker Cup teams of 1926 and 1930, Jones would thus have had the USGA pay his travel expenses across the pond. And the Walker Cup was scheduled so as not to conflict with either the British Open or British Amateur in those years, so Jones and other Walker Cuppers could play in all three events.

Golf historian Jeff Martin has an article from 1917 that lists the PGA Championship, the US Open, the Western Open, and the Met Open as majors. Martin notes that by the late 1930s there was a two-tiered structure of tournaments, at least in the minds of players, promoters, and fans. The first tier included the four majors of today, as the Masters had quickly established itself as one of the foremost events on the golf calendar. The second tier included tournaments like the Western Open, which many of the players back then considered to be a major, and the North-South, a tournament in North Carolina that also was seen as a big deal.

But while other tournaments came and went—George May's big-bucks tournaments in Chicago were definitely majors in the eyes of one Lloyd Mangrum—the top four spots remain unchanged. Ben Hogan's remarkable performance in 1953, when he won the Masters, US Open, and British Open, was called the Triple Crown. That year, the British Open was held July 8–10, but there was a mandatory 36-hole qualifier on July 6–7. The PGA was held July 1–7 outside Detroit. So there was no way anyone could conceivably play in both tournaments, yet they are both considered majors.

The four majors of today are all run by independent organizations. The Players Championship, which usually draws the strongest field of the year, is run by the PGA Tour and, because of its field, can make a valid claim to be a major. The Masters runs its own tournament. The USGA runs the US Open, and the R&A (Royal & Ancient Golf Club of St. Andrews) runs the British Open. The PGA of America, not to be confused with the PGA Tour, runs the PGA Championship as well as the Ryder Cup.

It really wasn't until Arnold Palmer won the Masters and the US Open in 1960 that the modern Grand Slam came into focus. Martin and other golf historians generally credit Palmer's agent, Mark McCormack, and a Pittsburgh sportswriter named Bob Drum (who followed Palmer almost as much as O. B. Keeler followed Bobby Jones) with the concept. "One thing led to another," Palmer told ESPN in a 2008 interview. "Drum got me all excited about it. He wrote about it. He got the British press all excited about it. And they picked up on it."

Until Palmer started doing it with regularity, American professionals tended to stay in the United States during British Open week. The Open purses were small, most of the courses were links-style, which the American pros rarely played, and the travel to and from Great Britain was onerous and expensive.

Palmer had never played in the British Open until 1960. He nearly made it three straight "major" titles that year, finishing second to Kel Nagle by one shot. Palmer returned to Great Britain the following year and won the Open title. He repeated in 1962. Soon, the R&A, the British version of the USGA, was increasing its purses, changing its dates (the British Open ran Wednesday through Saturday for a while) and was welcomed into the rotation as a major.

Other Americans would follow Palmer, and PGA regulars were soon coming back to the United States with the coveted Claret Jug. There were 56 British Opens before Walter Hagen became the first American-born player to win the tournament in 1922. (Scottish-born Jock Hutchinson won in 1921, a year after becoming a naturalized US citizen.) Since then, the tournament has been claimed by a Yank on 43 occasions, the most of any country. Tom Watson won the British Open five times. Hagen won it four times, all in the 1920s, while Bobby Jones, Jack Nicklaus, and Tiger Woods each have won three.

Barbara Nicklaus recalled when her husband won the 1973 PGA Championship, someone told her he had broken Bobby Jones's "record" of 13. "I think that's the first time that was ever brought to my attention," she said. Maybe the reason was because it was only her husband's 12th major title. Those who said it was his 14th were including the two US Amateur championships he had won. Now, only the four professional majors count, which is unfortunate for Nicklaus but even more so for Woods, who won three consecutive US Amateurs.

Scheduling for the majors became an issue, especially when television got involved. The Masters was firmly planted in the first week of April, and the US Open was almost always contested in mid-June. The R&A preferred July for its signature event, due to weather and lighting being at a premium in the summer. The PGA was moved from August to May in 2019. It has been the nomad of the majors, having been contested in nine of the twelve months (every month except January, March, and April).

Back when Hogan, Snead, Nelson, Demaret, and Mangrum were racking up victories, there were tournaments that naturally had more cachet than others. The British Open, for instance, wasn't considered an especially important tournament if for no other reason than it was difficult to travel to England, qualify for the event, play 72 holes, and then return to the United States. Lloyd Mangrum, like Hogan and Demaret, played in only one. Mangrum finished 24th the year Hogan won it in 1953.

There also were years when the British Open conflicted with the PGA, which, as a match-play event, generally took seven days: two for qualifying and five for matches.

When Hogan won the Masters and US Open in 1951, no one belittled him for not going for either the PGA or the British Open. He had stopped participating in the PGA after his serious automobile accident in 1949. His legs couldn't handle the possibility of seven consecutive days of golf. As it was, he had to be convinced by Jimmy Demaret, Tommy Armour, and others to give the British Open a try at venerable but difficult Carnoustie in 1953.

As Demaret told the story in *My Partner, Ben Hogan*, he told Hogan, "You owe it to the game. You're a legend over there." Hogan ran off all the reasons why it made no sense—travel, subpar cuisine, small hotels, bad weather—and then asked Demaret why he, Demaret, wasn't going. Demaret replied, "Why, Ben, a fella like me has to work for a living. We all can't have that sockful you carry around." As Demaret subsequently explained, "The last thing in the world Ben Hogan has to worry about is money."

So Hogan went, won his first and only British Open, and came back to a ticker tape parade in New York City. Perhaps inspired by Hogan's performance—and maybe deciding he should heed his own words—Demaret made his only British Open appearance the following year. He finished 10th at Royal Birkdale.

Bobby Jones is still seen today as the only player to win golf's Grand Slam in a single year. Jones historian Sidney Matthew, whose *Life and Times of Bobby Jones* beautifully encapsulates Jones's life, said Jones never even thought about the so-called Grand Slam until 1926. That year, he won the British and US Opens. "That was the first time he thought he might be able to win all four in one year," Matthew wrote. That was the year he had been upset by Andrew Jamieson in the quarterfinals of the British Amateur. He did not compete in the tournament again until 1930.

It was O. B. Keeler who used the term "Grand Slam" to describe Jones's feat in 1930. It was a bridge term then. It was also used to describe a bases-loaded home run in baseball, and would be co-opted by the tennis establishment for use.

Since 1960, only three players have started the year with victories in both the Masters and US Open—Jack Nicklaus in 1972, Tiger Woods in 2000, and Jordan Spieth in 2015. Of the three, Nicklaus and Spieth came the closest to winning the British Open, each finishing one shot behind the winner. Nicklaus lost out to Lee Trevino, while Spieth finished a shot out of a three-way playoff. Woods was in the hunt after 36 holes, but fell out of contention in the third round by shooting an 81 in wretched weather conditions.

So the definition of a major has changed over the decades, but has remained stable since 1960. It also has come to define a true winner. A major win can make a player's career. To some, like Nicklaus and Woods, winning majors became their raison d'être. Nicklaus would start mentally preparing for the Masters in January. Woods has been consumed with majors since turning pro.

Tom Weiskopf summed up the feelings of many of the pros when he discussed his career prior to the 1973 US Open. He had arrived at Oakmont having won three tournaments over a span of five weeks and finishing second in another. But he didn't consider himself a favorite. "Let's back up a minute," he said in an article from *World of Professional Golf.* "In the first place, I consider myself good, but not great. I'm not in a class with Nicklaus or Lee Trevino. Why? They have proven themselves by winning major tournaments. I haven't. I think the US Open is the premier tournament in the world—more important than the Masters. I'd rather win the US Open than any other tournament."

As it turned out, Weiskopf did win a major, but it wasn't the Masters or the US Open. A month after finishing two shots behind Miller at Oakmont in 1973, he won the British Open at Royal Troon in Scotland by three strokes. Miller tied for second.

So would it be unprecedented to add the 1942 Hale America as a one-time major tournament? And who would make the call? There is no overall governing body which makes these decisions.

That is why Dey's split-the-baby verdict on the tournament has its supporters. The USGA has made it clear it won't revisit its decision.

It's not as if the USGA tries to hide its involvement in the Hale America. On the contrary, it has reams of information about the tournament at its library and museum in New Jersey. It devotes a single display case to the tournament, with programs, pictures, and assorted factoids. The USGA even has an entire room devoted to Ben Hogan and his four "official" US Open victories. But when one looks at the plaques on the wall in the museum for the winner of the 1942 US Open, there is none. There is none for 1943 or 1944. All that is written is World War II. The same is true for 1917 and 1918 with World War I listed. The Hale America might merit its own showcase, and Hogan might merit his own room, but the two shall never meet on any USGA plaque denoting who might have won a certain USGA-sanctioned tournament in the summer of 1942.

That was the USGA's stance the day Dey announced the tournament in January 1942. That was the PGA's contention later that same year when it mentioned in its official magazine that the Hale America was not to be "considered a championship event in that the USGA has decided that its usual title play should not be held in war time when so many young men are engaged in armed service and unable to compete."

It goes without saying that had Otey Crisman won the Hale America, there would not have been a groundswell of Crismanistas urging the USGA to give Otey his first US Open. The same could probably be said for the runners-up at Ridgemoor, Mike Turnesa and Jimmy Demaret.

But Ben Hogan won the USGA's main event in 1942. And it was Ben Hogan's victory that gave the tournament the prestige it may have otherwise lacked while also providing the USGA with a shot of much-needed adrenalin. It was a certifiable event. Dan Jenkins remembered following the play over the radio. The tournament was covered by most of the major newspapers that covered golf in those days.

In April 2020 the CDGA wrote to the USGA requesting a restating of its position that the tournament was not an official US Open. It was for an article that was to run in the organization's June 2020 publication. The USGA responded with a lengthy statement outlining its reasons.

It read in full:

The answer lies in the historical context of the tournament and the tournament's auspices, format and field, rather than Hogan's gold Hale America medal.

In early 1942, the USGA made a very clear announcement to the world: there would be no USGA championships for 1942. The USGA canceled its four championships in order to devote its full efforts to war relief, as the usual events would be "hollow and improper." The Association declared the main aim of golfers and golf organizations would be to contribute the greatest possible service to the nation for the duration for the war.

The Hale America National Open Golf Tournament was billed as a singular tournament held in July 1942 to raise money for the war effort and celebrate "the American spirit." Its purpose was not to determine a national champion. It was co-sponsored by the USGA, PGA of America and the Chicago District Golf Association in support of a larger movement.

Even before the United States officially entered World War II, the Hale America Program existed as a national campaign intended to have all civilians become more involved in athletics, as well as to improve morale across the country. It involved not just golf, but many other sports. John B. Kelly, the Assistant U.S. Director of Civilian Defense in Charge of Physical Fitness suggested to the USGA that they host a series of "Hale America" Tournaments on Memorial Day Weekend, Independence Day and Labor Day, to further physical fitness and raise funds for the Red Cross.

In January 1942, the USGA Executive Committee resolved to follow Kelly's request. This was a special request under unusual circumstances that aligned with the USGA's intentions to serve the nation during war.

The Hale America Open was just one of many ways the Association aimed to serve the country in 1942. Using its position as the game's governing body, the USGA coordinated with local and national government agencies and public and private golf clubs to support the war effort. For example, the USGA also sponsored a series of Pearl Harbor Tournaments in 1942 to raise money for war relief in Hawaii (eventually using a portion of the funds to purchase an ambulance for the Hawaiian Chapter of the American Red Cross in 1943).

With this historical context for the tournament, as well as the USGA's clear cancellation of their official championships for 1942, the Hale America Open cannot be considered a U.S. Open.

The additional evidence is that the auspices, field and format were inconsistent with a U.S. Open. The Hale America Open was hosted by the USGA, the PGA of America and the Chicago District of Golf, whereas every U.S. Open prior had only been hosted by the USGA. The field was unusual as celebrities such as Bob Hope and Bing Crosby were invited to participate as exempt qualifiers (they did not participate), and Bob Jones emerged from a 12-year retirement to assist in boosting entries and ticket sales. The tournament's format did not include a 36-hole cut, but did include several side events such as a long drive competition and trick-shot exhibition.

The prizes are perhaps the most telling. Much of the confusion regarding the tournament being considered a U.S. Open is due to Hogan's Hale American gold medal appearing nearly identical to the gold medal presented to U.S. Open champions. This is because the medal was intended to be presented to the winner of the canceled 1942 U.S. Open. The medal had already been created and there were many wartime cutbacks and rations in place, so it was repurposed for the Hale America. The engraving on the back of the medal reads "Hale America National Open Tournament" and notes the purpose of the tournament.

The U.S. Open trophy, emblematic of the championship and presented to every U.S. Open champion since 1895, was not presented to Hogan. It remained with the 1941 U.S. Open champion, Craig Wood.

In conclusion, the Hale America Open has never been considered a U.S. Open. When one looks at the historical context for the tournament, the auspices, format, field and prizes, it is difficult to consider it more than what it was: a collective effort by golf organizations to support a nation at war. However, the Hale America was successful in its purpose, delivering funds for the war effort, inspiring participation in golf and boosting morale among Americans. The Hale America, and all other activities conducted for the greater good during World War II should be celebrated and serve an example for our generation that every sacrifice and contribution during times of suffering is valuable.

Finally, Hogan's victory at the Hale America should still be considered a great achievement. His impressive performance against some of the decade's top players should not be diminished though the Hale America was not a USGA championship. His participation and his victory elevated interest in the tournament and its historical importance.

Hogan later served in the U.S. Army Air Corps and became one of the USGA's greatest champions, a player with immense skill, focus and courage. Consistent with that, Hogan's Hale America Open medal is on permanent display in the USGA Golf Museum's Ben Hogan Room. His dog tags, flight book and other materials used during his military service are also in the collection, preserved so future generations may discover the life and achievements of one of golf's greatest players.

There are any numbers of ways to unpack and dissect the USGA statement and point to inconsistencies or convenient omissions. But the place to start is the part that mentions the USGA medal. For Hogan, it was the five medals that, to him, symbolized five US Opens. He never directly criticized the USGA and, over time, he even wondered if the Hale America should count as a US Open title. He was, however, insistent that the five medals represented five victories, and all five medals looked the same on the front.

It is impossible to determine when, exactly, the call to classify the Hale America as a US Open began. It was 10 years later, as Hogan was preparing for the 1952 US Open (which he would not win) that he mentioned to a sportswriter for *Golf World* magazine that he was really going after his fifth US Open championship. He had won the US Open in 1948, 1950, and 1951. So, if he counted the Hale America, he would be going after his fifth.

The difference in the medals is the inscription on the back. The medal for winning the Hale America has the tournament name on the back as well as the initials of the three sponsor organizations. It also notes that the tournament was played for the "benefit of Navy Relief and the USO."

In his 1983 interview with Ken Venturi, held on the 30th anniversary of his Triple Crown year of 1953, Hogan made reference to the medals when queried about his US Open experiences. "I already have five medals and the president of the USGA has presented each one of them to me," Hogan told Venturi. "That was the Hale America National Open in Chicago. It was 1942. I went into the service in 1943. I played the last 36 holes with Bobby Jones and I won the tournament. Jimmy Demaret was second." He then mentioned that he was presented the medal by the USGA president (he got the name wrong in the interview; it was George Blossom, not Dick Tufts) and then said, "and it's identical to the other four."

Venturi responded, "Then we'd have to call it number five, wouldn't we?"

Hogan said, "Well, Joe Dey does."

Except, as we know, Joe Dey *does not*. But Hogan always believed that the Hale America should have counted as a legitimate US Open. Dan Jenkins wrote, "I say a man who owns five gold medals for winning US Opens has won five US Opens." Golf writer Charles Price took up the cause in a 1975 article in *Golf* magazine titled "The Hawk." (It was one of many Hogan nicknames.) The article was published five years before Jack Nicklaus added his fourth US Open title.

"Speaking of Bob Jones, it has been said that he, Willie Anderson and Ben have won four National Opens. This is a lie. Ben has won five. Even the USGA, if pressed, would have to admit this," wrote Price. (Price would do an about-face 17 years later in an article for *Golf Digest* saying the Hale America bore little resemblance to actual US Open conditions or competition.)

The USGA has been pressed, many times, and has been unyielding in its position. The Hale America was, what, a National Open? A wartime substitute for the US Open? An ersatz US Open, which is what golf writer Herbert Warren Wind called it? Or was it really a US Open in every way except in name? "If it walks like a US Open and talks like a US Open, isn't it a US Open, no matter what name it carries?" wrote golf writer Ron Sirak in 2017, urging the USGA to reconsider.

There are a number of reasons why the arguments of Jenkins, Price, Sirak, and others (yes, even Hogan) should be heard and respected. The USGA's April 2020 statement will be examined here, both for what it contained and what it omitted.

We've already dealt with the medal situation. Hogan has five. There's a portrait of him with all five in the Ben Hogan Room at Colonial Country Club in Fort Worth. The USGA's response is that the medal was already made, the inscription on the back was not the same as other US Open medals, and Hogan was never presented with the silver, 18-inch jug that is the official championship trophy. US Open winners get to keep the trophy for a year and return it to the USGA before the next US Open.

Then there are the tournament's "auspices, format and field," which the USGA statement mentioned at the outset. We will start with the first.

AUSPICES

While it is undeniably correct that the USGA was one of the Hale America Tournament's three sponsors—and not the sole sponsor, as is the case with the official US Opens—it is also undeniably correct that the USGA ran the tournament almost exactly like it runs a US Open.

Hale America started with the two rounds of qualifying, the local qualifying in May and then the sectional qualifying at around a dozen sites in June. That is what happens every year around the country for those who are not exempt from qualifying. (There was no qualifying for the 2020 US Open due to the novel coronavirus.)

The USGA enforced its rules and regulations at the tournament, which it typically does only at major events. That led to Sam Byrd's clubs being deemed unusable due to unacceptable grooves. Did the organization check the grooves of all the participants?

The organization also deemed Bobby Jones to be a professional for the tournament, a designation that would have miffed the Grand Slam champion, who always considered himself an amateur.

The USGA runs only one professional men's championship a year—and in 1942, it ran the Hale America. The PGA agreed to make sure its members participated—the players undoubtedly would have regardless—and the CDGA handled local logistics so that the USGA could concentrate on raising war relief money, an admirable undertaking. But to use the "more than one sponsor" argument as a way to say the Hale America was not solely a USGA-run event, and thus not a US Open, is, again, a distinction without a difference.

FORMAT

The US Open has had a variety of formats since it first launched in 1895. The first three years it was played, it was a one-day, 36-hole event. For the next six years, it was two days of 36-hole day. The present four-day, four-rounds format didn't come into play until 1965, and much of that was due to television.

In the 1940s, the US Open followed a familiar script—two rounds of 18 holes on the first two days and then two more rounds of 18 holes on the final day, a Saturday. The 36-hole day was deemed to separate the golfing wheat from the golfing chaff. It usually worked. There were no Orville Moodys (1979) or Lucas Glovers (2009) crowned as US Open champions in Hogan's time. The most significant exception was Jack Fleck's stunning win in 1955. From 1946 through 1954, Hogan won four US Opens. The other five winners were Lloyd Mangrum, Lew Worsham, Cary Middlecoff, Julius Boros, and Ed Furgol. Mangrum, Middlecoff, and Boros are all in the World Golf Hall of Fame.

The sponsors of the Hale America wanted to raise as much money as possible, so it made sense to make it a four-day tournament with four separate gates. The tournament also had no cut, which meant that there were plenty of golfers on the course over the weekend without a chance at winning. But one of those was Bobby Jones. He likely would have made the cut anyway, but he was well out of it by the fourth round.

The addition of the so-called "side events"—if unseemly by US Open standards—did not detract from the quality of play. But you can't attend a US Open in the twenty-first century, or any PGA tournament for that matter, without getting overwhelmed by commercialism run amok. There are tents for *everything* these days, which sometimes make the actual golf look like a sideshow or an afterthought. So a golf clinic or a long-driving contest, while not regular staples of a tour event, were included in the Hale America package. This didn't seem to bother Hogan or Demaret.

FIELD

This is perhaps the most disingenuous argument of all. The field for the Hale America was exceptional. Maybe organizers were concerned at first about who might show up, which explains the early logic (ultimately disbanded) of inviting Bing Crosby and Bob Hope. Bobby Jones bemoaned the fact that newly minted PGA champion Sam Snead and "Bud" Ward, the defending US Amateur champion, were not in the field and thus "it wouldn't be fair to call it a championship tournament and put the results in the record books."

Come again? By that logic, the 1949 US Open should not be considered a major because Hogan was unable to participate. Or every major that Tiger Woods missed when he was injured shouldn't count. By that logic, pretty much every British Open until the mid-1960s shouldn't count because the great American professionals didn't participate. What about all the PGA Championships that Hogan missed after his car accident? Do they count? And let's not forget that Ward was an amateur—a good one (he also won the US Amateur in 1939), but an amateur. The Hale America was a tournament for professionals.

Snead entered the Navy a month before the Hale America, while Ward was already in the service. You can make a case that Snead's presence would have livened things up, but you can't make the case that his absence diminished the field at Ridgemoor. Every other prominent pro was there—Hogan, Nelson, Demaret, Lloyd Mangrum, Little, Wood, the three Turnesas, Sarazen, Byrd, McSpaden. And, unlike both the 1942 Masters and the 1942 PGA Championship, both of which count as majors for their respective champions (Nelson, Snead), the field at Ridgemoor was a full one. The PGA eliminated one round of match-play in 1942. The Masters field was about half what organizers originally expected. However, both fields contained the big-name players. So did Ridgemoor.

Tim Scott, who worked with Ben Hogan from 1969 to 1982, mentioned a situation in his 2013 book, *Ben Hogan: The Myths Everyone Knows, The Man No One Knew* in which he, Hogan, and Hogan's secretary Claribel Kelly were in the golfer's office one day. They came across a list of Hogan's accomplishments and Kelly had added the Hale America as a US Open.

Scott wrote that Hogan grumbled, and then said, "The competition was as strong as any other Open and they did count Sam's PGA and Byron's Masters as major wins. And the head of the USGA presented me with exactly the same medal as my four other US Open medals.

"Oh," Hogan concluded, according to Scott, "the hell with 'em."

Hogan made a similar plaint to his wife, Valerie, as she recounted in a section written for Martin Davis's richly detailed coffee-table book, *Ben Hogan: The Man behind the Mystique*. "It's unfair," Valerie Hogan recalled her husband telling her, "for the PGA to count Sam Snead's PGA Championship in 1942 in Atlantic City with a smaller field and for the USGA not to count the 1942 Open that I won." The argument that the field was in some way compromised for the Hale America simply does not ring true. Hogan was right about that.

THE COURSE

Grantland Rice wrote, "Ridgemoor was not a championship course. It is a membership course." But at the end of the day, Ridgemoor produced an estimable champion and an entertaining and competitive tournament.

Ridgemoor gets a bad rap. Despite its founding in 1905, it has never been considered one of those elite, upper-crusty clubs that the USGA tended to gravitate toward for its signature events. But it prefers it to be that way.

The club moved quickly to signal its willingness to host the tournament and, by all accounts, did the best that it could to produce a worthy venue for a USGA-sponsored tournament.

The USGA's complaint, as Dey said, was that the organization lacked the time and manpower to sufficiently toughen up the course to its exacting standards for a US Open. But here's the fallacy behind that argument: so what? All the good golfers were there, and they all played the same course under the same conditions. To nitpick Ridgemoor because it wasn't tough enough, or that it had consecutive par 5s (as does Baltusrol, host of 16 USGA championships), or that the finishing hole was a par 3 (as is the case with Congressional, site of two US Opens) overlooks the simple fact that it was the same course for everyone. And after four rounds, more than 75 percent of the field could not break par.

And to say it wasn't groomed sufficiently to USGA standards also might lead to the impression that it somehow bore more resemblance to Otey Crisman's

9-hole municipal daily-fee course in Selma, Alabama, than to a challenging 18-hole, tournament-ready layout. Maybe Ridgemoor wasn't as well manicured as Oakmont or Oakland Hills. But it also wasn't Hazeltine in 1970. Or Chambers Bay in 2015. Or Erin Hills in 2017.

In 1970, the USGA held its Open at Hazeltine Country Club in Chaska, Minnesota, for the first time. The club apparently had the space and the willingness that Interlachen lacked for a US Open. Early reviews were almost uniformly negative.

Asked about the course, Dave Hill, one of the tour's most outspoken and colorful figures, said all it lacked was "only 80 acres of corn and a few cows to be a good farm." Hill thought course architect Robert Trent Jones had gotten the blueprints "upside down," while Jack Nicklaus said just before the start of the tournament that Hazeltine lacked definition and that "many players will need guides as well as caddies in this Open." Hill ended up getting fined $150 for his comments. But he easily covered the transgression fee by overcoming his hatred of Hazeltine and finishing second, seven shots behind champion Tony Jacklin. The second-place finish paid $15,000.

Hazeltine counted for Jacklin, and, after a redesign, hosted the US Open again in 1991 when it was won by the late Payne Stewart. Between 1966 and 2019, Hazeltine hosted eight USGA-sanctioned national championships. Most recently the club was showcased hosting the 2016 Ryder Cup, although that is run by the PGA of America.

The conditions at Chambers Bay, site of the 2015 US Open, also drew criticism from the contestants. Billy Horschel deemed the greens almost unputtable, saying, "I think a lot of players, and I'm one of them, have lost some respect for the USGA and this championship this year for the greens."

Chambers Bay, meanwhile, exemplified more of the new thinking that goes into selecting US Open venues. While still partial to its celebrated courses such as Oakmont, Shinnecock Hills, and others, the tournament has expanded to include several public courses, such as Pebble Beach, Bethpage Black, Chambers Bay, Erin Hills, Pinehurst No. 2, and Torrey Pines. Pebble Beach is scheduled to host the US Open for the seventh time in 2027, tops among the public courses selected for US Open competitions.

Even the venerable institutions have come in for harsh criticism. In 1963, the US Open returned to The Country Club in Brookline, Massachusetts, on the 50th anniversary of the 1913 victory by amateur Francis Ouimet over Englishmen Ted Ray and Harry Vardon, a seismic moment in the history of American golf. Many of the players complained about the conditions, with one unidentified golfer saying, "They ought to draw a white line around the course and call it ground under repair." A former PGA champion, Chick Harbert, called The Country Club "the Cadillac of golf courses—1911 model." Of the 470-yard, par 4 12th hole, Arnold Palmer had one word to describe it: "ridiculous."

A report by the USGA's Championship Committee at the organization's annual meeting the following January noted that because of weather conditions over the winter of 1962–1963, "the course was in playable condition. It was not in top condition." The winning score in 1963 was 293, the highest for a US Open in the post–World War II era.

A decade later, at what came to be known as the Massacre at Winged Foot in Mamaroneck, New York, the conditions were brutal. Touring pro Bert Yancey had a 30-foot putt on the first hole of his first practice round—and putted it off the green. He turned around and walked back up the first fairway, saying, "Where in the hell can I find a USGA director?" Steve Melnyk reporting quitting a practice round before he played eight holes because he lost all his golf balls in Winged Foot's thick rough.

Lee Trevino once said of Oakmont's slick greens, "The only way to stop a ball around here is to call a policeman." Tom Weiskopf did not appreciate the "improvements" made to fabled Oak Hill, a Donald Ross design, by modern architects George and Tom Fazio. "I'm going to organize a Classic Golf Preservation Society," Weiskopf said when the PGA Championship was played at Oak Hill in 1980. "Members get to carry loaded guns in case they see anybody touching a Donald Ross course."

There were no such harsh words for Ridgemoor in 1942. The only complaint came from those who thought the US Open should be a punishing, confidence-destroying, humility-building golf tournament.

SCORING

Here, too, Ridgemoor gets a bad rap—and it gets worse in hindsight. Everyone was stunned by the low scores of the first two rounds. And they were low, astonishingly low for a US Open. They aren't so much anymore—and that is why the ease-in-scoring argument becomes harder to defend as the new breed of golfers tear US Open venues to shreds.

Hogan's four-round total of 271, 17 under par, was breathtaking for the times. The existing scoring record for a US Open at the time, Ralph Guldahl's 281 in 1937, was a mere 7 under par. But that was the record. The USGA was just as content to see the pros flounder once a year under ultrademanding— some might say diabolical—conditions.

Three years before Guldahl set the scoring record, Olin Dutra had emerged victorious at Merion with a 293 total, 13 over par. Sam Parks' 11 over par the following year at Oakmont proved to be unbeatable.

But between the Massacre at Winged Foot in 1974 and the 2020 US Open at Winged Foot, the winning score has been over par only seven times, and four of those were 1 over par. Even esteemed Oakmont succumbed to the modern golfer, with Dustin Johnson's 4 under par triumphing in 2016.

Two of Hogan's "records" from the Hale America would still be standing in the USGA record books—his second-round 62 and his 17 under par total over four rounds. His seemingly unfathomable 271 for a US Open was matched by Martin Kaymer in 2014 as well as Gary Woodland in 2019. By then, however, it had been shattered by Rory McIlroy's 268 at Congressional in 2011. McIlroy, however, was a mere 16 under par, as Congressional played to a par 71. Brooks Koepka, who won at Erin Hills in 2017 with a 272, was also 16 under par.

So had Hogan's 271 counted, he would have held the US Open scoring record from 1942 until 2011, almost 70 years. As it was, his 276 at Riviera in 1948 lasted until Jack Nicklaus' 275 at Baltusrol in 1967. Nicklaus lowered it again in 1980, to 272. It was subsequently matched by Lee Janzen (1993), Tiger Woods (2000), and Jim Furyk (2003) until McIlroy's four-day demolition of Congressional.

But what the scores of McIlroy, Koepka, and Woodland illustrate is that Hogan's 271, while not reflective of the time, is more and more in keeping with the modern-day scores of US Open champions. And how much more difficult was Erin Hills in 2017 than Ridgemoor in 1942?

At Ridgemoor, 22 players finished under par. At Erin Hills, 31 players finished under par. At Pebble Beach in 2019, 31 players finished under par. So the scores at Ridgemoor, in hindsight, don't look so eye-opening. And that is one more reason why the USGA should reconsider. Maybe the course was easy then. But it proved no easier to the game's best players than did Erin Hills 75 years later or even celebrated Pebble Beach two years after that.

PLAYERS' VIEWS

We know how Hogan felt. We know how Bobby Jones felt, even with his illogical reasoning. But how did the others feel?

In 1992, a half-century after the Hale America, *Golf World* writer Geoff Russell talked to some of the participants as to whether the tournament should count as a US Open. He got mixed reviews.

Mike Turnesa told the magazine, "It definitely was a US Open. I know Ben thinks it should count as a US Open and I don't blame him. If I'd have won, I'd have felt like I won a US Open. The only difference was the name."

Paul Runyan, who finished at even par for the tournament, disagreed. He said, "Don't get me wrong. Ridgemoor was nice and well-conditioned. But it was not, by any means, an Open championship layout."

The man whose run of bogeys on the back nine on Sunday helped Hogan win the tournament preferred to pass the buck. Jimmy Demaret, in *My Partner, Ben Hogan*, mentions the controversy in passing. "Some of our statisticians and record holders claim that Hogan has already won five US Opens instead of four," he wrote in 1954. "But let's allow those nearsighted students of record books to stew over that one."

FIVE? OR FIVE*?

In 1953, the USGA welcomed Ben Hogan back after his victory at Carnoustie in the British Open with a dinner on July 23 at the Park Lane Hotel.

As pictured in *Ben Hogan: The Man behind the Mystique*, the menu for the evening, printed on the back of the program, featured jellied madrilène, prime rib of blue ribbon beef, string beans au beurre, and potatoes au gratin. The dessert was frozen macaroon cake with fresh crushed strawberries.

As tempting to the palate as that was, what was even more appetizing to Hogan fans was what was printed on the front page of the program. It listed all of Hogan's major tournament victories, including his four US Open titles, his two PGA championships, his two Masters victories, his one British Open victory, and the 1942 Hale America National Open Tournament winner. There was no qualifier. It was listed right up there with the other major tournaments.

If the USGA listed the Hale America along with the other majors Hogan had won, why hadn't it recognized the tournament as a US Open?

The front of the program was autographed by several of Hogan's contemporaries, including Johnny Farrell, Tony Manero, Gene Sarazen, Francis Ouimet, and—in the smallest signature of all—Joe Dey.

Nearly four decades later, Colonial Country Club member Jody Vasquez helped arrange a meeting at Hogan's office. Vasquez had shagged balls for Hogan and authored a touching memoir in 2004 titled *Afternoons with Mr. Hogan*. In it, he describes a meeting in the fall of 1992 between Hogan and Nick Faldo, the first time the two had crossed paths.

Faldo had been compared to Hogan for his attention to detail and meticulous work habits, and had been longing to meet the man. Vasquez got involved through a friend, and soon Faldo would take a private jet from Palm Springs to Fort Worth for this once-in-a-lifetime meeting. There was only one ground rule: Faldo was not allowed to approach the topic of putting.

The meeting got going and Faldo leaned on Hogan's desk and asked what everyone assumed to be an innocuous question: "How do you win a US Open?"

Coming from Faldo, it was heartfelt. He was four years removed from his best chance at winning a US Open when he had lost to Curtis Strange in a play-off at The Country Club. He won three Masters and three British Opens, but never won a US Open. Or a PGA championship; he finished second in 1992.

Hogan sized up the question and said, simply, "You shoot the lowest score."

Everyone in the room, which included Faldo's agent and the outgoing president of the Hogan Company, cracked up. Everyone, that is, except the man whose remark prompted all the laughter. He was stone-faced.

A confused Faldo looked at Hogan, who continued, "Seriously, I'm not kidding. If by Sunday evening, you have shot the lowest score, I promise you they will give you the medal. I know. I have five of them."

A half-century after Ridgemoor, Hogan was still convinced that the five medals he had in his possession constituted five US Open victories. Vasquez noted that the Hale America had not been considered a true US Open by the USGA. "I wish they would get over it," Vasquez wrote, "but it's the USGA, so no one is surprised."

Less than five years later, Ben Hogan died, 19 days before what would have been his 85th birthday.

8

OCTOBER 1945 TO AUGUST 1946

The End of Hostilities and the Return of the US Open

Hogan, great as he was, will never again be able to reach the peak it takes to play winning tournament golf.

—Fred Corcoran, PGA tournament director, in 1944

Following the surrenders of Germany and Japan in 1945, the USGA went back to work to get its tournaments ready for 1946. The formal Japanese surrender had taken place on the USS *Missouri* in Tokyo Bay on September 2, less than a month after atomic bombs leveled Hiroshima and Nagasaki.

It was too late in the year for any meaningful tournaments, so the USGA turned its attention to 1946. Interlachen still had the right of first refusal by virtue of being awarded and then losing the 1942 US Open. But by the time the USGA Executive Committee met in October, Interlachen was off the table.

The reason? The club had not once, but twice told the USGA it was no longer interested in hosting the US Open when it returned following World War II. Late in 1944, when it looked as if the Allies might end the war before the end of the calendar year, Interlachen held an emergency meeting and notified the USGA that it was not interested in hosting a 1945 US Open if there were one. Thanks to the Battle of the Bulge, the disastrous Operation Market Garden in the Netherlands (the subject of Cornelius Ryan's 1974 book, *A Bridge Too Far*) and other miscues, the war dragged on well into 1945.

After V-J Day in August 1945, Interlachen officials again let the USGA know that it had decided against hosting the 1946 Open. While Interlachen initially wasn't crazy about the decision to cancel the 1942 Open, by the end of the war it had decided to move on from the disappointment of three years earlier. The USGA still kept Interlachen on its list of approved clubs for future events, just not for US Opens. And just not at the top of its list.

Interlachen went 51 years between hosting USGA events, finally landing the US Senior Amateur in 1991. (It had last hosted a USGA event in 1936.) The competition went off without a hitch, leading to the club hosting the Walker Cup two years later. The USGA returned one more time, in 2008, this time for the US Women's Open, won by Inbee Park. The club also hosted the Solheim Cup in 2002, the women's version of the Ryder Cup.

With Interlachen out of the picture, the USGA, facing a time issue, returned to Canterbury Country Club, site of the 1940 US Open won by Lawson Little. The executive committee met on October 10 and unanimously approved Canterbury for its first showcase event after the war.

The club received official notification in an October 16 letter from USGA Acting Executive Secretary Josephine Korber to Canterbury President E. G. Meister. The dates specified were June 13–15. The USGA had its signature event on the 1946 calendar. The Masters would be up and running as well, in April. The PGA Championship, meanwhile, had taken a one-year break in 1943, but resumed in 1944. The fields weren't the greatest—Hogan, Demaret, Mangrum, and others were in the service—and it had been won by Bob Hamilton, a journeyman pro, who upset Byron Nelson, 1-up, in the 36-hole final. Nelson (1940) had been the only former champion in the depleted field.

There were a half-dozen former PGA champions in the field for the 1945 championship in July at Moraine Country Club in Kettering, Ohio. Nelson rebounded from his 1944 loss and picked up his second PGA title with a 4 and 3 victory over Sam Byrd.

Once again, Hogan, Demaret, and Mangrum were not in the field. For Nelson, it was the ninth of his eleven straight victories in 1945.

The question on the minds of players and fans alike was how long would it take the big names to get their A-games back in tournament shape. Hogan had been the dominant player before the tournaments were canceled and the players went off to the service. Fred Corcoran, the PGA Tour's tournament director, had predicted in March 1944 that Hogan would never again be the golfer he had been before the war. "You have to keep playing," Corcoran told the Associated Press. "Hogan, great as he was, will never again be able to reach the peak it takes to play winning tournament golf."

Corcoran was correct in one sense. Ben Hogan was not the same golfer he was before the war. He was better.

Hogan announced his return in the fall of 1945 by winning five tournaments in a span of four months. That set the stage for a remarkable run in 1946. He had more than reached the peak; he had planted the Hogan banner at the summit.

The first full year of PGA activity would also see Mangrum and Demaret return to prior form. Bobby Jones, meanwhile, settled back into civilian life in Atlanta, resumed his stewardship of the Masters, and began a long and lasting relationship with his boss from the European Theater, a man he would not meet until the war concluded—Dwight D. Eisenhower. They shared a love of golf and letter writing.

The 1946 tour offered events and riches unseen in previous years. There were more than 25 so-called "open field" tournaments and another handful of invitationals, most of them team match-play events. Also to the pros' liking—an increase in purses, more than $400,000 in total. The Masters would even have a new structure to greet the golfers as they came up the 18th hole—a photographer's tower. Players also were informed that the Masters would abide by new USGA regulations limiting the number of clubs in one's bag to 14. (The PGA allowed 16.) "This happens to be one of the few remaining places where golf tradition persists," wrote the *New York Times*. "And the pros are not only willing but anxious to abide by all the rules."

The winner of the Masters would receive $2,500, an increase of $1,000 over the winner's share from 1942. Second-place money in 1946 was the same as first-place money in 1942.

The season began with an old stalwart, the Los Angeles Open, and Byron Nelson picked up right where left off, winning the tournament by five shots. Ben Hogan finished second. Nelson won again the following week in San Francisco, while Hogan picked up his first victory of the year at the end of the month in Phoenix, in a playoff with Herman Keiser. That was a name Hogan would soon not forget. That tournament also marked the return of Lloyd Mangrum, who had just been discharged from the Army.

Jimmy Demaret won in Tucson in early February, and Hogan won twice more before the first important tournament of the year, the Masters. The last Masters had not ended well for Hogan; he had lost to Nelson in a playoff after holding a three-stroke lead. With the USGA still not dignifying the Hale America as a US Open, Hogan was winning everything but the "major" tournaments.

Hogan featured prominently in all three American majors in 1946. Until the final one, however, he faced the same familiar chorus of questions about being a bridesmaid. And these weren't just ordinary, second-place, tip-your-hat-to-the-champion finishes. These were gut-wrenchers of the highest order.

The so-called American Triumvirate of Hogan, Snead, and Nelson—they all had been born in 1912—were the tri-favorites heading into Augusta. Each had won three times prior to the Masters, which had 51 entries. What few saw coming was a wire-to-wire victory for the man Hogan had defeated earlier in the year in a playoff in Phoenix—Herman Keiser.

Keiser was nicknamed the Missouri Mortician for his serious demeanor and earned his keep mainly as a club pro. Two years younger than Hogan, Keiser had just taken over the head job at Firestone Country Club. He wasn't Otey Crisman. His had been one of the final invitations to the Masters, but he had two second-place finishes prior to Augusta and would win back-to-back later that year in Knoxville and Richmond, the latter by four shots over Hogan.

Most of the writers designated Keiser a dark horse. Keiser had one win to his credit, the Miami International Four-Ball in 1942, where he paired with Chandler Harper. He then spent three years in the Navy, serving as a storekeeper on the USS *Cincinnati*. His two second-place finishes had him ninth on the money list. He was confident enough to place a $70 bet on himself at 20–1 odds.

Keiser and Chick Harbert shared the first-round lead with 69s over what was deemed to be the most star-studded and strongest field in the 10 years of the Masters. Hogan had trouble with the gusty conditions and shot a 74. Snead also shot a 74. Demaret had a 75, while course record-holder Mangrum shot 76.

Keiser and Harbert were the only two rounds under 70. The following day, Keiser shot a 68, one of just three rounds in the 60s. He had a five-shot lead at the midway point and a five-shot lead after three rounds. At that point, Hogan had bounced back from his opening round and submitted rounds of 70 and 69. He was in second place.

The final round was a study in agony for both men. Despite having the five-shot lead, Keiser was three holes ahead of Hogan in the pairings. The Masters' folks paired Keiser with Byron Nelson while Hogan was with Demaret, who started the day at even par, eight shots off the lead.

By the time Hogan was on the 16th tee on the final day, he and Keiser were tied. Keiser had three-putted from 25 feet on the difficult 18th to take a bogey 5, missing a 5-foot comebacker after trying for a birdie to add to his lead.

All Hogan needed to do was par the last three holes to forge a playoff. It was similar to the situation Hogan and Jack Fleck would find themselves in nine years later at the US Open. In this case, however, Hogan was not in the locker room waiting for his opponent to finish. Instead it was a disconsolate Keiser, who was quite certain he had blown his best (perhaps only) chance at the Masters.

The two were still tied when Hogan got to the 18th tee. Keiser told report-ers he hoped Hogan would either birdie or bogey the finishing play, as he had no desire for a playoff. Hogan would make nearly identical remarks at Olympic nine years later, as he wanted to avoid a playoff as well.

Hogan hit his approach shot on 18 to within 12 feet. As he relayed to the *New York Times*, he tried to make the putt to win the tournament outright. "Sure I went after it," he said. "But I never expected the ball to keep rolling the way it did. The moment I hit the ball I knew it was going to miss the hole and I turned my head away for a moment. I was really amazed when it didn't stop within a foot of the cup."

It stopped nowhere near a foot of the cup. The *New York Times* estimated Hogan still had 3 feet left. Others have said it was 4 feet. David Barrett, who wrote a book on the history of the Masters, said it was 30 inches. It was no "gimme." And Hogan did exactly what Keiser had done earlier—he three-putted "to bring his magnificent uphill struggle to a sorrowful end," wrote Wil-liam Richardson for the *Times*.

It was left to Henry Picard to deliver the news to a "wan and lingering" Keiser in the locker room. "Congratulations Herman," Picard told him. "The little man really took the choke. Those were the worst putts I've ever seen him hit."

Hogan wasn't reaching for the hemlock—yet. He told Richardson the follow-ing morning at breakfast that "it just wasn't my time to win. However, there's another year coming."

Demaret ended up tied for fourth place, while Mangrum never broke par over four rounds and finished tied for 16th. The only consolation for Mangrum was that the Masters had increased its purse to now cover the top 21 and ties. So he picked up $138. Bobby Jones also couldn't break par over four rounds and finished tied for 32nd.

But it was Hogan's close call—again—that was the big story, Keiser's surpris-ing victory notwithstanding. For the second consecutive Masters, Hogan had not only lost, but lost in a most painful manner. Hogan shrugged it off. He spent some downtime in Texas, worked on his swing, and then won three straight tournaments in May and early June, the last victory coming two weeks before the US Open returned following its war-induced absence.

When the golfers arrived in Cleveland for the 1946 US Open, Hogan and Nelson were once again the betting favorites. Hogan now had six victories on the season, while Nelson had four. Demaret had won once. A Mangrum had triumphed in Pensacola in February, but it had been Lloyd's big brother, Ray, ousting Hogan in a playoff.

Lloyd Mangrum was still looking for his first victory since June 1942, when he had teamed with Lawson Little to win the Inverness Four-Ball a week before the Hale America. Earlier in the year he had finished second to Hogan at both the Western Open in St. Louis in late May and at the Goodall Round Robin in New York a week later. He had finished third in the Greater Greensboro Open in March, so he had been in the hunt.

The field at Canterbury mirrored the one at Ridgemoor, with one notable exception—Sam Snead. Lawson Little was back to see if he could replicate his 1940 title when he defeated Gene Sarazen in a playoff. That was the same year that Ed (Porky) Oliver finished tied with Little and Sarazen, but was disqualified for teeing off too early.

After the first two rounds at Canterbury, the oddsmakers looked prescient. Hogan was tied for the lead with Vic Ghezzi. Nelson was two shots back. After opening with a disappointing 74, Mangrum was tied for 26th, then recovered to shoot 70 and was at even par, four shots off the pace, tied with Snead. Demaret was at 145.

The final, 36-hole day produced some wild golf, wild weather, and a leaderboard that seemed to change by the minute. Nelson had taken over the lead with a morning-round 69, which left him at 211, one shot ahead of Mangrum and two ahead of Hogan. Nelson managed the 69 despite getting penalized one stroke when his caddy accidently kicked his ball while it was in the rough on the 13th hole. An ever-alert USGA rules official named Ike Grainger spotted the infraction and notified Nelson immediately. Grainger was the official who penalized Mangrum two strokes for marking his ball incorrectly in the 1950 US Open playoff, and who would not let Snead finish putting on the final hole of his 1947 US Open playoff with Lew Worsham.

Demaret had slumped to a 73 in the third round and trailed Nelson by seven shots. But during a chaotic fourth round, any one of the top seven finishers, and that included Demaret, were at one point in contention. The round ended in a three-way tie for first, which could well have been a five-way tie. Demaret made a late rush with an eagle followed by two birdies on the back nine, but ran out of holes. He closed with a 68, the lowest score of the round, and finished at 286.

Nelson and Mangrum, who had shot a 68 in the morning, were in the same group for the final round. Nelson appeared to one and all to have the title in his grasp when he stood on the 17th tee with a two-shot lead. But he bogeyed the final two holes, three-putting the 17th and then ran into trouble off the tee on 18. He finished at 284, which is what Mangrum totaled as well. Ghezzi also was in at 284 and, for a while, it appeared that the 4 under par aggregate would not be low enough to win.

That's because Hogan was still on the course as was his partner, Herman Barron. With three holes remaining, each was 5 under par. For Hogan, that was almost a miracle in that he had taken a triple-bogey 7 on the eighth hole when he nearly hit his second shot out of bounds. At that point, he trailed Nelson by four shots.

But nine holes later Hogan was in the lead. He quickly bogeyed the 16th while Barron parred it, temporarily taking the lead. But Barron would bogey the last two holes to finish at 285, tied for fourth. He would be remembered as the first Jewish golfer to win a PGA tournament, the 1942 Western Open. But there would only be one Herman to win a major in 1946, and it was going to be Herman Keiser.

Hogan, meanwhile, parred the 17th. He was 4 under par, tied with Barron, Ghezzi, Nelson, and Mangrum. All Hogan needed was a par on the 18th hole to join the others in a playoff.

The 18th at Canterbury played out in strikingly similar fashion to the 18th at Augusta two months earlier. It was uncanny. Hogan once again hit the green in two and had about an 18-foot putt to win the tournament. What could possibly go wrong?

He again pushed the first putt past the hole. The *New York Times* said the putt for a par was about 2 feet. Other reports list it as slightly longer. It was similar in length to the one he missed at Augusta. And he would miss this one as well.

The three-way playoff was now set. It would be Nelson, who had won his only US Open title seven years earlier in a three-way playoff with Denny Shute and Craig Wood; Ghezzi, who had won the 1941 PGA championship (defeating Nelson in 38 holes); and the major-less Mangrum, barely six months out of the employ of Uncle Sam.

It was an odd pairing. There was the genial Nelson who, unbeknownst to pretty much everyone in the golf world, was on the verge of retirement. Ghezzi had the 1941 PGA title on his résumé, but most golf aficionados of the day remember Nelson being two up with two to play in that tournament and failing to close the deal.

Mangrum was, well, Mangrum. He could be gruff, aloof, and downright surly. And that was even if he happened to be your partner. Jim Ferrier recalled a match in a four-ball tournament against Mangrum and Bobby Locke, the fine South African player regarded as one of the game's top putters. On the final hole of the match, Mangrum missed a putt to force extra holes. Locke came over to his partner and said to Mangrum, "Don't you realize I'm the world's finest putter? Why didn't you ask my opinion on the line of that putt? You'd have holed it if I told you where to putt."

You can well imagine Mangrum's reaction. He was an excellent putter in his own right and he was having none of it from Locke, who had played himself out of the deciding hole. "You sonofabitch. I've put up with you for a week now. Never again."

And that, said Ferrier, "was a real twosome."

The playoff format in 1946 was for a round of 18 holes. If no winner emerged, there would be a second round of 18. No one wanted to contemplate what would happen if there was no winner after 36 holes. The three playoff participants had gone 36 holes on Saturday. They would do so again on Sunday.

Mangrum got the early jump in the morning. (The playoff started in the morning in case there needed to be a second 18.) At one point, he led Ghezzi by two shots and Nelson by four shots. But at the end of the first 18 holes, all three players had shot 72.

The key hole for Mangrum in the second round may well have been the ninth. He took a double bogey 6. It was as meaningful and important a double bogey as he ever made because he lay on the green in five, 70 feet from the hole. He had driven out of bounds, so he was playing his second ball. Mangrum was a firm believer that distance, not break, was the key to good putting, and his 70-footer hit the back up the cup, jumped up, and popped back into the hole.

Still, with seven holes left, Mangrum trailed Ghezzi by three shots and Nelson by two. But a birdie at the 12th, combined with bogeys by Nelson and Ghezzi, put him right back in the thick of things. As the golfers approached the final holes, a pounding thunderstorm hit Canterbury. There was pelting rain. There was lightning. It got so dark that the automobiles parked near the 18th hole turned on their headlights. Play continued.

One writer covering the tournament speculated that the thunderclaps and lightning bolts made Mangrum feel as if he was back in France with the 90th Infantry Division. What is undeniable is that Mangrum's play picked up considerably while the other two slipped back. Birdies on 15 and 16 gave Mangrum a two-shot lead. He was able to survive with a bogey at 18, only because Ghezzi missed a 4-foot putt.

Mangrum's second straight 72 was one better than his playoff partners. What better story was there? The ex-soldier returning home and winning the first US Open to be played after World War II. He had basically been idle from competitive golf for two years while Nelson had been playing regularly.

Bud Ward, the low amateur in the 1946 Open (he tied for 27th) said of Mangrum's victory, "It was the greatest demonstration of courage I ever saw on a golf course. Mangrum wasn't given a chance in the playoff. He needed a tricky 7-foot putt on a drenched green to win. He didn't even hesitate. He just stepped up like nothing was at stake and knocked it in."

We know how Mangrum felt about the victory. Yes, it was a big deal. It was an even bigger deal that he added $333 to his $1,500 winner's check because of the playoff. But would it lead to all sorts of endorsements? Yes and no.

Mangrum discussed why winning the US Open title is not all what people think it is in a *Saturday Evening Post* article from 1956, "I Say Pro Golf Isn't So Tough." He broke down his earnings from the weekend, estimating them to be $16,000, which included the Open purse plus exhibitions, endorsements, and bonuses. He estimated his expenses at $5,000. "My income from (winning) the Open Championship was about average," he wrote.

With the extra day, the 1946 US Open set a record for both attendance and gate receipts, surpassing the 1930 Open at Interlachen. Where Mangrum did benefit from the victory came in the form of a lucrative job offer. George May at the Tam O'Shanter in Chicago offered Mangrum the head pro job, and Mangrum quickly accepted. The Associated Press said Mangrum would receive a $10,000 salary.

The silver US Open trophy, which had last been awarded to Craig Wood in 1941, was back with the USGA and handed over to its 1946 champion. Mangrum took the 18-inch trophy with him back to Chicago and his new place of employment, where it was on display. Three months later, a fire ripped through the clubhouse at Tam O'Shanter and the venerable trophy, which had been awarded to winners since 1895, was destroyed. The USGA immediately commissioned a duplicate. A similar event in 1925 had destroyed the trophy presented by the USGA to its amateur champion. The winner that year had been Bobby Jones.

At the age of 31, Lloyd Mangrum had won his first major. He was one ahead of Hogan at that point, and tied with Demaret. He was several behind Jones, whether you include the amateur championships or not. Jones had won four US Opens.

There was still one more "major" on the calendar—the PGA Championship. In between the Open and the PGA, there were eight full-field, medal-play events and the Inverness Four-Ball, which was won by Hogan and Demaret. Sam Snead journeyed across the Atlantic to win the British Open at St. Andrews, the first British Open since 1939. It was Snead's second major championship. Hogan would add the Winnipeg Open to his list of victories a week before the start of the PGA.

The 1946 PGA Championship was being held outside Portland, Oregon, at the Portland Golf Club. It was a course Hogan knew quite well. The year before, at the Portland Open on the same course, he had shot an eye-opening 27 under par over four rounds, winning by 14 shots over Nelson. The four-round total of 261 was the lowest Hogan ever shot in an official PGA or USGA tournament. (He shot 259 in the 1950 Greenbrier Pro-Am, which was not an official event.) But the PGA would be a match-play event, and Hogan had never gotten out of the quarterfinals in his four previous appearances in the tournament.

Unlike the folks who ran the Masters and the US Open, the men entrusted with overseeing the PGA Championship had no qualms about staging the tournament during World War II. The PGA did pretty much shut down in 1943, and there was no championship that season. But the championship was held with a diminished field in 1944 in Spokane, Washington, and with a better but still incomplete field in 1945 in Kettering, Ohio.

By the time the tournament rolled into the great Northwest in the third week of August 1946, the field was as strong as the PGA could have hoped. The format returned to that of the prewar days, with 64 instead of 32 qualifiers and six rounds of matches instead of five.

The Portland Golf Club has a special place in PGA history, and not just for hosting the organization's first championship after the end of World War II. The following year, the club agreed to host the Ryder Cup. Or, to be more precise, a Portland businessman with deep pockets arranged for the club to host it, and made sure all the participants would be on hand.

There had not been a Ryder Cup since 1937 and, with the 1947 event scheduled to be hosted in the United States, there was a question if Great Britain, still reeling from the war and still under severe rationing, would be able to get a team to Oregon. There had been virtually no competitive golf in England during World War II, so whatever team did show up would be rusty compared to its American counterpart.

Up stepped Robert Hudson, a food magnate and Portland Golf Club member. He agreed to foot the bill for the Brits. He paid for their passage from England to New York aboard the *Queen Mary*. He held a lavish reception dinner for the players at a New York hotel. He then paid for the four-day train trip to Oregon. Hudson paid the entire bill for the 10-man team, from the time they left England until the time they returned. In doing so, he may have saved the Ryder Cup.

The event was played in November 1947, which is not the season for ideal weather in the Northwest. The American team routed the British, 11–1. The only point the Americans lost was when Herman Keiser lost his singles match.

There were 122 golfers attempting to qualify for the 64 match-play spots when the 1946 PGA began on August 19. All the big names made it through the 36 holes of stroke play. Jim Ferrier won medalist honors with a 134, which included a stunning 63. Mangrum and Snead barely made it, sneaking under the cut line by one shot.

The PGA likes to think of its championship as an Everyman Open. It encourages all those club pros—there were more than 4,000 in 1946—to try and compete with the big boys. For many of the club pros, the only two major events open to them were both by the qualifying route—the PGA Championship and the US Open. Thus, there are always some unknown names in the PGA, which can lead to some head-scratching results. There quickly was one in Portland.

Mangrum, who complained of being under the weather, faced a California club pro named Harry Bassler in the first round. Bassler played in some of the lesser known tournaments in California when he wasn't teaching at his Fox Hills Golf Course in what is now Culver City. (The course no longer exists.) He counted the 1944 Santa Anita Open as one of his victories. He would also win the 1948 Southern California PGA Championship.

Bassler had advanced to the second round of the 1944 PGA, where he lost to eventual champion Bob Hamilton. He made it one step further in 1946. He stunned Mangrum, only two months removed from his stirring US Open triumph, with a 1-up victory in the first round. He would defeat eventual US Open champion Lew Worsham in the second round.

Mangrum played in nine PGA Championships over the course of his career and made the cut into match play every time. The closest he came was in 1941 and again in 1949, when he reached the semifinals. The 1946 shocker was the only time he didn't make it out of the first round.

Hogan and Demaret, like Mangrum, faced little-known pros in the early rounds of match play. They fared much better. Demaret opened with a 3 and 2 victory over a Philadelphia-area club pro named Joe Zarhardt, whose claim to fame was winning the 1944 Philadelphia Open. Demaret then eliminated another obscure pro, Dave Tinsley, by the same score in the second round. Tinsley's big moment had come in 1940 when he won the Carolinas Open.

Hogan faced four relative unknowns in his first four matches with only one, his first-rounder against Charlie Weisner, a club pro from Oklahoma, being close. Weisner was credited with teaching future PGA Tour player Jimmy Thompson, who had shot a 66 in the final round of the Hale America. Hogan prevailed 2 and 1. He then faced Indiana club pro Bill Heinlein in the second round. Heinlein was a five-time winner of the Indiana PGA and a 1968 inductee into the Indiana Golf Hall of Fame. Hogan won that round 4 and 3.

Demaret and Hogan were in the same side of the bracket and destined to meet in the semifinals if everything went according to form. But Hogan had never reached the semifinals of a PGA championship, while Demaret's best showing had come in 1942, when he advanced to the semifinals.

But the pair's anticipated head-to-head meeting would come to pass. Demaret advanced to the semifinals with victories over two future PGA champions, Jim Ferrier (1947) and Jim Turnesa (1952). Ferrier would go on to win the 1947 PGA while Turnesa, the second youngest of the seven golfing Turnesa brothers, won the 1952 PGA.

Hogan's third-round opponent was Art Bell, who would become one of the top golf instructors later on, giving lessons to Tom Watson while serving as Pebble Beach's head pro. Bell and his amateur partner won the first Crosby Pro-Am in 1937. Bell also had eliminated Craig Wood in the second round of the 1944 PGA Championship. Hogan crushed him 5 and 4 and then did the same to Frank Moore, a Philadelphia-area pro who had been an assistant to Byron Nelson at the Reading Country Club in the late 1930s. Moore won two Westchester Opens in the late 1930s, was the medalist for qualifying in the 1938 PGA Championship (he lost in the second round of match play), tied for 7th in the 1938 US Open, and tied for 56th at the Hale America. So Hogan's opponents had gradually moved from nobodies to somebodies. And after dispatching Moore, Hogan was in the semifinals for the first time, facing his old chum, Demaret.

The two Texans were a terrific team together, both on the PGA Tour and when paired in the Ryder Cup. But on this day, they would go head-to-head, and it wasn't pretty.

The scheduled 36-hole match lasted 27 holes. Hogan hit Demaret with nine-hole scores of 33-32-31, and while scores in match play can be misleading or even meaningless, the numbers posted by Hogan illustrated how dominant he was. One writer referred to Hogan as "ruthless and cold-blooded" after the merciless pummeling of his good friend. Demaret, predictably, took it in stride, saying he thought the turning point had come when both golfers arrived on the first tee.

All that was left for Hogan was another 36-hole match. His opponent would be Ed (Porky) Oliver, who had eliminated Nelson 1-up in the quarterfinals, sending Lord Byron back to Texas for retirement to his cattle ranch. In Oliver's semifinal match, he came up against Jug McSpaden, one of the enduring personalities on the tour at the time. McSpaden was well known for being Nelson's sidekick, both as a partner in match play and as the runner-up in many of Nelson's victories in his historic 1945 campaign. "If you wouldn't have been born, I'd have been known as a pretty good player," McSpaden once told Nelson.

McSpaden *was* a pretty good player. His name has twice been submitted for enshrinement in the World Golf Hall of Fame, only to come up short. He holds two PGA records to this day: most second-place finishes in a season (13 in 1945), and most top-10 finishes in a season (31 in 1945.) He had 12 top-10 finishes in major tournaments.

Jug McSpaden was a Kansan by birth, and got into golf via the now-familiar caddy route. Four years older than Hogan and six years younger than Jones, McSpaden turned pro at the ripe age of 18. He played in the first Masters in 1934—he would play in a dozen more—and tied for seventh, earning $175. At the age of 38, he tied for fourth in the 1947 Masters.

McSpaden is credited with 17 PGA victories over the course of his career. The grandest was the 1939 Canadian Open, then regarded as a prominent, if not major, tournament. In 1944 he won the Los Angeles Open, the Phoenix Open (defeating Nelson in a playoff), and the Chicago Victory Open (in a playoff over Hogan.) While he is known for all those runner-ups, McSpaden did acknowledge that he beat all the big names at one time or another. He won five times in 1944.

He had no idea how he came upon the nickname "Jug." But it stuck with him. He and Nelson were nicknamed the Gold Dust Twins for their seemingly attached-to-the-hip narrative. They won two match-play tournaments as partners, the 1944 Golden Valley Four-Ball and the 1945 Miami International Four-Ball. Both players were given medical waivers during World War II, McSpaden's due to a serious sinus condition. He also had asthma. But the Gold Dust Twins, in addition to dominating the PGA Tour during the war, played more than 100 exhibitions from 1942 to 1944 to raise money for the Red Cross and the USO.

McSpaden had been a semifinalist at the PGA Championship before. In 1937, he had made it all the way to the finals, eliminating Sam Snead in the third round, before losing to defending champion Denny Shute in 37 holes. Given his propensity for second-place finishes, this was the only time McSpaden finished as a runner-up in one of the four recognized majors. (He never played in the British Open.)

Along the way to his 1946 semifinal match with Oliver, McSpaden had dispatched Claude Harmon, 1944 PGA champ Bob Hamilton, Dutch Harrison, and local favorite Charles Congdon, a club pro who won a host of lesser tournaments in the Northwest. But Oliver sent McSpaden packing, 6 and 5. That set the stage for a Hogan-Oliver final with each man looking for his first official major.

The final was a contrast in just about every way. Oliver wasn't called Porky for no reason; he weighed well over 200 pounds. He liked to dress garishly, more like Demaret than the buttoned-up Hogan. But Oliver was a legitimate threat, and if Hogan thought otherwise, the first 18 holes of the 36-hole final dispatched those sentiments. Hogan won the first hole, lost the second and the match proceeded to the 15th tee all square. Oliver went eagle, birdie, birdie on the next three holes, and the morning round ended with Hogan 3-down. His 73 marked the first time he had shot above 69 on the Portland Golf Club course. Another disappointment to match Augusta and Canterbury loomed.

Hogan took time between the two rounds to work on his game on the practice tee, and then absolutely hammered Oliver over the next 14 holes. Birdies on the third, fourth, fifth, and sixth holes turned the 3-hole deficit into a 1-up lead. Three more birdies on 9, 10 and 11 gave Hogan a 4-up lead, and he stretched it to 5-up with a par on the 12th while Oliver made a bogey. A birdie on the 14th settled things; Oliver conceded a 1-foot putt. Hogan won the match 6 and 4. He had played the first nine in 30 and was 4 under on the back nine when the match ended. He did not have a 5 on his afternoon scorecard.

"Ed Oliver is a great player and he was certainly not up to his game today," Hogan told reporters afterwards. "I was playing a little over mine. That's the reason I won." He later would admit, "It's impossible to explain how much this means to me." He had finally broken through.

Portland Golf Club would turn out to be one of the most important venues in Hogan's career. He shot his mind-boggling 261 there in 1945. He won his first major there in 1946. He captained the victorious Ryder Cup team there in 1947. At the regular PGA Tour stop there in 1948, he lost in a three-way playoff.

The PGA was Hogan's 10th victory in 1946. He won the following week in California and then twice more before the season ended, finishing with a stunning 13 victories and leading the tour in earnings with more than $42,000.

Fred Corcoran sure knew how to call 'em.

Hogan, Mangrum, Demaret, and all the other pros would soon come to appreciate life on the PGA Tour without the dominating presence of Byron Nelson. After losing to Oliver in the PGA Championship, he and his wife drove off to the Texas hill country, where Lord Byron would begin his life as a gentleman rancher. Nelson did show up for George May's ritzy tournament in Chicago later that summer, finishing second to Sam Snead. Nelson claimed he had not known it was a winner-take-all event, and Snead walked off with $10,000.

Bobby Jones tended to his business interests as the PGA Tour got up to speed. In his separation papers from the US Army, Jones listed his occupation as a vice president for the AG Spalding Company. He and Clifford Roberts collaborated to own some Coca-Cola bottling plants (Coca-Cola was based in

Atlanta), and soon he would start a friendship with a man he had never met, but who had long idolized him—Dwight Eisenhower.

It was during the early stages of the Battle of the Bulge in December 1944—the last great and ultimately unsuccessful German attack to stop the Allies—that Eisenhower had his first "introduction" to what would be a staple of his postwar life—Augusta National Golf Club.

Eisenhower's fondness for golf was well known. He was the classic recreational player who simply loved the game. He made sure that there was a golf course available to him when he scouted out potential headquarters sites in Europe. At one point, just before the surprise German attack in the Ardennes in December 1944, the British Chief of the Imperial General Staff, Alan Brooke, wrote in his diary that Eisenhower was playing too much golf and "taking practically no part in running the war." Brooke was a noted acerb; one of his most frequent targets during the war was his boss, Winston Churchill, whom Brooke filleted in his diary, published after the hostilities.

While the Allies were holding off the Germans at Bastogne, Eisenhower met at Reims—his headquarters at the time—with Bill Robinson, then the vice president of the *New York Herald Tribune*. Robinson had some questions about Eisenhower's operations in Paris and wanted the general's input. Robinson was also a member of Augusta National, which eventually would result in an invitation to the general to spend some R&R at the course. It would also result in the beginning of a decades-long friendship between the soon-to-be-president of the United States and the soon-to-be-named greatest golfer of the first half of the twentieth century, Bobby Jones.

9

1946 AND BEYOND

The Foursome on the Back Nine of Life

You must do two things: (1) Grip the club lightly and (2) swing slowly. Just take it easy and don't try to 'work on the ball' too much.

—Bobby Jones, in a July 20, 1951,
letter to Dwight Eisenhower

BOBBY JONES

Bobby Jones competed in his final Masters in 1948. He was only 46, and should have been able to play in many more. But he had been bothered by a pain in his shoulders, back, and neck, the same issue that had surfaced in Scotland when he had lost to Andrew Jamieson in the British Amateur at Muirfield in 1926. The pain had gotten progressively worse. In July of that year, after many efforts to cure the pain, Jones found he could no longer swing a golf club without feeling a burning sensation. Jones played his last round of golf in August 1948.

He had just begun a correspondence with General Dwight D. Eisenhower, who had written to "Mr. Jones" at the end of April, thanking him for arranging a 10-day stay at Augusta National for the general and his wife. "The interlude at Augusta," Eisenhower wrote, "was certainly one of the most pleasant that I have ever enjoyed."

For golfing company and male companionship, Eisenhower spent most of his time with Clifford Roberts, Bill Robinson, and another Augusta member, Bill Carlington. Jones did not get to meet Eisenhower over those 10 days, writing to the general on May 3 that "certainly your presence added to their enjoyment." Eisenhower had sent Jones a signed photograph of the general himself on the Augusta grounds. Jones promised to have it framed and hanging in the cottage where Eisenhower stayed.

Eisenhower "signed" his April 27 letter with a stamp. By the end of 1948, he would be signing his letters "Ike Eisenhower" while addressing them to "Bobby." Jones, similarly, referred to Eisenhower as "General Ike" in their correspondences.

In October 1948, Jones wrote Eisenhower, then the president of Columbia University in New York, to express his delight that the general (he would always be addressed as "the general") had accepted Augusta's invitation to become a member. "I cannot think of anyone that I would rather have as a member," Jones wrote. "It is a gross understatement for me to say merely that I am delighted."

Jones's deteriorating health prompted him to seek surgery and, at the end of October, he underwent a seven-hour fusion operation at Emory University Hospital. Initial reports were encouraging. A small growth had been removed, and Jones was expected to make a full recovery.

Eisenhower wrote to Jones three weeks after the operation, letting him know that he and his fellow Augusta National members "are pulling not only for a speedy but a complete recovery." He added that he would soon be mailing Jones a copy of his forthcoming book, *Crusade in Europe.*

Jones was delighted to hear about the book, writing back to Eisenhower that it will be "the most valued compliment I have ever received." (Jones never let hyperbole get in the way in his letters to Eisenhower.) When he did receive it, however, he was too weak to read it at the hospital. A few months later, Eisenhower sent Jones another book, this one by the prolific Winston Churchill.

In late June 1951, Eisenhower wrote Jones to thank him for a gift that was soon to arrive in Europe—a set of golf clubs that Jones could no longer use. The general had left Columbia to become the Supreme Allied Commander of the North Atlantic Treaty Organization. He was given operational command of all United States and NATO forces in Europe. But he still loved his golf: "I cannot tell you how touched I am by the news and how grateful I am for your thoughtfulness." Eisenhower then wrote Jones again, 11 days later, after the clubs had arrived: "I took them out to one of our toughest golf courses and promptly shot a one-over par on the first nine." Eisenhower added that "this astonishing performance is apt to work very adversely on my Augusta handicap which would be acceptable if I had any hope of making the habit a permanent one."

Jones responded that he was delighted his clubs "are now in such capable hands and that they will continue to perform on this level for you." They didn't, of course. Eisenhower reverted to form (his handicap was somewhere in the mid-teens), which Jones had anticipated when he wrote to the general on July 20.

"I hope you won't mind if, as one golfer to another, I pass along a little suggestion about their use," Jones wrote. He told Eisenhower the clubs were likely heavier than those to which the general might be accustomed. Toward that end, Jones told Eisenhower, "You must do two things: (1) Grip the club lightly and (2) swing slowly. Just take it easy and don't try to 'work on the ball' too much."

Eisenhower responded eight days later. "My constant prayer, these days, as I start my backswing, is 'oh, please let me swing slowly.' What I need more than anything else is about two weeks down at Augusta National with you sitting there to lecture me."

We have Eisenhower to thank for the passage in *My Greatest Day in Golf* that details Jones's thoughts through the general's recollection. The general was in town to watch the 1949 Masters, and the brother of the USGA president at the time arranged for the two notables to meet.

Eisenhower cut right to the chase. After the perfunctory introductions, he asked Jones what he considered to be his finest round of golf. Jones told Eisenhower, "I wouldn't know how to answer that question, General, but if you had asked what round of golf gave me more satisfaction than any other round, I would have said that it was a round of golf I played 25 years ago, not in a championship, and not a record-breaking score."

It is quite a stunning reflection by Jones, as he deemed his most satisfying day in golf to be not one of the many tournaments he won, nor his launching of Augusta National, but a round in 1924 on Long Island that meant absolutely nothing.

The National Golf Links at Southhampton, New York, had made arrangements to invite several members of the 1924 American and British Walker Cup teams to play its course. The United States won the cup in Garden City, New York, that year, 9–3, with Jones winning his singles match while losing his foursomes match. The National Golf Links had staged the inaugural Walker Cup in 1922 and this time arranged a special one-day tournament for the Walker Cuppers.

The course, Eisenhower recalled Jones telling him, was long, especially from the back tees. On the day of the tournament, which was wet, cold, and windy, the players were told to use the back tees. "On this particular day, the National

Links was a fitting test for the best golfers of Great Britain and the United States," Jones is quoted as telling Eisenhower. "It was a day to break the heart of any but the hardiest.

"In the wet and the cold and in the face of that wind, General Eisenhower, I shot a 73. I think it was the best round of golf I ever played. There was no title involved. It was just a round of golf with the player pitted against the elements. But that 73 gave me more happiness and satisfaction, I think, than any round of golf I have ever played."

Jones's health did not improve as hoped after the October 1948 operation, so he underwent another—a five-hour procedure—at the Lahey Clinic in Boston in May 1950. The clinic was famous for its work on spinal surgeries, and Jones was in desperate need of *something*. By that time, he needed canes and a leg brace just to walk.

Jones was soon to learn that he was suffering from syringomyelia, a degenerative disease of the spinal cord. The only cure is surgery, but after two operations, Jones was too far gone. He would soon be confined to a wheelchair. But while his body may have been deteriorating, his mind was still sharp. A lifelong Democrat, Jones helped organize Georgians in support of Eisenhower's presidential bid in 1952. While Georgia did not go for Eisenhower in 1952, the general still won the election. He was comfortably re-elected in 1956 but still did not carry Georgia.

Jones also showed off his keen concentration and memory skills in 1958 in a series of letters to the club captain of Royal Lytham & St. Annes, the English links course where he had won the 1926 British Open. As detailed in the wonderful book *Bobby's Open* by Steven Reid, Jones received a copy of a photograph showing his famous shot out of a fairway sand trap on the 17th hole at Royal Lytham during the final round. The captain, C. W. "Pincher" Martin, wanted Jones to verify that the photograph was legitimate.

In a two-page letter dated June 1958 Jones wrote that the photograph in question "does not quite ring true to me." He listed several reasons for his thinking, from the lie of the ball in the sand to the surrounding buildings, spectators, and others watching the match, including his opponent, Al Watrous. Then, in a particularly revealing postscript, he asked, "Have you studied the shadow?"

Two months later, Martin got back to Jones. He apologized for the delay; the club had hosted the 1958 British Open in July. He then told Jones that the photo had not been one of Jones's so-called miracle shot on 17, but one of Jones hitting out of a bunker on the 14th hole. "How very right you were about the shadow," Martin wrote. "We have successfully proved that the photograph is not that of the famous shot."

Martin invited Jones back to Royal Lytham in October, when Jones was scheduled to be the nonplaying captain for the US team competing for the first Eisenhower Trophy, a biennial World Amateur Team Championship. Over the years, such stars as Tiger Woods, Rory McIlroy, Jack Nicklaus, Tom Kite, and Ben Crenshaw have participated in the Trophy. In 1958, the tournament was scheduled for the Old Course in St. Andrews.

Jones wrote back that his health prevented him from making a return visit to Royal Lytham, adding, "I may even be a little rash in attempting a trip to St. Andrews." Still, the folks at Royal Lytham point proudly not only to Jones's memorable Open victory in 1926, but also to his round there in 1944, the last one he played in Great Britain. In 1960, Alec Barker, a Royal Lytham member attending an American Bar Association meeting, met with Jones and presented a letter on the commemoration of the plaque at the back of the 17th bunker. When Barker returned home, he received a copy of *Golf Is My Game* in the mail, along with an accompanying letter.

"You may be sure," Jones wrote, "that I often think of St. Anne's, not only of the Championship but also of the great pleasure I had visiting there on my way home from France during the war. I have been delighted to follow the continuing contributions of the club to the game of golf.

"With all good wishes and many thanks, Most sincerely, Bob Jones."

The 1958 trip to St. Andrews did prove challenging for Jones. Before arriving, he had received a telegram inquiring as to whether he would accept the honor of being named a Freeman of St. Andrews. Jones had already received two ticker tape parades through New York. What could be more than that? So he accepted the offer.

He soon realized upon arrival that it was no ceremonial honor, but a certifiable big deal. He was, as it turned out, being named a citizen of St. Andrews. The only other American to have been so honored was Benjamin Franklin, in 1759. Jones gave a heartfelt speech at St. Andrews University, telling the audience, "I could take everything out of my life but my experiences at St. Andrews, and I'd still have a rich, full life."

He had won his only British Amateur at St. Andrews in 1930. He had won one of his three British Opens at the Old Course in 1927. "I just want to say," he said, "that this is the finest thing that ever happened to me." He then gingerly sat down as the crowd responded with a chorus of "For He's a Jolly Good Fellow."

The syringomyelia advanced, and Jones died at his home on December 18, 1971. He was 69. (Eisenhower had died in March 1969.) The flags at East Lake, St. Andrews, and undoubtedly countless other courses were at half-staff. Jones is buried in Atlanta's Oakland Cemetery with a simple headstone noting just his name and the dates of birth and death. The great golf writer Herbert Warren Wind wrote of Jones: "As a young man, he was able to stand up to just about the best that life can offer, which is not easy, and later he stood up with equal grace to just about the worst."

LLOYD MANGRUM

Lloyd Mangrum battled health issues (and other assorted ailments unrelated to his health) for most of his career. It was said that when he died in 1973 at the age of 59, it was from his 11th heart attack. Like so much about Mangrum, however, the finer points remain murky.

What is clear, however, is that Mangrum went on a 10-year tear after World War II, elevating himself into the rarified air and company of Hogan and Snead. But all the successes, which included wins on three continents, were not enough to make Mangrum similarly memorable as Hogan and Snead. Or Nelson. Or even Demaret.

Byron Nelson wrote that at the 1996 Masters, he went around and asked a lot of the younger players if they'd ever heard of Mangrum. None had. "Lloyd's the best player who has been forgotten since I've been playing golf."

Mangrum was his own worst enemy in term of publicity. Maybe more people would know of Mangrum's achievements today if he had been more vocal, more accessible, more accommodating. Maybe he would have come across much differently had his life story been chronicled by a sympathetic biographer. But he was none of those, and never would be. "In tournament golf, where anyone not wearing chartreuse slacks, a heliotrope jersey contrasting with two-toned suede shoes and a crazy hat—or with the famed name of Ben Hogan—is practically invisible to the press and public, the wispy Texan with the neat moustache stands out as wry example of how to attain success without letting the folks know it," wrote Al Stump for *Elks Magazine.*

After World War II, Mangrum was every bit as aloof and standoffish as he had been before he set off for Europe in 1944. He struggled at first returning to the tour, which made his 1946 US Open victory so astounding. "He was like a ghost walking," said one of his tour friends, Cary Middlecoff. "He knew exactly what to do and he couldn't do it."

A *Golf World* profile of Mangrum in 2006 said he had become even more ill-tempered after his experiences in the war. If that was the case, he had plenty of company. He may have suffered from post-traumatic stress disorder, although it was called something much less sinister—battle fatigue—back then. "His personal history became dotted with stories of his getting into fights over card games, car accidents, barroom brawls and other incidents," the *Golf World* article said. The article also noted that Mangrum basically missed an entire year in the mid-1950s with what at the time were described as war injuries. It was more likely due to an attack by a pipe-wielding neighbor over a road rage incident.

Mangrum won no tournaments in 1955, only one in 1956 (his last one, the Los Angeles Open), and he did not participate in the US Open or the PGA Championship in either 1955 or 1956. He did play in the Masters both years, finishing seventh in 1955 and tied for fourth in 1956.

Mangrum's career basically ended at that point; he did manage to find his way to Augusta through 1963, never threatening, and missing the cut three times. He qualified for the US Open in 1957, 1958, and 1960, but finished no higher than a tie for 23rd at Cherry Hills in 1960.

The tragedy is that Mangrum was still a young man in 1956. He turned 42 that year and was two years younger than both Hogan and Snead. Yet while Mangrum's game was deteriorating, Hogan came close to winning three more US Opens and Snead continued playing into his 60s and had one remarkable stretch where he finished in the top 10 in the PGA Championship in 1972, 1973, and 1974.

Something, clearly, had happened. Mangrum basically disappeared, moving to Apple Valley in California's high desert and to a life of tranquility where no one bothered him. He built a house opposite the 18th tee and would occasionally be seen on Apple Valley's course. But if anyone was saying, "There goes Lloyd Mangrum. He used to be somebody," no one was listening.

It's a shame, really. Because whatever happened to Mangrum to cut short a career that would eventually lead to the World Golf Hall of Fame should not obscure all that he did to get there. Yes, the war stories are compelling, if nearly impossible to verify. But it was the golf that got him to St. Augustine. And for a 10-year stretch after World War II, few played it any better than Lloyd Mangrum.

The success didn't change who he was. The difference was that in the years following the war, he played so well that his results virtually demanded that people know more about him and want a bigger slice of him. He still kept to himself, his card games, and his devoted spouse. He lived well. He dressed impeccably. And he was near unflappable on the course.

Mangrum always preferred to let his play do the talking, and the numbers and results spoke at a deafening roar in the years after World War II. His body of work from 1940 through 1956 includes the 36 official PGA Tour victories as well as 9 others. He went 6–2 in four Ryder Cup appearances, including serving as the playing captain in 1953. The United States won all four Ryder Cups in which he played, dominating in the two held in the United States and just surviving in the two played in England.

In 1951—the year Ben Hogan won the Masters and the US Open—and in 1953—the year Hogan won the Masters, US Open, and British Open—it was Mangrum who won the Vardon Trophy for having the lowest scoring average. He won four times in each of those two seasons and placed in the top four in both the Masters and US Open in 1951 and 1953. In 1951, no one made more than the $26,000 Mangrum earned, although Hogan might have done so if he had been able to play in more events.

In 1948, Mangrum won seven PGA tournaments and four other unofficial ones. He made the cut in 30 consecutive majors starting with the 1942 PGA and continuing through the 1957 Masters. Even though he never won it, the Masters was his best major. From 1947 to 1956, Mangrum never finished lower than eighth, and he had six top-five finishes. He won four Los Angeles Opens, two Western Opens and two Bing Crosby Pro-Ams. He finished in the top five in the US Open on six occasions.

The victory at Canterbury was Mangrum's solitary win on the PGA Tour in 1946. He hadn't even returned to the tour until the Phoenix Open in late January. All the other big names had returned by the fall of 1945. He was still in Europe.

After his surprising US Open victory at Canterbury, Mangrum added a second title in 1946 when he won the Argentine Open. He and Vic Ghezzi, who also had been in the Army in World War II, went down for the tournament, which is a prestigious one in South America, dating back to its first year, 1905. Jimmy Demaret had won it in 1941, and Mangrum did the same five years later, besting Ghezzi by one stroke in a playoff. Their four-round totals of 271 were one off the record low score at the time. Other PGA Tour players who have won the tournament include Henry Picard and Paul Runyan.

Mangrum won twice more in 1947, and then in 1948 he had his breakout year. He won seven times on the PGA Tour and had that hugely profitable five days in Chicago where he won the All-American Open and the eight-man tournament the next day, eventually earning $22,500 in winnings and bonuses. Had all that counted, Mangrum would have led the tour in winnings that season. As it is, he estimated winning more than $48,000.

He won the Crosby Pro-Am in January, the Rio Grande Open in February, and the Greater Greensboro Open in March. Each win was worth $2,000. He won the Columbus Invitational in July (it was also called the Zooligans Open, after the sponsor) and then had his big payday in Chicago. His last PGA victory came at the Utah Open in late August. He finished second to Hogan in two other tournaments later in the season.

For someone who didn't care to say much, Mangrum had announced to the golfing world that he was here to stay. No less an authority than Gene Sarazen offered that if he had to choose one player to win a specific tournament, it would be Hogan. "But over a long season's pull, however, I'd have to take Mangrum. That skinny guy just freezes the boys up by never having a real bad day."

He didn't have many bad ones during this run. He won four times in 1949. But he still could be the ornery Mangrum. In the quarterfinals of the 1950 PGA Championship at Scioto, Mangrum went up against Chandler Harper. The two were all square heading to the 17th hole of the afternoon 18, and each player had a birdie putt of about 15 feet.

Harper was forced to chip his putt—the PGA didn't allow players to mark their balls for opposing players until 1952—and knocked it in the hole for a birdie, the ball bouncing over Mangrum's. Harper was now 1-up going to the 18th hole. He made a 15-foot putt for a birdie to match Mangrum's birdie and won the match. "I'll never forget it," Harper said. "There must have been 5,000 people out there. Lloyd took off his cap, bowed, and said, 'Take the goddamn game!'"

Harper went on to win the tournament. But Mangrum still won five times in 1950 and came very close to capturing his second US Open title. The tournament that year, at fabled Merion, produced a three-way tie at the end of 72 holes—Mangrum, Hogan, and George Fazio. An 18-hole playoff ensued on Sunday, and when the threesome got to the 16th green, Hogan led Mangrum by one shot. Fazio was well behind. It was a two-man race.

Mangrum needed to make a 6-foot putt on the 16th to stay one shot behind Hogan. Cary Middlecoff called Mangrum "Whirlaway" for Mangrum's ability to come from behind down the stretch. (Whirlaway was the name of the racehorse that won the 1941 Triple Crown.) But when he was lining up the ball, he noticed a bug had settled on it. So Mangrum marked the ball, lifted it off the green, blew the bug away, replaced the ball, and made the putt.

But the USGA did not allow you to mark your ball as Mangrum had done. When Mangrum got to the 17th tee, still one shot behind Hogan, he was informed that he would be assessed a two-stroke penalty for the marking incident.

When told of the infraction, Mangrum shrugged and said, "Oh, well. We'll all eat tomorrow." That was a magnanimous response given that his miscue had come so late in the playoff. Mangrum ended up four strokes behind Hogan's winning 69. Fazio shot a 75. Mangrum later said he was unaware of the rule. But it cost him a chance at his second US Open.

Mangrum won four times in 1951 and four times in 1953. He triumphed at the Phoenix and Western Opens in 1952 while also finding success again in faraway lands.

That is the year Mangrum extended his reach to the Pacific. He won the Philippine Open, which had the distinction of being Asia's oldest golf tournament. Mangrum also traveled to Australia that year along with Demaret, Porky Oliver, and Jim Turnesa for what was known as Lakes Cup Matches, a competition between PGA members and pros in Australia. Mangrum helped the Americans to a 7–5 victory over the Aussies—the format was similar to the Ryder Cup in those days—and then won a special tournament in Adelaide as well as the Ampol Tournament, billed as the richest golf event in Australia. Those were the kind of tournaments Mangrum enjoyed the most, and his first-place haul was 625 Australian pounds.

He then returned for his banner year in 1953, winning four more times. He won once in 1954 and then not again until the Los Angeles Open in 1956. And then not at all.

Mangrum never saw the lack of publicity or notoriety as an issue or concern until three weeks before he died. He called Jim Murray, the sports columnist for the *Los Angeles Times*, telling Murray that he felt as if no one knew who he was or what he had done. It was a revealing statement. Mangrum had never cared about any attention while he was playing and winning. But now, 17 years removed from his last victory, he thought it was time that someone let the world know what he had accomplished. Who better than Murray?

"He wanted me to do a resume of his career. He wanted to get out of the bag of anonymity," Murray wrote. The two met for lunch at Riviera Country Club where Mangrum detailed his achievements. Murray coined Mangrum "The Forgotten Man of Golf."

"Lloyd was as good as any of them in his day," Murray wrote. "There were Hogan, Snead and Nelson. And then, by golly, there was Mangrum. Push one in the rough and he went right by you. But life never seemed to lean over and knock his ball away and say, 'that's good.'"

Murray wrote that Mangrum was even thinking of moving from Apple Valley closer to Palm Springs. But before Murray could put his words into print, Mangrum had yet another heart attack and died on November 17. He never made it to Palm Springs. Murray wrote his column as an appreciation four days later, concluding with "Here's to a new life that's all fairway, straight putts and open shot to every green. He never got it. But wherever you are Old Pro, it still goes."

Twenty-six years later, Mangrum was inducted into the World Golf Hall of Fame. On the 1999 PGA Tour ballot, he received the required 75 percent of the votes while no other player that year cleared 66 percent. So in enshrinement, as in much of his life, Lloyd Mangrum cut his own solitary path.

JIMMY DEMARET

If 1946 was Ben Hogan's breakout year and 1948 was Lloyd Mangrum's breakout year, then 1947 belonged to the Human Rainbow himself, Jimmy Demaret. He had predicted it would take a couple of years to get his A game back after his years in the Navy, and he couldn't have been more correct.

He matched his win total from 1940 by taking six tournaments, including his second Masters. He won two four-ball competitions with Hogan as his playing partner and added the Tucson, St. Petersburg, and Miami Opens to his list of victories. He topped off the year by leading the tour both in money earned—with nearly $27,000—and as the recipient of the Vardon Trophy, edging out Ben Hogan.

His good friend Hogan said of Demaret, "This man plays shots I haven't dreamed of. I learned them. But it was Jimmy who showed them to me first."

Demaret had already won three times in 1947 when he pulled up the newly paved Magnolia Drive for the 1947 Masters. This was the 11th Masters, and if the first postwar one had been won by a relative unknown—Herman Keiser—Demaret made sure that no one would be scratching heads over the identity of the second postwar Masters winner.

He became the first player in the history of the tournament to break par in four consecutive rounds, shooting 69, 71, 70, and 71 for a 281 total, 7 under par. That was one shot higher than his winning total seven years earlier, but it was two shots better than the supposedly retired Byron Nelson (he continued to play in the Masters) and amateur Frank Stranahan, and three shots ahead of Ben Hogan and Jug McSpaden.

In his first round, paired with Byron Nelson, Demaret had executed a stunning shot on the par-5 15th hole, the same hole on which Gene Sarazen had scored his double eagle 2 in 1935. This wasn't quite that dramatic, but it was good enough to be featured in a book called *Great Shots* by Cal Brown and Robert Sommers in the 1980s.

Demaret thought he had cleared the pond in front of the 15th green with his second shot, but the ball rolled down the slope and into the water. He could have taken a penalty shot and tried to get up-and-down for his par. Instead, he took off his golf shoes and socks and, with one foot on land and one in the water, he blasted away. Out squirted the ball, rolling to within 4 feet of the hole. Demaret made the putt for a birdie 4.

Demaret was tied for the lead after the first and second rounds. He held a three-shot lead after the third round, prompting *Atlanta Constitution* columnist

Johnny Bradberry to write that the "the gay, colorful Jimmy Demaret" not only led by three shots "at the three-quarter pole and from here it looks as if there is no one in field who can catch him in tomorrow's stretch drive."

Bradberry may have mixed his metaphors but he was on target. Demaret felt the same way. On his way to the course for the final round, Demaret was given a lift by famed golfer Louise Suggs who, like Demaret, had an endorsement contract with MacGregor. Suggs had use of a MacGregor courtesy car, so when she dropped off Demaret at the course, he turned to her and said, "Shake my hand." Suggs did so.

Demaret said, "Feel that? My fingers are thin. I'm going to win today."

Dressed in yellow on this Easter Sunday—an *Augusta Chronicle* writer said Demaret looked like "an Easter egg rolling along the greensward"—Demaret was never seriously threatened. He had started the day at 6 under par and only one other player, Jim Ferrier, managed to get that low. But no sooner had Ferrier gotten to 6 under than he proceeded to shoot out of the top money with two bogeys and a double bogey.

Even a bogey at 16 didn't deter Demaret, who parred in and took home a tidy $2,500 for his efforts. Nelson took home $1,500 for his second-place finish, which he did not have to share with the amateur Stranahan. (Stranahan was one of the great amateurs of the post-Jones era, winning two British Amateurs while nearly winning the Masters, the US Open, and the US Amateur. He eventually turned pro in 1954 immediately after losing in the US Amateur to Arnold Palmer in the round of 16.)

Right after his Masters victory, Demaret made a career choice of sorts. He had bounced around in the early 1940s as a club pro before winding up back at River Oaks in Houston just before entering the service. He moved to a position as the "touring pro" affiliated with the Ojai Valley Inn in California. (This was similar to the move that Mangrum made after he won the 1946 US Open and took the head job at Tam O'Shanter.) The resort was a favorite among the glitterati in Hollywood, with guests including Clark Gable, Lana Turner, Rita Hayworth, and Crosby and Hope. It was nestled in a valley surrounded by mountains and was used for the golf scenes in the movie "Pat and Mike" starring Spencer Tracy and Katharine Hepburn.

Ojai was a place that didn't need a "name" head pro to man the shop or give private lessons. It could benefit immensely from its connection to a successful touring pro, especially one with the outgoing personality of Demaret. So it was a win-win for both sides.

Claude Harmon and Sam Snead won the next two Masters, but a new decade loomed in 1950, and Demaret was ready for his third victory at Augusta. No one had ever won three Masters up to this point—Hogan hadn't even won his first—but Demaret was his usual prankster self prior to the tournament, asking his fellow pros which one was going to finish second.

It wouldn't be entirely accurate to report that Demaret backed up his words. It would be more accurate to report that Demaret backed into his third Masters title thanks to Jim Ferrier's implosion on the back nine in the final round.

By the halfway point, Demaret was five shots off of Ferrier's pace and, after three rounds, was tied for third, four shots behind Ferrier. He closed with a 69 on Sunday. At one point, he was seven shots behind Ferrier. Demaret birdied the 15th and 16th holes to finish at 283, 5 under par. Ferrier was 8 under par with six holes left. He proceeded to bogey five of the last six holes, shooting a 41 on the back nine, effectively handing the tournament to Demaret, who ended up winning by two.

At the green jacket ceremony, Demaret took the microphone and started singing, "You Don't Know How Lucky You Are."

Demaret never won another major, so, understandably, he referred to his three Masters victories as the "proudest and most satisfying, competitive victories in my career." He said his three Masters medals (which the winners receive) were "the most meaningful awards of my competitive golf life." He skipped the PGA from 1951 to 1955, lost in the second round in 1956, skipped 1957, and was disqualified for signing an incorrect scorecard in 1958, the first year the tournament was a stroke-play event, as it has been ever since. That was his last PGA. His best US Opens were his 1948 second-place finish to Hogan and, nine years later—at the age of 47—finishing third, one shot behind the co-leaders, Cary Middlecoff and eventual champion Dick Mayer.

Demaret wasn't beyond self-effacement, especially when it came to one memorable performance in the 1952 Tucson Open. On the 18th hole at El Rio Golf Course, he hit five straight shots out of bounds and made a 14 on the hole. As he teed up his sixth, Lew Worsham, his playing partner, told him, "for your information, you are shooting 11." The sixth tee ball was in play and Demaret made a birdie four on the hole. "I have no idea to this day what I did wrong," he wrote later. "By the time the fifth tee ball left the course, I was seriously considering giving up the game. When I blow, man, I really blow!"

Demaret won the Tucson Open twice, but his favorite nonmajor event was, without question, the Bing Crosby Pro-Am. The tournament had relocated in 1947 to its now familiar perch on the Monterey Peninsula, and Demaret loved everything about it. He called it "one part golf, two parts party." He won it only once, in 1952, but vowed to always return to the tournament he so loved. "In

1985, I'll attend Bing's shindig leaning on a cane, sitting in a wheelchair or flat on a stretcher. But I'll be there," he wrote.

The last of Demaret's 31 PGA victories came in 1957. It was 19 years after his first victory at the San Francisco Match Play Open, when he had defeated Snead in what Demaret thought was as flawless a round of golf as he had ever played. But by now his attention was turning to other areas.

There's a generation of golf fans who know Demaret as the host of *Shell's Wonderful World of Golf*, a television show featuring top golfers at the time playing a match on one of the world's top courses. He was a natural for the new medium, having appeared as himself in a 1954 episode of *I Love Lucy*. He also played himself in the 1951 movie *Follow the Sun*, a Hollywood-esque look at the life of Ben Hogan up to that point in Hogan's life.

In 1966, Demaret joined Gene Sarazen as the cohost of the show. Unsurprisingly, he was a natural for television, which started broadcasting golf after Demaret had passed his prime.

Sarazen and Demaret literally traveled the world for the show. There were matches in several countries, including the Philippines, Spain, Malaysia, Panama, Norway, Greece, Venezuela, and the Netherlands. Tom Weiskopf played a match in Morocco. Demaret was a constant, roving the fairways, talking to the players and offering his insights to viewers. The show ended in 1970 before being revived in 1994.

By this time, Demaret also was helping design and start Champions Golf Club in Houston along with Jack Burke Jr., who had, to Demaret's delight, won both the 1956 Masters and PGA Championship. The club was established in 1957, and its Cypress Creek course opened in 1959. The club hosted the 1967 Ryder Cup, the 1969 US Open, the 1993 US Amateur, five PGA Tour Championships, and the 2020 US Women's Open.

In May 1983, Demaret was inducted into the World Golf Hall of Fame. To celebrate the occasion, he wore a bright apricot sweater with white knickers, argyle socks, and orange-and-black golf shoes.

Seven months later, Jimmy Demaret's fun-loving heart gave out, fittingly as he was getting ready to play a round of golf. He was 73. Comedian Phil Harris told stories at Demaret's wake. Friends recalled Demaret's litany of one-liners, the most memorable probably being "Golf and sex are about the only two things you can enjoy without being good at them." Another was his line after waking up one year at the Crosby and seeing there was snow on the ground: "I know I got loaded last night, but how did I wind up in Squaw Valley?" Others remarked that Demaret lived life to the fullest, abiding by his own credo, "Get out and live. You're dead for an awful long time."

A memorial service was held in Houston a month later. Hogan wrote a letter to be read at the service, addressing it to Jimmy Demaret, My Dear Friend and Playing Partner:

> I know you are here with us today in spirit for this deserving effort in your honor. Your warm, happy smile can be seen and felt by everyone present. As partners, you and I never lost a four-ball match and, although I will be a little tardy in joining you, I want you to keep practicing so that one day we can win another four-ball together. I send to you my admiration and thanks for all the nice things you have done for me and others. You helped make my bad times bearable and my good times better. You were my friend and I miss you. May you sleep in peace and I will join you later.

In 1990, Demaret was honored at Jack Nicklaus's Memorial Tournament in Dublin, Ohio. Dave Marr, a close friend and former PGA champion, wrote a remembrance of Demaret for the program that year. Two sentences stood out: "He got along with everybody and I never heard him say a bad thing about anybody. He genuinely cared about people."

BEN HOGAN

In late September 1949, Ben Hogan was aboard the *Queen Elizabeth*, returning from England with the US Ryder Cup team. Hogan had been a nonplaying captain for the victorious Yanks. Demaret, a member of the team, remembered one particular bumpy night on the ship, which prompted him to wake up early and head to the bar. He ran into Hogan, who was walking around the deck, still in discomfort from an automobile accident nine months earlier.

He and Hogan noticed a group of shipmates who were conducting a burial service for one of their colleagues who had just died. The flag-draped body was gradually being pushed into the sea. Demaret said Hogan grabbed him by the arm and said, "Jimmy, please. Whatever happens to me, don't let them do that. You're my friend. Don't let them do that to me if I die on this thing."

Demaret, trying to lighten this rather heavy moment, told Hogan, "Don't worry. The water here is too cold for you. If anything happens, we'll wait until the ship gets into warmer waters."

For Hogan, the year 1949 was about as painful as one could possibly imagine. He was back at the top of his game, having bounced back from major-less 1947 to record his second and third major triumphs, the 1948 US Open at Riviera and the 1948 PGA Championship, an authoritative 7 and 6 victory over Mike Turnesa at Northwood Hills in St. Louis. Then came a foggy February night in 1949.

Hogan already had two wins and had just finished runner-up to Demaret at the Phoenix Open. He had been on the cover of *Time* magazine, where he was quoted as saying, "If you can't outplay them, outwork them." He and Valerie were headed home to Fort Worth when a Greyhound bus, passing a truck, rammed head-on into Hogan's Cadillac. At the last moment, Hogan dived across the front seat to protect his wife and, in so doing, probably saved his life.

The injuries he suffered were massive—a double fracture of the pelvis, a fractured left ankle, a chipped rib, a fractured collarbone, and near-fatal blood clots. He waited 90 minutes for an ambulance and then spent nearly nine weeks in an El Paso, Texas, hospital where he received blood transfusions and a special vascular operation performed by a New Orleans surgeon flown in by military transport specifically for the procedure.

Hogan was told he might never walk again. He was told that he would, in all likelihood, never play golf again. (He had asked his wife after the accident if his golf clubs were accounted for. Valerie, who was not seriously hurt in the crash, made sure they were.)

While recovering, he came to understand something he had not previously known: people liked him. He received hundreds of get-well letters and telegrams from golf fans across the country. Newspapers marveled at his gut reaction to save his wife. Ben Hogan had always been respected, admired, and popular. Until now, however, it wasn't clear to him *how much* he was respected, admired, and popular.

He began to rehabilitate, and it was quickly apparent that Hogan was not only going to walk again, he was also going to play golf again. He missed the rest of the 1949 season, unable to defend his Open and PGA titles. Cary Middlecoff won the US Open that year, while Sam Snead added another PGA title to the one he had won in 1942. Snead also won the Hogan-less Masters that year.

When the calendar turned to a new year and a new decade, Hogan pronounced himself fit to return to the PGA. But he would have a limited schedule, which grew more limited as the years progressed. He played in eight official tournaments in 1950, starting with his comeback in January at the Los Angeles Open. There, less than one year after his horrific crash, he lost in a playoff to Snead.

The eight tournaments in 1950 would be the most Hogan would play in any one year until he stopped competitive golf in the late 1960s. His year would focus on the Masters and the US Open. He would never again play in the PGA

Championship; the week-long grind was simply too much for his legs. He suffered from circulation and other physical issues in the years after the accident.

He tied for fourth at Augusta in 1950 (Demaret's third Masters title) and then shocked the world with his sole official win of the year at Merion in the US Open. The iconic picture of Hogan hitting his 1-iron to the 18th green on the final day adorns the cover of David Barrett's *Miracle at Merion*. It is one of the most famous golf pictures in history. The shot enabled Hogan to par the hole, thrusting him into the three-way playoff with Lloyd Mangrum and George Fazio that he would win the next day. His only official appearance the rest of the year was at the Motor City Open, where he tied for 12th.

There were two constants to the next several years. Hogan didn't enter many events. And he usually won the ones he did enter.

He played only in four official events in 1951, the Masters, the US Open, the World Championship of Golf (George May's extravaganza in Chicago), and the Colonial at his home course in Fort Worth. He won three of them, finishing fourth in the Colonial.

In winning his first Masters and his third official US Open (and third in as many years, given that he had missed the 1949 US Open), Hogan duplicated Craig Wood's achievement from a decade earlier. A final round, bogey-free 68 enabled Hogan to rally from third place. That was the first year the Masters awarded medals to both the tournament winner and runner-up.

His US Open triumphs following the car accident would be memorable if for no other reason than the 36-hole finish on Saturday. They were grueling endurance tests for even the fittest of golfers. Hogan frequently took Epsom salts baths for his damaged legs. His US Open victory at difficult Oakland Hills outside Detroit featured one of his greatest rounds in tournament competition. He trailed by two strokes entering the final 18—Demaret and Bobby Locke shared the 54-hole lead—and then authored a magical 67 in the afternoon, long considered to be one of the finest rounds in the history of the tournament. Even with that round, he still finished 7 over par for the tournament and won by two shots. It was at the trophy presentation ceremony that Hogan is credited with the memorable line, "I'm glad I brought this course—this monster—to its knees."

The following year, 1952, Hogan played only three tournaments, winning the Colonial while placing third at the US Open and tying for seventh at the Masters. But he made a lasting contribution to Augusta National's main event; at his suggestion, the first Champions Dinner was held in 1952. The tradition continues to this day, with a menu supplied by the defending champion served at a dinner before the start of the tournament.

And then there was 1953. Hogan entered six tournaments. He won five of them. He tied for second in the one he did not win. This included another Masters win, a fourth official US Open and, for the first and only time, his one British Open title at Carnoustie, where he mesmerized the transfixed Scots with his shot-making and demeanor (leading to the moniker "Wee Ice Mon.")

At Augusta, Hogan shot 70 or better in all four rounds and shattered the Masters' scoring record by a stunning five shots. The record stood until Jack Nicklaus bettered it in 1965. Ed (Porky) Oliver was a distant second, five shots behind. At the US Open at ultradifficult Oakmont, Hogan was the only player to finish under par and won by six strokes. Snead finished second and, yes, this was one of those US Opens he would have won had he shot a 69 on the last day. He instead shot a 76.

It really isn't a surprise that Hogan's major haul included twice as many US Opens as the others. What is surprising is why it took him until 1948 to win his first "official" US Open. Generally, US Open courses demand precision, patience, and an understanding of the course and its layout. Hogan excelled in those areas. There's a premium on accuracy in US Opens. Who was a more superior shot-maker than Ben Hogan?

Hogan played in 22 official US Opens from his debut in 1938 until his finale in 1967. He finished in the top 10 in 15 of those, all consecutive Opens in which he participated, from 1940 to 1960. (The missing 6 tournaments are the 4 from World War II, the 1949 Open, and the 1957 Open.) On eight occasions he finished in the top three, and from 1940 to 1956, he never finished lower than sixth.

Following the dominating win at Oakmont in 1953, Hogan started getting some advice from his fellow pros who thought he should give the British Open a shot. It wasn't just four rounds; everyone had to play a 36-hole qualifier just to get into the tournament. And the stakes were ridiculously high; he simply had to win.

He ended up setting the course record at rugged Carnoustie with a 68 on the final round to win by four shots. It was even more impressive in that he was battling an illness. The course record of 69 had been set that very morning in the third round by Argentina's Antonio Cerda, and would be matched in the fourth round by US amateur Frank Stranahan.

A ticker tape parade in New York City greeted him when he returned home from Scotland. He was 41. He was named PGA Player of the Year for the fourth time (he also won in 1948, 1950, and 1951.) The Associated Press named him as its Male Athlete of the Year. His limited schedule dovetailed with a decision in 1953 to start his own club-making company in Fort Worth. He eventually sold it, and the company was sold and resold many times over the years.

He never won another major. And over the next dozen years, he would have only one official tournament victory, the 1959 Colonial, for the fifth and final time. It was his 64th career PGA victory. (He did win the 1956 Canada Cup with Sam Snead and had the lowest score over four days.)

But the story of Hogan from 1954 to 1960 is also one of the near misses in the big events. He already had botched chances in 1946 at the Masters and US Open when he three-putted the 72nd hole to fall one shot out of a playoff. There were other indignities to come, the first in a one-stroke playoff loss to Snead in the 1954 Masters followed by the loss to Jack Fleck in their US Open playoff at Olympic in 1955.

He tied for second the following year, missing a 4-foot putt on the 71st hole and finishing one shot behind champion Cary Middlecoff at Oak Hill. He withdrew from the 1957 Open due to a back ailment, tied for tenth in 1958, and tied for eighth in 1959. Then came 1960.

In what was a confluence of the greats from the past (Hogan), present (Arnold Palmer), and future (Jack Nicklaus), Hogan, at the age of 47, nearly pulled off an improbable victory that would have rivaled any of his majors. Partnered with Nicklaus, then a strapping 20-year-old amateur, Hogan stood on the 17th fairway during the final round with a wedge approach to a green fronted by water. He was tied for the lead with Palmer, who was two groups behind him, and was in great position to make a birdie four.

He hit what he thought was an ideal third shot, but it had too much backspin and skidded into the water. He ended with a bogey 6 and then found water on 18 and had a triple bogey 7. He ended up tied for ninth. "I find myself waking up at night thinking of that shot, right today," Hogan told Ken Venturi in their 1983 interview at Shady Oaks in Fort Worth. "There isn't a month that goes by that that doesn't cut my guts out. I didn't miss it. I just didn't hit it far enough."

Hogan was similarly inconsolable after missing that short putt in 1956, and missing the US Open playoff at Oak Hill by one shot. Harold Sanderson, a teaching pro in the greater New York area who had attended the tournament, described watching Hogan agonize over the short putt even before he struck the ball.

Sanderson and Hogan were on the same plane out of Rochester. Hours after the miss, Sanderson said Hogan still had not come to grips with it. "He had the look of the most abject misery on his face," Sanderson wrote. "So I thought to myself, 'boy, oh boy. What price glory?' What is it? This game? You never lick it."

EPILOGUE

Preserving the Legacy: The Hoganistas

Why do a chosen few live for so long after they die?

—Kyle Chandler, narrator of the documentary
Hogan on the Golf Channel

THE COLLECTOR

In June 2019, shortly after Gary Woodland won the US Open at Pebble Beach, the Golf Channel ran a two-part documentary on the life of Ben Hogan. The producers could have selected any number of events from Hogan's life to open the documentary—the car accident, the ticker tape parade, the 1950 US Open, the 1953 Triple Crown, or even some words of wisdom from the man himself.

They did none of the above.

They opened instead with a shot of a home in Arlington, Texas, belonging to a proud Hoganista—John Seidenstein. To say his home is a shrine to Hogan would be an understatement. The rooms on the ground floor, as well as the main hallway, are adorned with Hogan memorabilia. There's a poster of *Follow the Sun*. There's a photograph of Hogan and Arnold Palmer. Seidenstein figures he has more than 2,000 pieces of Hogan memorabilia, ranging from a replica of the Hogan statue outside Colonial Country Club to a pair of Hogan golf shoes (complete with the extra spike) to one of Hogan's trademark white caps.

Seidenstein also has artwork that belonged to Hogan, and personal letters Hogan wrote to friends. But the items that he cherishes above all others relate to a certain golf tournament in 1942—the Hale America National Open.

He has an original program from the tournament. He has a ticket stub. He has a pairing sheet. "Mr. Hogan became my sports idol in the mid-70s," Seidenstein said.

The men who knew Hogan, and those who did not but wish they had (like Seidenstein), *always* refer to him as Mr. Hogan. Every time. It's not Hogan. It's definitely not Ben. It's Mr. Hogan.

Whether it's Robert Stennett at the Ben Hogan Foundation or Karen Wright at the Ben Hogan Museum, Tiger Woods, or Dow Finsterwald Jr. in the Colonial Country Club pro shop—it's always, always, always, *Mr.* Hogan.

Seidenstein discovered Hogan as a youngster in El Paso, Texas, some four decades ago. His family belonged to a local country club that later would become a stop on the Hogan Tour, the name given to the first tour targeting aspiring PGA players. It's gone through various name changes and is now called the Korn Ferry Tour. The pro at his club played with and sold Hogan clubs. So Seidenstein learned to play using Hogan clubs.

His Hogan collection started when he was in his 20s. He continues to this day to peruse websites, auctions, and any other places that might have a piece of paper, a photograph, a ticket stub, *something* to fill in a missing piece from Hogan's life. His goal, he said, "is to have either a program, ticket, or pairing sheet from every tour event Mr. Hogan ever played in." (He declined to participate in the auction for Hogan's 61 scorecard, which went for more than $29,000. "Nope. Not for me.")

Glancing through his books and papers and getting a tour of his Hogan-themed downstairs makes one understand why the Golf Channel chose this particular way, and this particular individual, to introduce its Hogan documentary. It did so to illustrate the reach and appeal of Hogan, even a quarter-century after his death.

"I'm very lucky to have a patient wife who tolerates my Hogan obsession," Seidenstein said. "The walls of our house are filled with Hogan items and we even have a den type room that the family calls the Hogan Room. There are two miniature copies of the Hogan statue at Colonial in different rooms and a multitude of Hogan knickknacks throughout our home."

THE CLUBS

There are two country clubs in Fort Worth that celebrate Hogan's life and career. Both were built by Marvin Leonard, the Fort Worth businessman who bankrolled Hogan's early (and unsuccessful) forays on the PGA tour. To this day, Hogan is probably more well known for his association with Colonial Country Club, site of an annual stop on the PGA Tour. But in his later years, he was often across town at Shady Oaks Country Club, sitting at a huge round table with a spectacular view of the course, cigarette in one hand, libation in the other.

"I heard him say 'welcome to my club' when he had someone at Colonial," said Jody Vasquez, a Colonial member and author of a book on Hogan. "He felt tied to Colonial emotionally. But later in his life, operationally, it made more sense for him to go to Shady Oaks."

Colonial is a veritable Hogan shrine. He is omnipresent at the 85-year-old club, from an 8-foot statue that greets visitors to the Ben Hogan Room, 225 square feet of displays, and mementos of all things Hogan.

The statue greets visitors just outside the clubhouse, and on the four sides of the base are his major golf achievements. The US Open panel notes his four official victories as well as the 1942 Hale America National Open. There's a section in the pro shop that used to sell women's clothing, but was converted into a replica of his office, complete with an immaculate desk, two sets of golf clubs, a coffee mug, a leather chair, and numerous pictures.

The Ben Hogan Room has displays recounting all his triumphs (including his five victories at Colonial as well as a picture of him holding the US Open trophy with the five medals), a display with pictures from his car accident (there's one of the demolished Cadillac he was driving), a replica set of clubs, and a model of the statue given to the recipient of the Ben Hogan Award. It honors the top player in collegiate golf.

Colonial was founded in 1936. Marvin Leonard wanted Colonial to have the smoother, bentgrass greens common to courses in the Northeast. Texans were used to playing on the bumpier Bermuda grass greens. Five years after the club opened, Leonard had convinced the USGA to stage the first US Open in Texas at Colonial. It is the one that Craig Wood won. One of the ways Leonard was able to get the USGA to come to his new, Texas course was a guarantee of $25,000 from the Fort Worth business community.

Leonard sold the club to its members in 1942 and then moved on to build Shady Oaks, a lavish and spectacular club 7 miles from downtown Fort Worth and 6.5 miles from Colonial. Leonard hired golf architect Robert Trent Jones to design the course. It opened in 1958 with bentgrass greens and the imprimatur of none other than Ben Hogan, who at first advised against building a course in that location because of all the hills. Leonard didn't listen to Hogan then, and Hogan was happy he did not. "Anyone who is building a golf course anywhere in the world and doesn't come down to see what has been done here at Shady Oaks will be making a big mistake," Hogan said.

While not as Hogan-centric as Colonial, the ghost of the man is everywhere. There is a reproduction of his locker, with clothes, clubs, ointments, shoes, and golf balls. There are plaques on the wall commemorating Hogan's victories. The pro shop is stocked with books about Hogan.

And then there is the table. It is large, round, and on many occasions would have been occupied by one person—Ben Hogan. In the 1960s, *Town and Country* magazine ran a feature on Shady Oaks. A picture of Hogan adorned the cover with the headline, "My Favorite Country Club."

As was the case with Colonial, Leonard sold Shady Oaks to its members. Leonard died in 1980 at the age of 75.

It would be remiss not to include Ridgemoor in this group, as no other club in the United States—outside of the two in Fort Worth—has more pictures of Ben Hogan on its walls. Ridgemoor is alive and thriving in the same locale as in 1942, boasting about 360 member families. The golf course has changed very little. The 18th is still a par 3 over a pond, but it was redesigned by the golf architect A. W. Tillinghast, whose course designs include Baltusrol and Winged Foot. The course still plays to around 6,500 yards. It still has the elegant clubhouse.

There are more than a dozen pictures of Hogan from the Hale America both upstairs and downstairs, including one of him showing his scorecard to Bobby Jones. That came after his 62 in the second round. If a prospective member of Ridgemoor was unaware of the club's ties to Hogan, and to golf history, all he or she had to do was take a stroll through the clubhouse.

Hogan made several trips to Chicago after the Hale America, but there is no record of him visiting Ridgemoor. His 62 is still the course record, but he shares it with Bob Zender, a three-time Illinois state Amateur champion and Ridgemoor member who had a brief fling on the PGA Tour in the 1970s and 1980s. Zender had the distinction of winning the PGA Tour's six-round qualifying tournament in 1971; he was paired with Tom Watson in the final round and beat him by six shots.

Zender's 62 at Ridgemoor came on a cool Sunday afternoon in October 1984 and featured three eagles, five birdies, and one bogey, a 5 on the par 4 first hole.

In a book commemorating Ridgemoor's 100th birthday in 2005, Zender said he had shot a few 63s, but had never shot a 62 until that day. He wasn't about to compare it in importance to what had happened on the same course 42 years earlier.

"What he (Hogan) did was really good. I looked at what I did as a really great round," Zender said. "The big difference is that he did it in the equivalent of the US Open, and I did it with three friends."

THE CHEERLEADER

The Ben Hogan Museum opened on the 100th anniversary of the golfer's birth in the town where he spent the early years of his life—Dublin, Texas. It is one of a handful of museums in a town of less than 4,000. Since opening in 2012, the museum has become a must-see for Hogan fans everywhere. Karen Wright, who calls herself a Hogan cheerleader but is more curator than pom-pom girl, has been on the scene since the doors opened and is a bottomless repository of Hogan lore. She can relate the story of Hogan growing up, the son of a blacksmith. She can go over the Triple Crown season of 1953 in detail. And she can recite numerous examples of Hogan's resiliency and resourcefulness in overcoming personal and professional setbacks.

The museum features displays of Hogan's victories, sets of club faces designed by the Ben Hogan Company, Hogan's "little black book" where his expenses were detailed, and a replica of the Hickok Belt.

Wright loves to tell the story of the belt, which from 1950 to 1976 was awarded yearly to the best male athlete of the year at a dinner in Rochester, New York. Hogan won it in 1953, was unable to attend the dinner, and accepted the belt in a presentation in Los Angeles. The presenter was Bob Hope.

The Hickok belt is almost obscene in its opulence. According to Wright, the belt is made of solid gold with a 6-carat diamond, a ruby, a sapphire, and a surrounding of 36 diamond chips.

Hogan's Hickok Belt story involves not one, but three thefts, which explains why there is a replica in the museum rather than the original.

Hogan stored the original Hickock Belt in the Ben Hogan Room at Colonial Country Club. It was stolen, quickly recovered, stolen again, and subsequently was destroyed. The family made a replica and sent it to the USGA Museum in New Jersey, which never had a break-in. But someone did break in and stole the replica. So a second replica was made, and is on display in Dublin.

Wright and two other women, Pat Leatherwood and Mary Yantis, worked closely with the Ben Hogan Foundation in Fort Worth to get the museum up and running. It generally is open on weekends and by appointment. And while Dublin isn't a big place, the museum itself is impossible to miss. Its exterior is painted yellow-gold; the actual name of the color is Straw Hat. "It's a small museum, but it is packed with Hogan stories and the real aficionados want to know them all," Wright said.

A recent visitor had to hold back tears as he left, telling Wright that he felt as if he had been to the Ben Hogan shrine and that he was grateful to have made the trip to Dublin.

"We get that a lot," said Wright.

THE CALIFORNIAN

Ten times every year, Mark Baron sends out a reminder of sorts to his estimated 20,000 followers on his Ben Hogan Facebook page. They are the anniversaries of Hogan's victory in his 10 major championships. And yes, Baron counts the Hale America as a major.

So twice in April, once in May, five times in June, and twice in July, Baron has a "This Day in Hogan History" item that celebrates the major titles that Hogan won. There's a lot more, as Baron bills the site as "the most comprehensive and popular Facebook Page, where you will find one or more posts a day about quite possibly the greatest golfer ever."

You can find accounts of Hogan's come-from-behind victory at the 1948 Reading Open, where he shot a final-round 64 to erase a five-stroke deficit and won for the fourth straight time. The streak would eventually reach six. There's an article from the *Chicago Tribune* in 1952 written by Ed Sullivan, who would later go over to television and host his popular variety show on Sunday nights (and introduce America to the Beatles.) Sullivan relates the story about asking Hogan to appear on his TV show, *The Toast of the Town*, at the conclusion of the 1950 US Open. He offered Hogan $1,000, and Hogan accepted. After Hogan won the tournament, a competitor of Sullivan's offered Hogan $1,500. He turned them down. Sullivan wrote, "Perhaps this story will give you an idea of his integrity."

Baron has a room of his own dedicated to all things Ben Hogan at his San Diego home. It has war records acquired from the estate of a secretary to Ben and Valerie Hogan, Hogan's Screen Actors Guild card, clubs, posters, and other memorabilia, including a copy of nearly every magazine and periodical from the 1940s and 1950s that has a photograph or article about Ben Hogan.

But it's the Facebook page to which he devotes so much time and attention. Every day, you can find posts about Hogan's life experiences and, at times, there are multiple posts a day. When there is no anniversary to note, Baron will sometimes post a thought from Hogan himself on any number of topics.

Hogan is an inspiration to him.

THE CLINCHER?

Also in John Seidenstein's possession is a single sheet of paper signed by Hogan, which lists all the golfer's major victories. Under the category of US Opens, it lists the four years Hogan won an official US Open. Hogan proceeded to write in *1942* before the other four dates, and then affixed his familiar John Hancock at the bottom of the page.

"He signed the paper," Seidenstein said. "So, I can definitively say that Mr. Hogan considered the Hale his first major and first US Open win."

BIBLIOGRAPHY

BOOKS

Atkinson, Rick. *The Guns at Last Light*. New York: Henry Holt, 2013.

Barkow, Al. *Gettin' to the Dance Floor: An Oral History of American Golf*. New York: Atheneum, 1986.

Barrett, David. *Miracle at Merion: The Inspiring Story of Ben Hogan's Amazing Comeback and Victory at the 1950 U.S. Open*. New York: Skyhorse, 2010.

Barrett, David. *The Story of the Masters: Drama, Joy and Heartbreak at Golf's Most Iconic Tournament*. Croton-on-Hudson, NY: Tatra Press, 2021.

Companiotte, John. *Jimmy Demaret, The Swing's the Thing*. Ann Arbor, MI: Clock Tower, 2004.

Concannon, Dale. *Bullets, Bombs and Birdies: Golf in the Time of War*. Ann Arbor: Clock Tower, 2003.

Cronin, Tim. *Reflections on Ridgemoor*. Chicago: Ridgemoor Country Club, 2005.

Darsie, Darsie L. *My Greatest Day in Golf*. New York: A. S. Barnes, 1950.

Davis, Martin. *Ben Hogan, The Man behind the Mystique*. Greenwich, CT: American Golfer, 2002.

Demaret, Jimmy. *My Partner, Ben Hogan*. London: Peter Davis, 1954.

Dodson, James. *Ben Hogan, An American Life*. New York: Broadway, 2004.

Fleck, Jack. *The Jack Fleck Story: The Legacy of the Playoff of the Century and the Greatest Upset in Sports History*. Portland, OR: JC Publishing Ltd., 2002.

Frost, Mark. *Grand Slam: Bobby Jones, America and the Story of Golf*. New York: Hachette, 2004.

Graffis, Herb. *The PGA: The Official History of the Professional Golfers Association of America*. New York: Thomas Y. Crowell, 1975.

Jenkins, Dan. *Jenkins at the Majors*. New York: Anchor, 2010.

———. *His Ownself: A Semi-Memoir*. New York: Anchor, 2014.

———. *Unplayable Lies*. New York: Anchor, 2015.

Jones, Robert T. *Golf Is My Game*. New York: Doubleday, 1960.

Keeler, O. B. *The Bobby Jones Story*. Chicago: Triumph, 2002.

Lowe, Stephen R. *Sir Walter and Mr. Jones: Walter Hagen, Bobby Jones and the Rise of American Golf*. Chelsea, MI: Sleeping Bear, 2000.

Mangrum, Lloyd. *Golf, A New Approach*. New York: McGraw-Hill, 1949.

Matthew, Sidney. *Life and Times of Bobby Jones*. Tallahassee, FL: Impregnable Quadrilateral, 1995.

Middlecoff, Cary. *The Golf Swing*. Upper Saddle River, NJ: Prentice-Hall, 1974.

Rapaport, Ron. *The Immortal Bobby: Bobby Jones and the Golden Age of Golf*. Hoboken, NJ: John Wiley & Sons, 2005.

Reid, Steven. *Bobby's Open: Mr. Jones and the Golf Shot That Defined a Legend*. London: Corinthian, 2012.

Roberts, Andrew. *Churchill: Walking with Destiny*. New York: Viking, 2018.

Sampson, Curt. *Hogan*. New York: Broadway, 1996.

Scott, Tim. *Ben Hogan: The Myths Everyone Knows, The Man No One Knew*. Chicago: Triumph, 2013.

Strege, John. *When War Played Through: Golf during World War II*. New York: Gotham, 2005.

Symonds, Craig L. *World War II at Sea: A Global History*. Oxford: Oxford University Press, 2018.

Towle, Mike. *I Remember Ben Hogan*. Nashville, TN: Cumberland, 2000.

Vasquez, Jody. *Afternoons with Mr. Hogan: A Boy, a Golf Legend, and the Lessons of a Lifetime*. New York: Gotham, 2005.

SPECIAL CHAPTERS AND DISSERTATIONS

Gordin, Richard D. "Robert Tyre Jones Jr.: His Life and Contributions to Golf." Dissertation. The Ohio State University, 1967. https://etd.ohiolink.edu/

Nickson, Edward Anthony. "The 1926 Open." Chapter 7 in *The Lytham Century: A History of Royal Lytham and St. Anne's Golf Club*. St. Annes-on-Sea, UK: E. A. Nickson, 1985.

Shefchik, Rick. "Crossroads of History: Interlachen Country Club." Chapter 4 in *From Fields to Fairways: Classic Golf Clubs of Minnesota*. Minneapolis: University of Minnesota Press, 2012.

Watson, Ryan. *Shinnecock Hills Golf Club History*. www.golflink.com

PRIMARY NEWSPAPERS AND MAGAZINES

Atlanta Constitution

Atlanta Journal

Augusta Chronicle

Chicago American

Chicago Sun-Times

Chicago Tribune

Golf Digest

Golf World

Minneapolis Star-Journal

Minneapolis Tribune

New York Times

Saturday Evening Post

Sport

Sports Illustrated

Washington Post

PODCASTS

"The Life and Career of Ben Hogan." *No Laying Up*, episode 2017, May 21, 2019. https://nolayingup.com/podcasts/no-laying-up-podcast/nlu-podcast-episode-217-the-life-and-career-of-ben-hogan

"Supernova in the East, Part 4." *Dan Carlin's Hardcore History*, June 3, 2020. https://www.dancarlin.com/product/hardcore-history-65-supernova-in-the-east-iv/

ARCHIVES AND MUSEUMS

Augusta National Golf Club, Augusta, Georgia

Eisenhower Presidential Library and Museum, Abilene, Kansas

Office of Military Personnel Records, St. Louis, Missouri

Stuart A. Rose Manuscript, Archives and Rare Books Library, Emory University, Atlanta, Georgia

United States Golf Association Museum and Library, Far Hills, New Jersey

World Golf Hall of Fame, St. Augustine, Florida

INDEX

Note: Images in photospread are designated by letters *A* through *P* in italics.

ABOUT THE AUTHOR

Peter May has spent the last four decades covering sports for the *Boston Globe*, the *New York Times*, ESPN, and the *Hartford Courant*. He is the author of three previous books about the Boston Celtics—*The Big Three*, *The Last Banner*, and *Top of the World*—and helped craft the narrative for the autobiography of Baylor University's Kim Mulkey, *Won't Back Down*. May has spent the last eight years teaching in the journalism program at Brandeis University. He lives in New Hampshire with his wife, the journalist Eileen McNamara, and his miniature schnauzer, Fauci.